BETWIXT
AND BETWEEN

A Memoir of New China

Margaret Sun

EARNSHAW BOOKS

Betwixt and Between

By Margaret Sun

ISBN-13: 978-988-8552-36-8

This book has been reset in 10pt Book Antiqua. Spellings and punctuations are left as in the original edition.

BIOGRAPHY / Autobiography

EB111

Published by Earnshaw Books Ltd. (Hong Kong)

CONTENTS

NOTE

In this narrative, some people's names are given only as initials, in order to protect them. But their names can be traced, if needed. Although many will now be dead and gone, there are still others living, I hope.

PREFACE

THERE HAVE NOT been many books written by people who weathered the several decades of upheaval in China, from the 1950s onwards. The few that have been written and published in the West are by authors now living abroad, who therefore do not have to face the consequences, if there be any, of having said things which might have been considered 'offensive' to the system. Personal accounts of what transpired during those years differ depending on each person's experience, on their own points of view, and most importantly, on the social status and background of the individual, which determined to what degree and how he, or she, was affected.

Many friends have encouraged me to write my story, and I have been weighing the pros and cons of doing so for many years. I procrastinated for a multitude of reasons, until I realized that procrastination was not only a thief of time, but also a thief of memory, and I became convinced that if I waited any longer, I would have difficulty recalling the past. It is true that a lack of time has been a major factor, but most important of all, it has also been the fear, or the lingering fear of past experience, that kept me from beginning the project. I am still in China, and I will be here until the end of my days.

Another reason for procrastination was a reluctance to emotionally relive those years. The experience was so harrowing, and I am not as resilient as I used to be. And yet, if the story is left unwritten, I would be deprived of the healing process which has been too long overdue, and it would be too late to get the weight off my mind as it gets heavier with the years, So now I have finally come to the conclusion that perhaps whatever will happen after this is written and read will not be worse than whatever has already happened.

I have given myself another good reason to write this, and that is the noble idea of bearing witness to history so that posterity can identify the signs of something bad about to happen, and so avoid a repetition. But since human nature is so hard to change, and human beings are so forgetful (otherwise why would history keep repeating itself?), this feeble attempt might be just something else that goes in one ear and out the other, and all my tears, trials and tribulations will have been to no avail. But "forgetfulness equals betrayal" and I don't want to be a traitor. I believe that nearly every Chinese who lived through those crucial years has a story of their own to tell, but there aren't many who have done so. One reason could be that they, like me, think that someone else's story is more worthy, and that whatever they went through wasn't that bad. After all, they survived, didn't they? Horror stories from the Cultural Revolution days abound, and while during that period many sacrificed their youth and much of their lives, and the lives of their dear ones, for the cause, the real heroes, the founders of the new system, literally heads of state, were persecuted to death. Those who survived, then, must have had a much, much easier time, and therefore must have little that is worth writing about. All this is still part and parcel of the Chinese mentality of 'self-effacement' that is still in many older people, whose numbers are now dwindling with the passage of time.

Only the people of that age group who went through it all, whether as persecuted or occasionally as persecutors, will be the ones to write and only those from the former group will write truthfully. With time, the memories of the Cultural Revolution days will fade away because not enough has been written about it, and before long it will be totally forgotten.

Another reason is that people of my father's generation and many of my generation, are convinced that we will not see another Cultural Revolution, that we can be assured that we will not have to go through the same ordeal twice. But what about posterity? Is there anyone to guarantee that history won't be repeated in future years? In view of the fact that even people at the very top were treated like criminals and toppled during the Cultural Revolution, whose word is good enough? No one's, that's for sure.

To many young people, even the Second World War is ancient history and still younger ones know nothing about what happened following that, in the world or in China, their own Motherland. They are not interested in history at all. To them, the past is dead, never to return. Whereas to older people, we remember the saying "Know the past and you can explain the present, know the present, and you can predict the future" If there had been no past, there would have been no present, much less a future.

It is questionable how many persecutors have had to answer for their shameful behavior during those years. If no direct deaths resulted from their persecution, there is no responsibility, and even if there had been deaths, the persecutors can always push the responsibility on to the political climate of the time or on to anyone who had ordered them to do what was done. There is little responsibility in carrying out orders, it seems. As for the persecuted who out-lived their persecutors, most kept mum. The few who were eventually rehabilitated during their lifetimes, or even after their demise, were credited to the unswerving endeavors of their family members who were convinced that several arms could out-twist a leg. The more timid souls left the past to the belief that "heaven has eyes," and "those who do bad things will come to no good end." What many did not realize was that that heaven's vision is also dimmed with time.

It is not appropriate to think that the atrocities, especially the persecution of intellectuals, which took place during the Cultural Revolution were isolated from what had been taking place after 1949. Things had been snow-balling with the first "Thought Reform" movement in the early 1950s, and the countless political movements that followed Liberation. With the Anti-Rightist Movement in the late 1950s, the persecutions gained momentum. Many took the view that it was understandable, that nearly all the political movements that had taken place after 1949 were necessary for the new system to take root. But if innocent people are treated like enemies, then a movement loses its real objective. The system's capacity to antagonize the people it could dispense with the least has always been difficult to understand. "Treat a child like an animal, and he will grow up behaving like one," is an old saying. It seemed then that anyone who had lived in the "old society" (the days before the 1949 Liberation) had some kind of confession to make, especially if he could not claim to be a member of the "exploited" class. How ridiculous!

Current Chinese history is incomprehensible if divorced from its ancient cultural heritage. Some rulers in the past were obsessed with xenophobia while others had other forms of phobia. These maladies have been manifested during different times in the past history and usually stem from insecurity, from ignorance, from lack of confidence, and therefore from an underestimation of self and an overestimation of the opposition. They are expressions of an inferiority complex expressed in a superior way. Such a collective inferiority complex is lethal to the society.

Many years have passed since I first began to write this. It has been shelved again and again, with stories and comments added here and there as memories have surfaced. I hope you find it worthy of your time.

Margaret Sun
Urumqi
January 2019

BETWIXT AND BETWEEN

1

THE SHANGHAI YEARS PRIOR TO THE LIBERATION OF 1949

I WAS BORN in a Cantonese-speaking family in Shanghai, in 1935. All my life, I thought that both my parents were adopted children who did not know their birth parents, until quite recently when a first cousin in Vancouver contacted us and sent us a copy of the 'family tree' he had drawn up, showing that we shared the same paternal grandfather, Sun Gaifook, who had worked on a ship which plied the route between Shanghai and Hankow. He had a wife in Zhongshan County, Guangdong Province, and another one in Shanghai, who was my grandmother, also a Cantonese. She could not have been from a well-to-do family because she did not have bound feet. In fact, her toes fanned out and she was only comfortable in cloth shoes. So she could have been from a family that lived near the water. My father had never been to his ancestral home, and we only found out recently that his and his mother's name were not in the family ancestral hall.

My father, Sun Chuksam, like most Chinese of his generation, had been taken to a private tutor when he was around six years old, to learn to read and write Chinese. Like all other students who studied with a tutor, on his initial visit he would carry an ink bowl, a stick of ink, a brush pen, and a few green onions, which are called *tsoong* in Cantonese, sounding like the character in the phrase *tsoong ming*, meaning bright and clever. He would first kowtow three times to the teacher in the ritual marked the establishment of their relationship.

After several years with that private tutor he mastered basic Chinese and learned by rote many of the classics which were required of students of that era. Any misbehavior on the part of the student, including failure to recite the required passages, called for an upturned palm for the teacher to hit with a ruler, if not a caning, which would leave the boy in bruises and tears. Girls were not privileged to have an education except in the very enlightened and moneyed families.

When my father was eleven or twelve years old, some of his mother's *mahjongg* cronies advised her to send him to a foreign school, believing if he knew English he would be able to get a job with one of the many foreign companies in Shanghai. So my father left his Chinese teacher and enrolled in the St. Francis Xavier's School which was run by Jesuit priests. The school was located near where they lived, in Hongkew, near the Sanjiaodi Market, a section of Shanghai which is on the other side of the Soochow Creek from the heart of the International Settlement.

The teachers there gave him the English name of Charles. Just as he was adjusting to learning English and French and doing well in his studies, his father (my grandfather) abruptly died. Charles was forced to leave school because his mother was unable to afford the tuition with the breadwinner now gone. My father would perhaps have to find an apprenticeship to learn a trade and earn his own keep. The pension my grandfather's shipping company paid to the widow was certainly not enough to see him through school.

When my father told his Jesuit teachers of his plight, they were sympathetic. They knew what a good student he was and told him that they would help him by waiving his tuition fees so he could stay on to finish his studies. Their generosity did not change his mother's mind because attending St. Francis Xavier's School meant that he had to dress, not well, but cleanly, and she was reluctant to spend 'unnecessary' money when she needed to put aside some for a rainy day, for his eventual marriage, and for her own old age. But my father would not consider being an apprentice when he was sure that with a good education, he would find a good job. So the 'dress' problem was solved when the parents of some of his foreign classmates, many of whom, Germans, Danes or British with names like Beirwirth, Limbaugh and Artindale, gave him their 'hand-me-downs.' My father was smaller in built than most of his classmates, so his clothes hung loosely off him as he made his way to and from class.

My father stayed on at St. Francis Xavier's until he finished school and then got a job working for Siemens, while taking evening classes at the Lester Institute and La Salle correspondence course to continue his education. His mother came to realize that his decision had been the right one since working for Siemens meant he was earning much more than he would if he had been just an apprentice to a local shopkeeper.

My mother, Poon Mayling, also a Cantonese, was an orphan who did not know who her birth parents were except that there was a woman whom she called her 'godmother' who was a Buddhist, or Taoist, nun. My mother was taken into a Eurasian family with the last name of Hawes. She was treated better than a maid, but not nearly as well as a member of the family. There she learned to speak English, but she was not given an education in either Chinese or English. When she was of marriageable age, different relatives of the Hawes family tried to get her introduced to different Eurasian men. Nothing worked out because she was Chinese, and illiterate, to boot. When she was in her late twenties or early thirties, a Mrs Johnston introduced her to my father. It was love at first sight. But when his mother learned that this woman her son loved was around thirty years of age, she put her foot down saying any woman that age would be too old to have children. My grandmother did all she could to introduce her son to younger girls, but he would not even look at them and vowed that he would not marry unless it was to my mother. This 'cold war' went on for at least a couple of years, and my grandmother was worried that if it continued any longer my father would be too old to find a wife. When, eventually, my grandmother buckled, the bride and groom were both in their thirties. Being the only child, my father had no choice but to stay with his mother after he married. So my mother had to make the adjustment of living with a mother in-law who did not really like her, in addition to living in a totally different world from the Eurasian home, which was all she had known until then.

One unwritten 'law' among the Eurasians I knew was that if they married at all, it was never to a Chinese nor to anyone who had more Chinese blood than they did because they were afraid of a 'throwback', meaning to have Chinese-looking children. Most of the Eurasians I knew, stateless or otherwise, were very Chinese-looking and mostly married other half-Chinese.

Despite my grandmother's worry that any woman older than her late twenties would not have children, my mother was already expecting me! So my grandmother busied herself asking her mahjongg cronies for recipes that would ensure an expectant mother would give birth to a boy instead of a girl. The foods recommended included steamed quails with gingko and other medicinal herbs and jelly made from donkey hide extract with dates and walnut meats. In addition to all that, she also sought the help of fortune-tellers, asking them if her daughter in-law was going to have a boy, as she fervently hoped. The fortune-teller she trusted the most told her that if her daughter in-law's firstborn was a boy, he would not live. But if the firstborn was a girl, and if she could survive the first three years, she would live on. She never told either her son or his wife about what the fortune-teller said, but did acquaint all her friends about it.

I think my mother must have reeked of steamed quails and donkey hide extract by the time she delivered me. I was a big fat baby when I was born, looking more like an over-ripe tomato than anything else. I had what appeared to be boils all over me, especially under my left arm and on my right buttock. I had to be operated on immediately. I was bleeding badly and the bad flesh and pus had to be cleaned away with cotton and gauze-covered sticks inserted into the wounds to clean them out. I have around a dozen scars from these operations performed right after birth that I will carry for life. But in spite of the ordeal, I survived and gained weight, and stayed roly-poly into my twenties and later life.

My mother was relieved that her mother in-law did not show any disappointment in having a female firstborn grandchild. On the contrary, she found that the old lady was quite a good grandmother and was proud that the baby was so fat, saying that the nutritious prenatal diet of steamed quails and donkey hide jelly that she had so carefully prepared for so many months was to thank for the baby's good health.

Being a fat baby was a 'painful' experience. Neighbors, friends, and relatives would pinch me and pretend to bite and gnaw at my fat arms and legs whenever they saw me, even though I had no legs because they were thighs all the way down. Some even asked if I was bloated, to which my mother responded with a typical Cantonese *"daigatleisee"* and touched wood. Pictures taken during that time showed that I was thriving. But my grandmother still kept in mind what the fortune-teller had told her -- that if the female child could survive the first three years, she would live on. otherwise....

The old Chinese way of calculating age was that a child is one year old when born, which is quite reasonable since it had already developed for nine months before birth. We gain a year in age on Chinese New Year's day. So, if a child were born on Chinese New Year's Eve, he would be two years old the following day even though he is only 2 days old according to the old way of counting age. I was born on the twenty-eighth day of the first moon (month) of the Lunar Calendar, I would be two years' old by the time my first Chinese New Year came around, and three years old the following one.

The family dinner on Chinese New Year's Eve is the one important gathering for any family, very much like an American Thanksgiving. Unknown to my parents, my grandmother had been keeping her fingers crossed, because I would be three years' old the following day, and if nothing bad happened to me I would survive for years to come. During the meal, my mother sat me on her dressing-table to feed me, and when she turned around to get me more food, I toppled and fell, cutting my forehead on the jagged edge of an old Standard Oil Company kerosene tin which was used as a garbage bin. I began to bleed like a pig.

Being Chinese New Year's Eve, the streets were not full of empty rickshaws as they usually were, but my mother eventually found one and took me to the General Hospital by Soochow Creek, run by Catholic nuns dressed in gray or grayish-blue habits with starched hats shaped like huge *wontons*. My cut was taken care of by the doctor and we were sent home with my head all bandaged up in white gauze, like a chief mourner at a Chinese funeral.

My mother braced herself for what her mother in-law would say for not taking care of me, but to her great surprise, not only did my grandmother not blame her for the accident, but she

6

also kept muttering "good, good" which greatly infuriated my mother. They quarreled then and there, with my mother crying and saying that just because the child was a girl, the grandmother had no feelings for her. My poor father, a very filial son, was caught in the middle. He could not condemn his wife and neither could he condone what his mother had said. He always said that the back of his hand and the palm were made of the same flesh. It was only after several years following my grandmother's death that one of her close friends told my mother about what the fortune-teller had said about me.

The history of Shanghai as an international port began in the mid-1840s after the Opium War, and it grew to be a metropolis that has been used as a backdrop for many a book and Hollywood movie. To the world and the people who knew it only superficially, the Bund was a microcosm of that city. Along the Bund were the offices of world-class foreign banks and companies, and the consulates of foreign countries. The Garden Bridge, in Chinese called Waibaidu Qiao (meaning 'the outer bridge which can be crossed for free') was the first of many bridges which spanned the Soochow Creek, running perpendicular to the Whangpoo River, which divided the city into what was known as Hongkew, the British or International Settlement and the French Concession. Our family lived in Hongkew for a short time before we moved to the International Settlement.

The many stately buildings along the Bund facing Pootung (Pudong) with the Whangpoo River running between, housed the many foreign banks and companies, such as the Hongkong & Shanghai Bank, and companies such as Jardine Matheson, Butterfield & Swire and Glen Line. Further on was the French Concession where the French Consulate stood. That part of the Bund was known as the French Bund.

The Power Company, the Water Works, the Telephone Company, the Gas Company and the Telegraph Company, and other companies which provided the essential services of the city were all foreign-owned. It seemed as if all world-class foreign companies and banks had an office in Shanghai at that time.

The city also had its share of Chinese people from other parts of the country. The true natives of Shanghai were the Pootung people and people who lived on the outskirts of the city such as Kiangwan (Jiangwan) and Chapei (Zhabei), almost all farmers.

People from the northern part of Jiangsu Province, sometimes referred to derogatively, provided the cheap labor for the city in doing menial work, such as garbage and human waste collection and disposal, while others worked as barbers, coolies and other forms of manual labor of the 'lowest' order. There were even 'manure lords', thugs who monopolized the sewage outlets, and sold the human waste to farmers from the nearby countryside who came for it in boats. The human waste from the more affluent parts of town was more expensive than that from the poorer parts and slums. I presume its quality is closely related to what food the people consumed. All that was before anyone had heard of chemical fertilizer.

Generally speaking, societies are divided into the Haves and the Have-nots, and a closer look at the old Shanghai society showed it also to be, politics aside, racist, to say the least. Shanghai, being a world of its own, had little in common with the rest of China, except in the stark, naked poverty which could be found in some hidden corners of the city. The city had smaller societies within itself, and these smaller societies were subdivided into yet smaller societies on the different rungs of the social ladder. A good example was the staff structure of a foreign bank or company, or the many associations formed by people from the different parts of the country.

8

The very top rung of the social ladder of that foreign-dominated time and place was allocated to the English, or to be more exact, any 'pure' Caucasian from their native birthplace, be it the British Isles, the United States, Canada, or any European or Scandinavian country, who were sent by the home offices as chief executive officers of their Shanghai offices, or the consuls of the different countries. A rung below that were the Caucasian staff from the home offices working as departmental heads, and after that came the locally-employed Caucasian or Eurasian staff with foreign last names — with or without passports, for many were stateless. Then came the locally-employed Chinese staff who were either overseas-born or with foreign last names because some had foreign passports, many gotten by hook, but mostly by crook — by bribing corrupt consulate officials. The locally-employed Chinese staff with Chinese last names, like my own father, lay between the above-mentioned categories and the janitorial workers at the very bottom of that specific social ladder.

People who were employed as doormen of good hotels and watchmen of foreign companies and warehouses were mostly Sikhs from India, popularly referred to as the "Red-headed Number Threes", "Red-headed" because most of them were turbaned with red or orange colored cloth, and "number threes" because they were people of little consequence, or perhaps because the Shanghai dialect equivalent sounded very much like 'yes, sir'.

In competition with the secular world, in which the different banks and companies efficiently served the material needs of the city, were the missionaries of the different Christian denominations and the Catholic church orders such as the Jesuits, the Carmelites, the Franciscans, and others, each of which built their own churches and missions to serve the city's spiritual needs, even though most of the Chinese were either Buddhists,

9

Taoists, or atheists. There was the China Inland Mission, which later became the Overseas Mission Service, based in Singapore; the Free Christian Church, a church with an English-speaking congregation, and the Endeavourers' Church, formerly known as the Endeavourers' Sunday School which grew from the Ragged Sunday School, started by the Reverend H.G.C. Hallock of Rochester, New York. There was also the Trinity Cathedral which was an Anglican and English-speaking church attended by the English-speaking people of the social upper rung. The Moore Memorial Church and the Community Church and many others had services in Chinese, and there were other Protestant churches which had services in Cantonese. The German Lutheran Church, meanwhile, had its services in German. There were also Jewish synagogues, plus a Greek Orthodox Church. The number of Chinese-speaking church-going people far out-numbered the English-speaking ones.

The Protestant and Catholic missionary influence also extended to the fields of education and medicine. There were numerous missionary schools covering all ages and convents. In higher education, the two best known Protestant universities were Shanghai University and St. John's University, while St. Francis Xavier's College and Aurora College were the Catholic ones. The General Hospital, St. Luke's Hospital, St.Mary's Hospital were run by the Catholics.

But between the Caucasians and the Chinese, there was another group, the Eurasian community. Shanghai would also not have become as successful as it did had it not been for the people suspended between the two worlds. Many were English-speaking people, and many of mixed ancestry. But there were also many local Chinese who fitted into the category - missionary school-educated, literate in English but illiterate or semi-literate in their own native language of Chinese. These people served as a bridge between the foreign and local cultures. It was that community into which I was born.

There are no records to tell us how the Eurasian community of Shanghai came into being. From what I was told by older people, it could have branched out from the Eurasian communities of Canton and Hong Kong since nearly all the Eurasians of Shanghai at that particular time were Cantonese-speaking, whereas the natives of Shanghai spoke only Shanghai dialect, with a very strong rural accent. It also could have been that when some Chinese females found themselves giving birth to foreign-looking babies, they were looked down upon, if not actually becoming outcasts from Chinese society. And as outcasts, they could have moved together to give each other support, and slowly formed a community of their own.

From stories that I had heard as a child, there was a community of "boat people" or "boat women" - *tengdzaipaw* literally meaning 'sampan woman' in Cantonese. The younger females were known as *hahmsuimui* or 'salt-water lasses,' and they could have had babies from visiting sailors, and had branched out from the south China ports to Shanghai, being the thriving port that it was. Some of the men could have returned to claim their mates and children, and eventually settled down, multiplied, and formed a community of their own.

The Chinese side of society was also stratified, and in addition, clannish. Like New York City, Shanghai is a city of immigrants. People from the same birthplace banded together to form different associations while various guilds and associations looked after their own kind. The Cantonese were considered 'outsiders' in Shanghai, and so they banded together and even bought a big piece of land to bury their dead. It was known as the Cantonese Cemetery. The Cantonese were mostly engaged in the restaurant business, running grocery stores. Later on, the more educated ones, some of whom had returned from foreign countries, were engaged in the department store business. The four biggest department stores in Shanghai, the Sun Company, the Wing On Company, the Sun Sun Company, and the Sincere Company were all owned by Cantonese, some of whom had been laborers in Australia and returned to China with a fortune. The Swatownese were engaged in the lace and embroidery business. The Ningpo people were mostly involved in banking, shipping and tailoring.

Foreign companies, big and small, abounded in the city, and provided employment for local Caucasians, Eurasians, and the English-educated Chinese population. Anyone employed in a foreign company consider himself lucky. For any Chinese, to be employed as a clerk in Customs House or at the Hongkong & Shanghai Bank, or any other place of equal caliber, was good fortune. Having a job in a company of good standing was like having a "golden rice bowl" even if that bowl was not always full.

However, there was the seamy, and often sleazy, side of the city that few foreigners knew of, or cared to learn about. Shanghai society then was a polarized one. The rich had more money than they knew what to do with it while the poor did not know where their next meal was coming from. The distribution of wealth in the society was in the shape of a diamond, racially separated at its widest, to make two pyramids. One was foreign, the other Chinese. At their tips were the very rich foreigners and the wealthy Chinese, and at their bases were the very poor Chinese and non-Chinese such as the Greeks, the gypsies, the Sikhs, and many of the Jews and Russians. It was into such a society that I was born.

I cannot trace my roots back further than my grandfather. My father, Sun Chuksam (1905-1993), had a name which could be taken to mean "Blessed by the Trinity" even though he was not a Christian at birth. In his Siemens and Caltex (Texaco) records, he is known as Charles Suin. My mother Poon Mayling, or Fanny, (1905-1991) grew up as something between a housemaid and an adopted child in the home of a Cantonese and English-speaking Eurasian family with the last name of Hawes, who lived in a house in Frenchtown, on Avenue Victor Emanuel. The head of the household was Mr Hawes (1868-1943 ca.) whom we affectionately called "Ah Gung" (Grandpa). He was a kind old man, short in stature, and quite deaf. He had a job with the Shanghai Water Works. His sister, Kate, married a Mr Wood who was a manager of the Works. Mrs Hawes, also a Eurasian, was a member of the Pomeroy family and she died before I was born. Mr and Mrs Hawes had three children. A son, James Pomeroy Hawes, worked for the Standard Oil (Socony) Company until it was liquidated in the early 1950s, and two daughters, Lily and Violet. Of the three of them, only Violet married, to someone by the name of Ollerdessen. After she married, she left for the US and settled down in the Bay Area of San Francisco.

Like many Cantonese and English-speaking Eurasians of that generation, Mr Hawes and his wife were very Caucasian in appearance, and many of their children were blue-eyed and blond. Families like theirs made up the Cantonese and English-speaking Eurasian community of Shanghai, and they were likely to be the second or even third generation of mixed ancestry. Strangely enough, nearly all the women in that community dressed like their Chinese sisters of that time, and a few of their husbands also dressed like their Chinese brethren, especially if they were not employed by foreign companies, perhaps due to poor English.

Deafness prevailed in quite a few of the offspring of the

related Eurasian families, and most of the males and females from those families of my mother's generation stayed single, for various reasons. A Eurasian with a non-Chinese name would not condescend to marry a Chinese with no foreign blood, nor would a Chinese, male or female, from a well-to-do family think of marrying someone of mixed ancestry. And since many families were related to each other one way or another, the younger generation tended not to intermarry.

Shanghai was a very tolerant city toward 'outsiders' and foreigners. With the possible exception of American Indians or Eskimos, Shanghai had people of every race and creed. It was an immigrant city, and aside from its international population, its population was made up of people from other provinces of China, especially Zhejiang and Guangdong. A person's accent could often put him or her in a very disadvantageous position. Anyone who spoke with a Jiangbei accent would immediately be mentally assigned to the bottom rung of the social ladder. A man, however masculine and virile in appearance, speaking in the Soochow dialect would immediately be tagged a sissy. The Ningbo dialect, on the other hand, is blunt and harsh. So we have this saying, "One would rather quarrel with someone from Soochow than converse with someone from Ningpo."

As children, we liked to make fun of our Ningpo playmates by mimicking them. The most common mimicry was the "Doe Lay (Ray) Me", a dialogue between a mother and son.

Mother: Lay (ray) Fa! (the son's name)

Son: Sew Si La? (What's the matter?)

Mother: Me sew si doe lay. (Pass me the cotton thread)

Son: Sew me sew si?(Which kind of cotton thread?)

Mother: Lay me sew si. (The blue cotton thread.)

Son: Lay me sew si doe lay (The blue cotton thread is here.)

The other one was
Mother: Lay Fa!
Son: Sew si la? (What is the matter?)
Mother: Doe me. (Go wash some rice.)
Son: Doe sew me? (Wash which kind of rice?)
Mother: Doe doe me. (Wash the good kind.)
Son: Doe me fa doe? (How do I go about doing it?)
and so on and so forth.

The educated people, and especially those working in foreign companies, had a habit of mixing English words into their Chinese conversations, or else spoke entirely in English. These people were often ridiculed by others who could not speak a foreign language. I remember hearing "eat Chinese, fart foreign" behind my back more than once when I was out shopping with someone who spoke no Chinese. The resentment was not against the individual, but built up over the years, tracing back to the Opium War when some foreigners treated Chinese like animals, on their own native soil.

Shanghai was a city of extremes. Aside from the very poor Chinese, there were many gypsy squatters in French Town, especially near Rue La Tour and Rue Remi. These people all spoke Shanghai dialect fluently and had big families with many children. The grownups had no permanent employment, but survived on what they could beg from foreigners and Chinese who had something to spare.

There was a place called the Jewish Camp in Hongkew. It was not a camp in the real sense because it was not surrounded by walls or barbed wire, but rather a community where many Jewish families were concentrated. The Jewish people lived there in peace while their fellowmen were being persecuted in Europe. Many of the richest people in Shanghai were also Jews, and many of those in the Jewish Camp were professionals and intellectuals and were able to find a foothold in the city. They had their own places of worship and their own schools for their children to receive a traditional education.

As for the Eurasian community, families with parents who were Eurasians themselves were mostly Cantonese-speaking, but families with one Chinese parent and the other Caucasian of whatever nationality were not. In families where the father was Chinese and the mother European or American, the children had Chinese names and often attended Chinese schools. Such families were almost all highly educated. In many cases, the Chinese father had been a student who had earned his doctoral degree in a foreign country and married a local girl before returning to China. The children were also highly educated and tended to become professionals in their own right, and nearly all of those who remained left the country in the early 1980s and established themselves either in Europe or the United States, after experiencing the abominable Cultural Revolution. But with families where the father was European or American, and the mother Chinese, the children attended non-Chinese schools. No one from such families remained in China after the late 1950s and early 1960s.

The Cantonese-English-speaking Eurasian community was not big but some of its members were very influential and rich. These people were different from the Cantonese-English-speaking Eurasian community of Hong Kong, as represented by the late Sir Robert Ho-Tung, who was proud to call himself Chinese. Such people in Shanghai all had foreign last names, and would never call themselves Chinese even though the Chinese genes were obvious in the way many of them looked. If they had no passports, they would much rather be referred to as 'stateless' than Chinese.

One thing these two communities had in common was their wealth and influence. Most people of my parents' generation know of a man—let's call him 'Tam'—who was a Cantonese-English speaker, and how he became one of the richest of that community. He started as a lowly office boy working in the Shanghai Municipal Council in the the International Settlement. One of his jobs was to go around the conference room filling the tea cups of the participants during meetings. He was not well-educated but he was bright and quick on the uptake, quite Caucasian in appearance and eager to please. He understood enough English to know what was being discussed at those meetings, and as the city councilors reviewed city development plans, red circles were made on the city map and he was clever enough to identify the locations. He found people who would pay for such information. As time went by, he became wiser, and under an assumed name, bought property in the about-to-be developed areas himself and then sold to the city government for a handsome profit. No one surpassed him in business savvy and eventual wealth. He was fluent in Cantonese, Shanghainese and English, and both the Chinese and foreigners trusted him, because he had what was needed to deal with both parties. He left his mark on the city as all old Shanghai people will remember there was a jail named after him. And at one time he owned most of the godowns (warehouses) along the river. He died in his late seventies, shortly after 1949. He still has descendants living in different parts of the world today.

After the Sino-Japanese War officially broke out in 1937, there were rumors that the Japanese would formally take over Hongkew and close the bridges that linked Hongkew with the main part of the International Settlement. Many residents in Hongkew panicked, especially those families with bread-winners working on the 'wrong' side of the Creek, people like my father. One day, some months later, the rumors proved true and the Japanese closed the bridges.

My father went to work that day as usual, and only my grandmother and my mother and I were at home. There was nothing to do except to escape to the International Settlement before it was too late. My mother, several months pregnant with a second baby, me in her arms and holding on to my grandmother, a prematurely old woman with a big belly and chopstick-thin legs, managed to make it across the bridge. My mother's 'valuables' had been taken to Uncle Jimmy's (James Pomeroy Hawes) house in Frenchtown several months earlier when the rumors first circulated.

My grandmother and mother looked up former neighbors who had moved into the British Concession earlier. They found them housed in the China Trust Company at 156 Peking Road, next door to the China Sunday School Union and the Chinese Christian Bookstore on the corner of Museum Road. The CTC was a four-story building. On the ground floor was the bank owned by an overseas Chinese (Cantonese) with the family name of Li. On the second floor were offices, small rooms each with balconies. On the third floor were the bank's dining hall and recreation room, and another big room partitioned into cubicles for offices. The fourth floor had tiny rooms with no balconies which served as a dormitory for single men, employees and college students.

The rooms on the second floor were now rented out to individual refugee families from Hongkew, people like our family. Several of the families were old neighbors of my grandmother's and childhood friends of my father's. There was Uncle Giles and his family of two wives, three sons and a daughter living in Rooms 16 and 17 which had verandahs facing Sichuan Road. Giles worked for the British American Tobacco

Company, otherwise known as B.A.T., located a block away. Giles was Cantonese like we were, but he, somehow or other, had managed to get a foreign name, and so earned foreign pay at B.A.T. The other family, also Cantonese, consisted of Jorge Gonzalez, and his wife and two daughters, were in Room 15 which was right next to the one and only toilet, public faucet and sink for the families on the entire floor. JG was my father's classmate at St. Francis Xavier's, younger by a couple of months. He had become a Catholic while he was at SFX and had adopted the surname of his godparents, worked in a foreign bank under that foreign name and therefore earned foreign pay.

Macau, like Hong Kong, was inhabited by Cantonese-speaking Chinese. It was a Portuguese colony and Cantonese women who had children with Portuguese men, sailors and others, could claim Portuguese citizenship for their offspring. Such people were referred to as Macanese, but known derogatively as 'haam ha tsaang', which means something like 'salted shrimp grub', a product for which Macau was known. In the 1920s and 1930s, there was a corrupt official in the Portuguese Consulate in Shanghai who sold passports to anyone with the money to buy them. JG was among those who had gotten their Portuguese passports that way.

My grandmother, on the basis of her age and her past relationship with these former neighbors, demanded that Giles' Wife No.1 find her a room on the same floor, and she was willing to pay the deposit and the first three months' rent in silver dollars. After a long haggling session, we were finally given Room No. 6 on the second floor, with a verandah facing Peking Road. The family stayed in this room for the following half a century and more, and until very recently was still occupied by my youngest brother and his family.

My parents' home in Hongkew was looted and occupied

by a family the very day we left it. All done by neighbors who had known beforehand that my parents were going to move to the British Concession because of my father's job. My parents did not return to their former place even after the bridges were reopened, nor did they once venture into that old neighborhood during the fifty-odd years following their departure. I think a visit would have been too painful because they had lost everything, everything that my grandparents and my father had accumulated throughout the years. Nothing much, perhaps, but it was all they had had. In the decades that followed, neither our parents nor any one of us children have ever had the desire of looking for our parents' first home.

So, life began again, almost from scratch, with three generations in one room. In a way, my mother was happy with the move because she was now nearer the Hawes, the Fords, the Johnstons and the Ward families, people who were good to her and for whom she cared a lot. Nearly all members of those families who were of my mother's generation had jobs working for firms along the Bund. Most lived at the other end of town, on Yuyuan Road, and brought their lunch to work. They would often come to our room at noon with their lunches and my mother would serve them cups of hot tea. Some would have Cantonese fried noodles from nearby food stands, and would always buy more than they could finish so that we would also have a treat. They would each give my mother some pocket money every payday, even after my mother was married and had a home of her own. My mother had no blood relatives, and these aunties and uncles were her closest friends and she treasured them. One of my uncles gave me the name Margaret, after the younger sister of the future Queen of England, Elizabeth.

We were on the same block as Ward Building on Sichuan Road, which is also next to the Navy "Y", and around the corner was the Banker's Club which faced the China Bible House on Hong Kong Road. We lived right next door to the China Sunday School Union and the Chinese Christian Bookstore which was on the corner of Peking and Museum Road, and Mr and Mrs 'T' were one street away, on Yuan Ming Yuan Road, on the top floor of a building which overlooks the grounds of the British Consulate. I remember, after V-J Day, at night from their verandah, with the help of a telescope, I could see movies on the decks of U.S. Navy ships anchored on the Whangpoo River.

Life went on in Shanghai pretty much as it always had, even though the rest of China was in turmoil because of the Japanese invasion. The city had always been a Mecca for beggars from northern Jiangsu and other nearby provinces where natural disasters were annual occurrences. But during the Japanese war there were even larger numbers of beggars flocking to the city. They usually came as families, sometimes of three generations. The father would be carrying a shoulder pole with a basket on each end, one holding a roll of tattered wadding, and in the other usually a young child or two holding out begging bowls for food. The wife would have a baby inside her jacket, kept in position with a rope tied around her waist, and supporting an old lady or old man, usually her in-laws, walking with the help of a bamboo stick. Such people had no clear destination, and would stop to sleep at night wherever they happened to be. The sticks served two purposes, one to support the elderly as they walked, the other for defense. These beggar sticks were referred to as 'dagougwun' in Cantonese, literally meaning 'hit dog stick.' The rich kept dogs to keep away beggars and that stick came in handy to keep the dogs at bay.

When the weather turned cold, these thinly-clad beggars died like flies, so there were always plenty of dead to be collected. Different charity organizations sent people out with shoddy coffins stacked on pushcarts to pick up the dead each morning. Some corpse, especially those of babies and young children, were not always whole because the dogs had feasted on them before daybreak. It never failed to send chills through anyone's spine to see the carts go by. The dead were treated like sides of beef, just picked up and dumped inside the coffin with a thud. Many corpses were so curled up to protect themselves from the cold that the coffin lids could not be closed.

There were Japanese soldiers in Shanghai and they were referred to as *'lobaktau'* in Cantonese, meaning turnip heads, because of their modest height. When children were naughty or refused to go to bed at night, they would be threatened with a 'The Japanese devils are coming!' or the 'bong-bong man is coming' meaning Japanese priests who went around with a leather drum which he hits with a stick. In a word, anything Japanese was abhorred, especially the sight of Japanese soldiers with their bayonets and swords. The grown-ups, those with spending money, boycotted anything that was made in Japan. In fact, in those days, any shoddy product was referred to as 'east ocean product' (*dongyuengfoh*), meaning a Japanese product.

Nearly every family living on the second floor of CTC was Cantonese, and we felt a lot closer squeezed together in that small space. The backdoor of the building led into Flying Phoenix Lane which was mainly occupied by Cantonese, Swatownese, and Ningpo families.

After the war began, Japanese soldiers stood guard on the bridges spanning Soochow Creek. Chinese men were to bow (90 degrees) to them whenever they passed on their way to and from Hongkew. My father avoided going to Hongkew because it meant crossing one of those bridges.

When I was old enough to go to school, I spent a week or two at a preschool near us, next to the Union Church across from the Rowing Club, at the far end of Yuan Ming Yuan Road. It was called Miss Molim's School, but it was too expensive for me to stay longer. My father taught me to read and write simple English and Chinese, but mostly by requiring me to learn by rote passages from a popular Chinese (Cantonese) almanac which was called the *'toongsing'* in Cantonese even though it was really the *'toong sue'*, but because the character *'sue'* for 'book' has the same sound as the word for 'to lose' (at gambling), that it was changed to *'sing'*, a homonym for the word 'to win'. This *'toongsing'* has not been seen in Shanghai for the last half century or so, but is readily available in Hong Kong and other places overseas where there are Cantonese communities. The almanac included many proverbs and wise sayings, nearly all of which I remember to this day, but I had no idea as to their meaning when I learned them by rote as a young child. Proverbs like *"It is better to save one life than to build a seven-tier pagoda,"* or *"It is better to lack in righteousness than to exceed in evil."*

Most Cantonese of my father's generation knew these sayings and many more, learned by rote as I did. The sayings were summaries of keen observation of human behavior and the *'toongsing'* was a "must" in every Cantonese household, frequently consulted. Many Chinese, and Cantonese, customs which were considered 'feudal' were banned after 1949, but they have remained intact elsewhere in Chinese communities. Whether they were 'feudal' or not, they were, and in many cases still are, part of Chinese culture, ancient and unique.

All the Chinese reading that was taught in Cantonese because my father spoke no Shanghainese even though he was born and raised there. But for me, Cantonese, Shanghainese and English were learned at about the same time, but Mandarin (Putonghua) did not come until much later in my life.

Soon after the Japanese bombed Pearl Harbor, Americans and British people in Shanghai, including Chinese with American or British passports were put into internment camps. It was the parallel of the internment camps in which people of Japanese descent in the United States were confined. The one difference was that the Japanese did not confiscate the property from the people who were interned, and so their homes were left untouched, at least the homes of those whom my parents knew, perhaps because they were still occupied by the parents of those interned, many of whom did not have foreign passports, and were considered either stateless or Chinese.

Nearly all our aunties and uncles had to go to the different internment camps, which were on the outskirts of the city, across the river in Pudong, in Lunghwa, and another in Chapei.

My grandmother died in her seventies in 1942 in St. Luke's Hospital, next door to the Trinity Cathedral. According to the Cantonese custom, the chief mourner, in this case, my father, was supposed to remain unshaven until the end of the mourning period, which can drag on for up to one hundred days. But since he was working at Siemens, he could not conform to the custom. The funeral was managed entirely by my grandmother's *mahjjong* cronies, and professional mourners were hired to cry whenever visitors came to pay their respects to the dead who was lying in an open coffin. The funeral was held in a rented hall of a temple to which my grandmother had made monthly donations. The initial funeral rite lasted three days, and on the third day the coffin was covered, nailed and a rooster was killed, his blood smeared on the lid of the coffin as it was taken to the cemetery. The funeral cortege was led by my father, the chief mourner, clothed in white and hemp, then came my mother and then came the grandchildren.

My grandmother was buried in the Cantonese Cemetery.

The Cantonese, being a very innovative people, had the unique custom of burying their dead twice. The first time is the normal burial, and the second burial is called *'japgwat'*, meaning 'the gathering of the bones', which occurs years after, when the body has thoroughly decayed and the bones are gathered and put in a clay container. I think the custom aims to make full use of the limited land because after the body and the coffin decay, the space is vacated if only a clay container is buried in its place.

The Cantonese commemorate the death of a loved one with seven Sevenths. The Initial Seventh is the first week after the death. My grandmother's Initial Seventh which was celebrated in a big hall at the temple where the funeral was held. Before the meal was served, there were plates of salted white pumpkin seeds and black watermelon seeds for the guests. Black and white were mourning colors, so there were no red watermelon seeds, usually served on festive occasions. All the food served was vegetarian including various dishes of bean products, such as bean curd *(tofu)* which is of mourning color. These dishes never lost their popularity with Shanghai people of different birth origins. In later years, there was a food shop right next door to the former Carlton Theater (next door to Hall & Holtz and across from the Park Hotel), by the name of *Gung De Lin* which sold exclusively such vegetarian dishes.

By this time, I had two siblings, my sister Betty, and a brother 'Junior'. My father was still working for Siemens as late as in 1943 or early 1944. Employees were encouraged to take their families to watch German documentaries at the German School near Bubbling Well Road. One day while we were waiting for my father to return home for lunch, a Chinese colleague from Siemens came running up, panting, and told my mother that ".Mr Sun has been bitten by a mad dog." I took it literally, and pictured my father being torn to pieces by a mangy dog foaming at the mouth. Without a word to us, my mother grabbed a coat and flew out the door with the messenger. She did not return until late at night, alone. All the neighbors came rushing in to inquire what had happened.

It seemed that just before lunch that day, a young man named Ah Leem G'aw who lived in another room on the same floor as ours had carried a big bundle wrapped in a bed sheet to my father's office and deposited it there, telling him that he would come for it at noon. My father stayed behind waiting for him, but Ah Leem G'aw returned with two policemen accompanying him, and he was in handcuffs, beaten black and blue, and bleeding profusely. It seemed he had taken cash from the safe of a company where he worked as a cashier, bundled it up in a bed sheet and left it with my father without telling him what was inside the bundle, then went back to open another safe when he was caught in the act. He was then taken to the police station and beaten half-dead. He confessed that the money from the first safe was "at Siemens with a Mr Sun". The police opened the bundle under my father's desk, and sure enough, it was money. My father was handcuffed and taken away to jail, without being given a chance to explain himself. Ah Leem G'aw died the following day from the torture.

There was no way my father could clear himself since there were no witnesses to prove his innocence. Siemens fired him without one cent of severance pay even though he had worked for them for many years and had a squeaky-clean record. All his Chinese colleagues vouched for his honesty, but to no avail. The German manager declared that the company had never been so disgraced. It was unheard-of to have one of their employees handcuffed and taken away by the police.

There was nothing my mother could do except to appeal to my father's Chinese colleagues for help because the German manager refused to talk to her. My father's colleagues found a good lawyer to defend him, but he still had to spend one night in jail. He was freed the following day.

For a long time after that, my father avoided walking on Nanking Road where Siemens was located. It was too painful for him to be near the place he had worked for so many years. The incident scarred my father for life.

When my father returned home the next day, at the advice of a superstitious old neighbor, he had to step over a basin with burning charcoal, supposedly to get rid of the bad luck brought from the prison cell. Although my father had only been away for one day, he had aged overnight. I noticed that his face was unshaven, but he was unscratched. I turned up his trouser legs to see where he had been bitten, but could find no wounds. I later learned that 'bitten by a mad dog' meant 'to be framed'.

Now we were without a breadwinner. There was no income whatsoever, and all our aunties and uncles on whom we could have called for help were interned in camps, and those who were not, had problems of their own. But, as the Chinese saying goes, "A live person will not let his bladder burst." My father found an old wooden box and attached four old ball-bearings to the ends of two wooden axles and made a 'cart' towed with a rope. He sat me in the box, and off we went to a dock somewhere near the Gas Company on Tibet Road, bought a sackful of sweet potatoes from the boat people. With my father towing the rope in front and me pushing from behind, we brought our load home. My mother scrubbed the sweet potatoes clean and boiled them and put them in an enamel bucket wrapped around with a blanket to keep them from getting cold, and told me to go down to the street with it, sat me on a little stool outside the building, hugging onto the bucket of sweet potatoes, to sell them.

My father had always gone to work in suit and tie, and my

mother had never gone out without wearing make-up, earrings, and presentable clothes. It is a Shanghai trait from which the old saying "鸡窝飞出金凤凰" (from the chicken coop emerges a golden phoenix) originated. Regardless of how humble your abode, you have to dress presentably to preserve 'face'. I think that lasted until the time of doing away with the 'four olds' in the 1960s. My mother, and lots of other women like her, never went out without make-up or earrings. She always said she felt 'naked' without them. (I think she got used to being 'naked' in later years).

It was just not possible for either of them to make the rapid descent overnight. There was no on else at home except three young children, and as I was the oldest among the three, the job fell to me. I reluctantly sat outside as told, crying as I hugged onto that bucket of sweet potatoes. The day passed and not one potato was sold. I don't think people knew what was under the blanket. Several passersby had mistaken me for a lost child because I was crying, and asked if they could help me. My parents came for me when it was dark. We went home and sat around that unsold, now cold, bucket of sweet potatoes, and washed them with our salty tears. In the following decades, whenever I got together with my parents, we would still remember that incident, and tears would still be shed. But while the first tears were of humiliation, these later tears were of relief that we had survived it all.

This was the first time my father experienced unemployment, and for him it was emotionally devastating. We were left high and dry, with no source of income whatsoever. My parents were really desperate. But, as the Chinese saying goes, "Heaven does not lead a man into a dead-end street", meaning that there is always a way out of difficulties, regardless of how big they are.

A fellow-Cantonese, a Mr Mak who was working for a doctor practicing medicine illegally after his license was revoked because he had performed an unsuccessful abortion on the daughter of a high-ranking government official, lent my father the money to buy half a carton of cheap cigarettes and a box of matches, and suggested that I sit on the doorstep of our building to sell individual cigarettes on a tray, providing a free match to light them. That way, I need not hawk what was being sold because they were clearly seen, and unlike sweet potatoes, cigarettes did not get stale overnight. My parents were grateful for Mr Mak's help and did as suggested. The 'business' was considered 'successful' on the very first try since all the cigarettes on the tray were sold out before the day was done. That started my business career which spanned over two years, lasting until several months after VJ-Day in 1945.

Most of the KMT policemen bullied vendors, rickshaw coolies, and beggars. They had to find money elsewhere to feed their families because they were so poorly paid. But since I was only a child, I was spared. In fact, the corner policeman who operated the traffic lights, knew us well because my mother would go down to him with a cup of hot tea once or twice a day in the winter, and begged him to keep an eye on me so that people would not bully me. My business thrived, and instead of using just a tray for my wares, my father bought a box with a glass front and sat it on a stool while I sat on another smaller stool beside it. I learned to read the characters on the cigarette and match boxes.

I was soon joined by a newspaper stand attended by a little Jiangbei girl around my own age. We became good friends. We would giggle and hug, compare our sales, and take turns hawking the newspaper by yelling out the headline which we could not read, but had learned to repeat after her uncle had taught us, when he delivered the bundles of newspaper each morning. We became close, so close that I soon had lice on my hair and body like she did. My mother was horrified. I can still remember how painful it was to have my hair fine-combed after being scoured with kerosene. I stank. Prior to that I had recovered from a bout of typhoid fever which caused me to lose all my hair, but it had now grown back to its former length.

From this newspaper girl, not only did I learn to speak, but also to swear, in Jiangbei dialect. It was evident that I had a talent for mimicking. So, to correct that problem, my mother found some old knitting yarn and made me knit a sweater for myself to wear when the weather turned cold, since my hands were mostly free the entire day while I sat at my stall. With knitting, I had to concentrate so as not to miss a stitch, and that kept my mind occupied.

As I recall it, that sweater was never finished. But the skill of knitting came in handy several decades later when I took in knitting for my Kazakh neighbors in exchange for eggs or milk, when we were again living from hand-to-mouth. After learning how to knit, I did most of the knitting for the family.

A cardigan of my Grandmother's, or rather the yarn that was initially used to knit it, would last for three generations. Each year it would be unraveled, washed and knitted over, switching the yarn from the sleeves to knit the body, and vice versa, so that the yarn would wear out evenly. My father's cardigan mostly wore out at the elbows because of his work. Knitted items were not washed unless first unraveled in order to keep the wool from matting so that the yarn could be easily unraveled. If a sweater is washed whole, it usually mats, making it impossible to unravel later on.

My mother was home taking care of my younger siblings, doing the housework, and queuing up for what the Shanghai people called "*wukou mi*" (rationed rice) in front of the rice shop on Sichuan Road. Supplies were always erratic, some days there was some, and other days there wasn't any. There were several good-looking young women who lived nearby and who were well-acquainted with the clerks that worked in the rice shop. Whenever there was queuing for rice, no matter how late they came, they would always be at the front of the line. They were dubbed the 'rice-queue queens' and they were hated by everyone else. I wouldn't be surprised if they had been 'reminded' of their 'glorious reign' after Liberation, if they were still in the neighborhood.

Sometimes a prankster would go around the neighborhood and spread the rumor that rice was coming to the shop, and before long there would be a huge crowd of people standing in line in front of it, each with a number written in chalk on their shoulder to mark their place in the line. If it was a practical joke, people would be queuing up for hours for nothing.

The amount of rice sold to each family at one time would be very limited, enough to last for only a few days, which meant that each week at least two whole days would have to be spent in queuing for our 'daily bread'. People who did not have little children to take care of would spend the night sitting in front of the rice shop to keep their places, but my mother could not, and neither would she let my father go in her place because she knew what a 'softy' he was. My mother was the feisty kind who would stand her ground, whereas my father would turn the other cheek, so she knew it was futile to let him go and queue as he would most likely return empty-handed. My father was the kind of person 'you can't get a squeak out of him even if you clubbed him three times' as the Chinese saying goes. He took everything in silence and with a bowed head, too.

The importance of rice, the main source of food for those living south of the Yangtze River is reflected in the Chinese vocabulary. The word *fan*, which means cooked rice, is also the generic word for food, or a meal. When a Chinese person meets someone, we don't say "how are you?" but rather "Have you eaten cooked rice?" There's a joke about a man meeting a friend coming out of a public outhouse, still hitching up his pants, and still greeting him in the usual way: "Have you eaten…"

My father was busy looking for a job, but never having worked for a Chinese employer prior to leaving Siemens, he was unsure if his Chinese was good enough. He finally found work given to him by a former Chinese colleague at Siemens whose English was poor, and who had started his own business selling motors and generators. The shop was on Avenue Edward VII, diagonally across from the Whangpoo District Police Station. It was called Yuan Tai. My father was not offered a regular job with a regular salary, but the work provided my father with a free noon meal and a little pocket money. Something was better than nothing. "Even a fly is meat", as the Chinese saying goes, and beggars can't be choosers.

Meanwhile, the family lived on what could be earned from my 'business', and it was 'thriving'. The first glass-front box was soon replaced by a bigger one on four wheels. In addition to cigarettes and matches, candles, laundry soap and toilet paper were added to the commodities sold. When air raids became frequent, we added cheap cookies and pastries. Whenever the air raid siren sounded, the planes would usually be first sighted by people on the streets as sparkling, silvery dots in the sky, before the sirens wailed. When they did, there would be a curfew and the streets would be cordoned off and everything would be at a standstill until the sirens sounded again to signal that the planes had left.

Sometimes several hours would elapse between air raid soundings. People waiting on street corners were hungry and my cheap cookies and pastries sold like hot cakes. There were different kinds of cookies, one had peanut pieces stuck on top, another had a hole in the middle filled with custard or jam, still another was dotted with raisins. When no one was looking, I would pick the pieces of peanuts off the cookies, scoop off some jam or custard, or pick off some of the raisins. I could not resist the temptation.

The first time I tampered with the cookies happened just before an air raid siren sounded and I found that with or without the 'decorations', they sold just as fast. Times were hard, and no one would buy a cookie unless they were too hungry to wait till they got home. People would pay for the cookie with one hand and immediately stuff it into their mouths with the other, never noticing how badly 'pock-marked' they were. The cheapest pastries and cookies I sold were bought wholesale from a bakery near where my father worked, and each evening he would bring home a fresh batch. For me then, the most welcome sound was the air raid siren because it meant money for the family, and snacks for me. But, my luck ran out because there weren't air raid sirens every day, and I was left with unsold, but not undamaged wares, much to my parents' dismay.

Air raid sirens were also frightening because of the bombings that would sometimes follow. I saw truck loads of dead people from air raids, most of them naked and covered in plaster, looking paler than ever. Whenever a truck carrying the dead met a red light at our intersection, it never failed to leave behind streaks of red blood, soon turned black by flies feeding on them. Air raids were most frightening when one or both of my parents were not home. My imagination would run wild. If they were not back by the time they had promised, in my mind I would have them all dead and buried. That panicky feeling, that feeling of utter helplessness was most enfeebling. My temples would start to hammer, and my heart would pop into my mouth, and no matter how hard I tried to swallow to get it down to where it belonged it would not work because the passage would be blocked. I was the eldest of the children, and I dared not cry, because if I did, my sister and brother would follow suit, and pandemonium would result. The frightening thought that I would have to be the sole breadwinner, and father and mother to my sister and brother if my parents were dead.... The longer they were away, the wilder my imaginings became until I was in a frenzy. But, thank God, my parents, or one of them, would always appear just before I lost control of myself.

There was a German man named Mueller or Moller who lived in an apartment in the building across the street and was friendly and always neatly dressed. Because he knew that both my parents and I spoke English, he would sometimes stop to speak to us, and bought candles, laundry soap and other things from us. He was repatriated to Germany not long after the war ended. In another apartment in that building was a tall Russian prostitute named Jane who later became bed-ridden, and the only person who took care of her was the skinny Chinese beggar who for years had slept under the staircase of that same building.

It is hard to believe that a family of six, for by then I had another baby sister, could get by with my father's token job and my stand. I was out on the street from early morning till dark. We were given leftover food now and then by Auntie Ellie's mother, and ration tickets for bread from Auntie Mabel who had a Danish passport and did not have to go into an internment camp like her sisters and cousins. She worked for the Swiss Red Cross during the war dispatching care packages to the people in the various internment camps, and was rewarded for her efforts with an overseas trip after the war ended. Auntie Mabel and her family later left for Denmark where she was widowed. She stayed in a very good nursing home in Copenhagen until she died at a ripe old age.

Uncle Giles died, in the Country Hospital as befitted a 'foreigner', not long after Pearl Harbor. I think he died from drink as much as from shame. Up until then, he had passed for a British citizen, and earned foreign pay, too, even though he was Chinese (Cantonese) like we were. After Pearl Harbor, when all the people with British and American passports were registered and put into internment camps, he had nothing to show for being 'British' as he had claimed to be. It was not so much that he was afraid to go into camp—although he might have been—but rather the fear of being exposed for drawing foreign pay under false pretense for so many years. He was afraid he would be required to reimburse the company for all those years of 'extra' money that he had been getting, and there was no way he could do so, not with two wives and four grown children to support. He drowned his shame in drink, and drank himself to death.

My mother later told me that he had the surname of Giles because his mother had been a wash-woman who worked for someone with that name and who had paid for the boy's education at a local missionary school. When he finished school and applied for a job with the British American Tobacco Company, he used the name John Giles as he had in school, and he was never questioned about it. At that time in history and in that society, it was taken for granted that many Chinese had foreign names, and among them few were literate in their native language. Giles was one of them.

Even as a very young child I never liked Uncle Giles, and later that feeling was reciprocated. I did not like him because of his frequent pinches on my fat fanny and his affectionate bites on my fat arms and legs which really hurt. He always smelled of alcohol. He was referred to by his Wife No.1 as Drunken Cat. But, when he was tipsy, he was more likable than when he was sober.

One day, he came back from work with a dixie cup of ice-cream in each hand and approached me and my sister, Betty, and he said if we would call him "Good Uncle" he would give us each one of the cups. Betty was quick to respond, but I did not. He would not leave it until I called him "Good Uncle" even though I lied and said I did not like ice-cream. The ice-cream soon melted and Uncle Giles was very angry, and told my mother that if she did not do something about my 'behavior', I would be heading into trouble when I grew up. From that day on, I was permanently liberated from Uncle Giles' affectionate pinching and gnawing. If I had been older at that time, I would have known the right response to anyone's request to have 'good' as a prefix to his name. Good? A 'good' man has no belly button, as the Shanghai saying goes.

Uncle Giles' Wife No.1 was an arranged marriage and she was intensely disliked by all in the neighborhood. She was given a long nickname which literally meant 'when pricked with a needle she will not shed one drop of blood' because she was so pale. She was an anemic, sickly, whiny, and zombie-like thing who had with her an equally whiny, widowed sister who did her hair for her every day. This sister had married a Portuguese passport-carrying Cantonese with the last name of Costa and had two children, a son by the name of Albert, and an adopted daughter. They were Catholics and the son received a Jesuit (English) education, but the daughter did not.

Uncle Giles' Wife No.2 was a delicate-looking woman, the sister of a very close colleague of Giles at B.A.T. and also his *mahjongg* crony. Giles had gotten this young lady pregnant and he married her at the insistence of her parents because at that time there was no law against a man having two wives, and richer men had more.

Even though at that time Giles' had been married for several years, his Wife No.1 had had no children. So his first-born, a son named Frank, was by Wife No.2. He was followed by a daughter. A few years after these two children were born, Wife No.1 gave birth to two sons. Wife No.2 was am amiable and quiet person whom everyone in the neighborhood, especially the children and women, liked. She was a marvelous seamstress, and would offer to do the sewing for women who had many children because her own children could afford to have their clothes made by the tailor. All three of Giles' sons studied at St. Francis Xavier's School.

Unlike Wife No.2, Wife No.1 was scheming, mean, and venomous. The women in the neighborhood used to say that 'even a fertilized egg cannot hatch if she has touched it.' Wife No.2 took to her bed with asthma and another ailment for which the Chinese doctor prescribed drinking little boys' early morning urine. I remember I would follow her back and watch with wonder as she drank from a freshly-collected bottle of my brother's urine. My brother was just a toddler, and my mother would collect his first urine in the morning with the bottle that Wife No.2 left with us the night before. Little boys' urine is called 'tongzi niao'. She seems to have suffered from a form of hormonal imbalance, and there were elements of steroid in the urine which was supposed to do her good. She recovered and ended up out-living Wife No.1.

After Uncle Giles' funeral, the company he worked for, B.A.T., had to decide on his widow's pension, and in this case there were two widows. His eldest son, by Wife No.2, had an uncle on his mother's side who was also a B.A.T. employee, but he spoke no English. So Wife No.1 called upon my father to represent the family in the negotiation because it had to be done with an English-speaking foreign manager. She asked my father not to include Wife No.2 and her son, Giles' eldest son, who was not yet an adult. My parents were shocked at Wife No.1's request, and my mother cautioned my father not to have anything to do with the matter unless it was to aim for a fair settlement. There was no one that Wife No.1 could go to outside of my father, and the eventual settlement turned out to be reasonable, with the three sons and the two wives each having an equal share, which also meant that two-fifths went to Wife No.2 and her son, and three-fifths to Wife No.1 and her two sons. The daughter of Wife No. 2 had meanwhile eloped with some man and so had no share.

In the richer families of the Cantonese community in Shanghai, and elsewhere, were female domestic help called '*daimatse*', which literally means 'big-mother-sister', often called Amah in English. They were all unmarried and all dressed alike, in black pants and light blue, or white, Chinese jackets buttoned down on the right. They wore their well-lacquered hair in one long, thick braid down their back. Almost all were spotlessly clean and very faithful servants. There were whispers that these people were 'different', meaning lesbian, just because they were single, even though most had passed marriageable age. Most were not hard up, and some of them had a side business as money-lenders. There was one in *Tengfenglay* who was an avid Cantonese opera fan of a certain male opera singer by the name of Leung Gum Sing who was performing in Shanghai, and this woman spent all her savings on him. Many of these middle-aged women had once been housemaids, sold by their parents to rich households in childhood, and often accompanied their masters' daughters in marriage as part of their dowry.

Few families in our building had radios. Those who did would listen in the still of the night, and rumors floated around that the Japanese were heading toward defeat. Needless to say those rumors eventually proved true. When the Japanese surrender was official, my father rushed out and bought wholesale a big bunch of shoddily-dyed Chinese (KMT), American, British, French, and Soviet flags and told me to sell them on Nanking Road. They were sold out in no time. It seemed that even the poorest wanted to buy a flag, not necessarily a Chinese flag, and wave it as they jumped and shouted along the streets in celebration of victory. My father went and bought some more, but unfortunately, when I went out again to sell the second batch, I was caught in a downpour with no umbrella or raincoat, and all the colors of the flags ran, so none was fit to be sold. I think we had pushed our luck a little too hard.

My youngest brother was born after VJ-Day, the fifth and last child in the family. From Pearl Harbor to VJ-Day was fewer than four years, but it must have seemed like a lifetime to those interned in the camps. There was much hardship for us outside of the camps to endure too. When VJ-Day finally came, everyone was overjoyed and before long all our aunties and uncles came out of camps and picked up their lives once again. Some people came out broken. Old Mr Hawes (Grandpa Hawes) had fallen seriously ill after he was interned, and was only let out when he was dying. Old Mr Ford, who was not interned because he did not have a British passport, also died around that time and his daughters came out of camp to arrange for his funeral.

I don't remember hearing any of my aunties or uncles describe any atrocities committed by the Japanese soldiers during their camp days. Nothing similar to what the Nazis had inflicted upon the Jews in the camps in Europe. Or it could be that those who had suffered such atrocities did not live to tell their stories. But few, if any, deaths occurred from maltreatment among the people whom we knew. The Japanese soldiers were cruel to the Chinese in Shanghai and other parts of China, without a doubt, but the Japanese people in Shanghai were different. They lived and let live. We were told that a lot of torturing had gone on in the Bridge House, the building behind the New Asia Hotel opposite the back of the General Post Office on the other side of Soochow Creek. But whether the tortured were foreigners or Chinese, I was too young to know.

Before long, our aunties and uncles came out of camp and returned to their former residences in different parts of town. The Americans had parachuted relief packages to the camps, and the parachutes, some white, others yellow or light blue, were divided among the internees. The parachutes were all made of nylon and they were taken apart to make curtains and bedspreads, and they just lasted and lasted because the material was so strong.

A Chinese friend of the family named Auntie Fanny was married to an American who worked for the Shanghai Customs House and was interned in the Pootung Camp. She, being Chinese and not registered with the American Consulate as his lawful wife, was not interned. Many a time she came to my parents to borrow an old Chinese jacket, buttoned on the right, which was left behind by my grandmother, and had my father write a letter for her in English on a piece of white cloth sewn to the inside of the jacket. She would smear her face with dirt and pretend to be scavenging for garbage outside the barbed wire fence of the Camp in the hope of catching sight of her husband so she could unbutton her jacket and let him read the letter. After VJ-Day our family was invited many times to their apartment for meals. They were childless and Auntie Fanny wanted to be godmother to my brother Junior. He had taken her to the United States on one of his home leaves, and she was very proud of having visited the U.S. because many Chinese female bed-mates of foreigners never had the privilege of visiting a foreign country. After Liberation in 1949, we lost touch with them.

In fact, prior to the end of World War II, most of the Cantonese-speaking Eurasians in our community had never ever left China. The one or two who had, were envied. Uncle Douglas (Kay), fondly referred to as 'Dumbfunkin', was the brother of Auntie Ella, who later worked in the British Embassy in San Jose, Costa Rica. He had visited England, and 'showed' it by the way he 'carried' himself. He always had a walking stick and wore a hat, and was meticulously dressed, but he was not too proud to visit us now and then in our small room. On the other hand, Uncle Jimmy was denied a visa because he was said to be infected with trachoma. He eventually went to England in the early 1950s along with everybody else in the group, and he died shortly after arrival while his sister, Auntie Lily, died at sea on her way to England.

My mother usually bought her eggs, big, brown ones, from a Pudong lady who frequented the neighborhood with her big basket of eggs. There was always a lot of good-humored bargaining and my mother became quite well-acquainted with this 'egg-lady.' Whenever she visited with her basket, the neighbors would come and buy from her, and if there were still eggs left, my mother would tell one of us children to run upstairs to the third floor and fourth floor to notify other neighbors that the egg-lady was here. My mother would ask her to stay for a bite to eat if the time happened to be meal time. We never saw her again after Liberation. I suppose Land Reform gave the land to the tiller and she had no time to cross the river to come to the city anymore. Her hawk was the same as other egg-ladies, in the familiar Pudong accent *"Lao bare niang, ji-dare yaova ji-dare?"* meaning, "Mistress, want any eggs?"

There were also other people who sold things from door to door, and among them were poor Jews or Greeks. One Jewish man who visited our building had a different commodity in each pocket of his jacket, vest, and pants, such as remnants of cloth, strips of lace in different colors, buttons in all shapes and sizes, pieces of elastic, shoelaces and other things. He seemed to be a door-to-door salesman for Baruch's, a store on Kiangsi Road, near Nanking Road, which sold exactly those things. This Jewish man spoke some English and some Shanghainese, and my mother could meet him half way in both. Whenever he came during mealtime, my mother would just get another pair of chopsticks and he would join us in whatever we had. The word 'kosher' was not in our vocabulary then.

Even though by now the war had ended, my father still had a hard time finding a job. First of all, he had no letter of reference from Siemens, his former employer, even though he was proven innocent in court. After all, if he had been an accomplice he would have made away with the big bundle and not have been so stupid as to wait for Ah Leem G'aw to come for it.

With his experience at Siemens, he knew he could perform well with a foreign company, but what foreign company would employ anyone without a letter of reference? He combed the Help Wanted columns in the newspapers, and eventually found a job with the U.S. Air Base in Kiangwan (Jiangwan), working as a mechanic.

Each morning he would leave the house with a lunch pail and cross the Sichuan Road Bridge to wait for the ten-wheeler truck which would take him to the Air Base. He worked with Sikhs, Russians and other stateless people, as well as fellow-Chinese. But the job at the Air Base did not last long because my father was more or less an office clerk rather than a mechanic. But a job was a job because he had a big family to support. Now and then, he would bring home some goodies from the PX, such as K rations, chewing gum, Hershey chocolate bars, M&Ms and other goodies.

Inflation was such that what he earned was not enough for a family of six. I still had to sit outside with my stand. Everyday, GIs and sailors would pass me by on their way to the Navy "Y" which was on the same block. Some of them would throw me chewing gum, mostly Wrigley's Orbita, Chiclets, or Dentyne, and Hershey chocolate bars. Whenever any of them talked to me, I would answer back in English, which usually surprised them. Pretty soon, word got around among them that 'that little girl around the corner can speak English'. The Navy Headquarters then was in the Glen Line Building, right next door to the British Consulate, which was a minute's walk away from where we lived, and so was the Navy "Y", but in the other direction. Most servicemen who went to the "Y" from the Bund passed by where I was. One day, one of them took a picture of me, sitting and knitting by my stand. That picture was confiscated by people from the China Petroleum Company during one of the very early political movements in the 1950s. I came across a copy of it which my father had sent to a friend in the United States when I visited him there in 1987, and he gave it to me when I told him that our copy had been confiscated and lost.

One rainy Sunday, the streets were deserted and I was hiding from the rain under our verandah, looking after my stand. Two GIs went up to the policeman who operated the traffic light on the corner and asked him where the biggest hotel in Shanghai was. The policeman, who knew no English, referred them to me because he knew that I spoke English, having seen me speak to Auntie Mabel whenever she passed by.

"Park Hotel," I told them.

Were they surprised! When I gave them detailed directions of how to get there, they were even more surprised, and insisted that I go along and be their guest. I couldn't leave my stand even though there was no business. I called up to my mother and told her that the two "uncles" wanted to take me to Park Hotel. It was my mother's turn to be surprised. She gave them the once-over and decided that they were trustworthy people and said it was okay for me to go with them, but they had to bring me back by a certain time. The two GIs helped us push the cart inside the entrance of our building, and off we marched down Nanking Road, with me in the center holding on to each of their hands.

When we finally reached Park Hotel, the doorman tried not to let me in because I was almost in rags, my toes were coming out of my old rubbers, and my clothes were badly faded from sitting out in the sun. I suppose I was taken for a beggar, as beggars were plentiful in those days. But I was with American soldiers, and in the early days after World War II, American soldiers had a certain status. We rode up in the elevator and came to a big dining-room. We were shown a table and seated. They ordered.

"Sundae?" one of them asked me, which sounded like "Sunday", and thinking that he was asking me if that day was a Sunday, I nodded. A little later, a waiter came with a big bowl of ice-cream with assorted fruit, nuts, and whipped cream on top. It was not until years later that the word "sundae" entered my vocabulary. After we finished eating, the two soldiers bought a box of tea cakes and took me home. They gave the cakes to my mother and thanked her for my company. They never left their names, and we never thought to ask, so to this day, I don't know who they were and cannot remember their faces. But the experience was an indelible one.

I had a bad, bad tummy-ache that evening. I guess my system was used to the very poor diet of the war, and then this big bowl of ice-cream with all the trimmings all of a sudden was just too much.

The Park Hotel, built in 1934, remained the highest structure in Shanghai for many years until recently, although it is now dwarfed by, and practically lost in, the present skyline of the city. Nevertheless, it was prophetically named. Until the early 1950s, it faced the former Race Course, until the Race Course was turned into the People's Park, which it has been facing for the last half-century. Really a 'Park' Hotel.

Mr Li, son of the owner of the China Trust Company where we were staying, returned from overseas. He must have been shocked to find the building in such a shambles. Instead of offices, it was now occupied by families from Hongkew, or refugees as we had been called. Each room, only big enough to hold a desk or two, now housed a family of at least five people, or in our case, six, and later, seven. One day, on his way out from the bank, Mr Li bought a pack of cigarettes from me, and he did not want the change!! It was totally unheard of. To me, he was too generous for words.

Jorge Gonzales' wife, a childhood friend of my mother's married to a former classmate of my father, lived in Room 15 on the same floor as us. As neighbors we got along, especially since the children of both families were about the same age. Materially speaking, they fared much better than we did because Uncle Li (JG) was employed during the war, and after VJ Day he was promoted and could afford to have his children study at the Shanghai British School where tuition had to be paid in pounds sterling. His wife, a lady of leisure comparatively speaking, decided to set up a stand of her own on the street next to mine, selling at competitive prices because her family didn't really need the money the way we did. She just wanted to earn pocket money for her *mahjongg* games.

My parents, and other Chinese in the building had never felt comfortable with the Li family because they called themselves 'Portuguese' when we knew they were just as Chinese (Cantonese) as we were. But her putting up a stand next to ours was like grabbing our bowl of rice from right out of our hands! My mother was furious and confronted her. When her husband returned from work, she told him what had happened, and he stormed into our room and told my father to 'go to hell'. My father, always a man of few words, answered calmly that he would meet him there.

Not long after Liberation, the JG family left for Guangzhou (Canton) and bought their way into Hong Kong using 'yellow oxen' - people who made money by smuggling illegal immigrants out of the country, and never returned to the mainland. After 1949, Big Uncle Li soon found himself without a job. Regardless of how handsome a severance pay he must have had from his former foreign employer, it would not have lasted forever. Later, people like him and those who had worked for foreign companies were rounded up and put into Thought Reform where they had to write their own histories over and over again, and not in English, either. So, it must have been very trying for him. His son, Robert, must have had an equally hard time. When Robert and his cousins were attending the Shanghai British School, the boys and girls in blue serge blazers, pants and pleated skirts, school ties and caps, and I was sitting by my stand selling cigarettes. How I had envied them!

Years later, either in 1965 or 1973 when I visited my parents in Shanghai, I one day saw Robert standing on a street corner, shabbily dressed, carving names on pens for people, and demonstrating the use of an embroidery needle that was made from a hypodermic needle. I did not greet him because he would not have recognized me. I thought to myself, what a terrible waste of talent for him to be doing what he was doing! If he had been bright enough to attend the Shanghai British School, why couldn't he have picked up Chinese? He spoke Cantonese and Shanghai dialects, so what was so difficult about learning to read and write in Chinese? It was heartbreaking and incomprehensible, for me to see someone with his expensive education earning his living doing something that menial even though when I was a young child I had done something no less menial, albeit under altogether different circumstances. But here was a grown man who had had a good and expensive education in English. It was pathetic.

The sad thing about many Chinese who had had all their schooling in English was that they had felt it was beneath them to learn to read and write in their own mother tongue, Chinese. Many of them did not even use their Chinese names even if they had one. Some like the Li's, who had claims to Portuguese passports, managed to get them, either by hook or by crook, and mostly by the latter. They considered themselves one rung higher up the social ladder than their own countrymen. Before 1949, China was a doormat made up of her own people on which anybody could step and rub their feet at will. The "Chinese and Dogs Not Allowed" mentality was prevalent among both foreigners and fake foreigners then. The mentality underwent an evolution after 1949 and became an allegedly less insulting approach of "Chinese Not Allowed" in such places as top hotels catering exclusively to foreigners. This lasted to as late as the 1980s. Bad habits take a long time to die off.

All news was good news concerning the Liberation War which had been taking place after V-J Day, and little was said about the battles that the KMT had lost, and they had lost nearly every one of them. The foreigners and wealthy Chinese were getting out of the city with their valuables. In December 1948, a passenger steamship named the *Kiangya* sank off Woosung, downstream from Shanghai. The casualty rate was high, and for two years after there were very good catches of carp for the fishermen. It was said the fish had fattened themselves on the bodies of the victims of the tragedy and some fishmongers and their customers came upon jewelry, rings, necklaces and even watches in the intestines of fish.

In Shanghai fish markets, the bigger fish are cut up and sold in pieces by weight, and the insides which include intestines, roe, and air bladder are sold separately as a set, and they were much cheaper than usual because they were plentiful. My mother ate a lot of it in the noon meals that were provided for the employees at the Sun Company during the time she was working there, and before long she and some of her colleagues broke out in countless little, sesame size pimples on their faces which bled as though each pimple had been pricked by a needle.

My mother went to our Cantonese lady doctor who prescribed Chinese traditional herbal medicine that would detoxify her system of the 'poisonous' fish that she had eaten, which supposedly had been fattened on human flesh. From that day on, my mother did not touch carp, and cautioned others against doing it, especially expectant mothers.

The fake foreigners, Chinese who had unrecognized foreign passports or those who preferred to be stateless rather than being Chinese, were scared of the Liberation because the real foreigners started to leave, and foreign companies were closing down, and so their livelihood was in jeopardy. There was no way that they could function without the foreign companies they depended on for employment, as many of them knew little or no Chinese. I think they realized that the real foreigners would not help them to get out of the country so they had to fend for themselves. And since they had always had the superiority complex of not being Chinese, their own kind had no desire to help them either. They had to find a way out for themselves. My father had always considered it treasonous of such people to deny their Chineseness, but the rest of our family only saw the material benefits that came with their being Portuguese, or anything other than Chinese.

Whenever I visited my parents in Shanghai after 1956, I would ask about Robert and his father. I was told that his father had remarried, and had moved to Guangzhou after he had been jailed once or twice in Shanghai. For what, we don't know. Political movements followed one after another after 1949, and it was nothing surprising to hear of anyone being jailed. Big Uncle Li's father, whom we all affectionately call Ah Gung, or grandpa, had taken the youngest grandson with him to Hong Kong to be with his other son, the boy's uncle. Robert later married, and if he is still living, he would now be a useful person with his knowledge of English, if it didn't rust away during the three decades or more that it would have been useless to him. Hopefully he picked up some Chinese in the meantime. I wonder if he kept his Catholic faith. I hope so, and I hope it sustained him through the long years of hardship.

We were told that one of Robert's male cousins became a well-to-do businessman in Hong Kong who regularly made business trips to Shanghai, but he was discreet and never once surfaced in the old neighborhood. Their surname of 'Gonzales' reverted to their Chinese name of Li, or perhaps they would now spell it "Lee" to make it sound less Chinese. The Portuguese passports they and other Chinese had bought from the corrupt official in the Portuguese Consulate in Shanghai were not recognized by the Portuguese Government. Such had been the history in those days, a Chinese was a second- if not third-class citizen in his own country, never mind if he had black hair, slit eyes, or a flat nose, which some people think are typical Chinese features. So long as his name was not Chinese, he was a class above the common man. How unfair!

The end of the Anti-Japanese War meant the beginning of the Civil War and while it raged in other parts of China, Shanghai suffered from unheard of inflation. The popular saying then was that it was cheaper to use banknotes as toilet paper than to use the real thing, an earthy Chinese version of the English phrase 'the money is not worth the paper it's printed on'. My father was again looking for an office job as the one at the Air Base did not last. But, again, without a letter of reference from a former employer, it was difficult to get a job with a good company. Our stand also have to close down because we could not compete with Mrs Li selling next to us at more competitive prices.

One hot summer evening, a university student named Mr Ji who lived in one of the dormitories on the fourth floor of our building, and his girlfriend took me to the Bund Park to 'catch the breeze' by the river. A sampan rowed up to us and the boat people were selling big cans of food containing corned beef hash and something like potato salad. Mr Ji asked them where the food cans came from, and the woman told him that she had done the laundry for American sailors on a ship anchored out in river, and received leftovers from the kitchen instead of cash. Mr Ji bought a can from them for very little, and shared it with us. He then had a bright idea, and asked my mother whether, since I was not going to school nor working at my stand, I could work with the sampan people as their interpreter so they could get cash for their labor instead of just leftover food, and I could also earn a little. My mother considered this and decided it could be tried.

Before sunrise the following day, Mr Ji and my father took me to the dock and handed me over to the boat people we had met the evening before and told them what the terms were. I think it was three meals a day plus a portion of what they would received in cash. We rowed out on the sampan to the US naval ship, which I think was numbered GC-804, and on the way I threw up because the river was so rough. I can't remember the conversations I interpreted that day, but there was one with a man named Mickey, who worked with the signaling lights. He was nice and took a picture with me on the deck of the ship which I have to this day. I went to that ship only twice and then it sailed away.

My father was still unemployed, and times were still very difficult, but again, Mr Ji was very helpful in finding a student for my father to coach mathematics in the mornings. The young boy's name was David and we were later told that he was the grandson of Dr Yen Hui Ching, the one-time Chinese ambassador to the Soviet Union. My father also taught in a night school to help make ends meet. But, as has always been the case, teachers were poorly paid. In China, poverty has always been linked to the teaching profession

My mother also found a job. A friend's friend who sold lace and embroidered goods had rented a counter at the Sun Company (now Shanghai No.1 Department Store), one of the four biggest department stores in Shanghai, and therefore in China. It was owned by a Cantonese, as were the other three (the Choi family owned the Sun, the Kwok family owned Wing On, the Ma family owned Sincere, and another family owned Sun Sun). Most of the sales people spoke no English and the friend recommended my mother, who did. Each extra cent was needed to keep a family of seven alive. Whenever we children were 'wasteful' my mother would remark that if we tore apart a bank note money, 'our parents' blood would drip from it'. I never knew what play was after my father lost his job at Siemens. I had to grow up in a hurry. I had been a very fat baby, and was tall for my age as a youngster, but I turned out to be the runt of the family. I guess the war and the hard times stunted my growth.

When my mother was working, I could go to school, and did. And at long last my father found a job with the Caltex Oil Company (Texaco). His office was on Avenue Edward VII, in the Wheelock Building. Uncle Jimmy was back working at his old job with the Standard Oil Company (Socony) and had written a letter of recommendation for my father. The job with Caltex was a good one, and once again, my father was in suit and tie, and had regular office hours, working in the Appropriations Department. My mother then left her department store job since it was no longer necessary for her to work. We had thought the good days had finally returned after what seemed like an eternity of hardships. Imagine, a family of seven people in a room meant to be an office with just enough space for two desks. My parents' double bed took up at least a third of the floor space, and we children always slept on the floor, head to toe, like sardines, the year around.

Even with a good job, my father could not afford to pay for our tuition in one lump sum, like the rich did, and we had to apply to the school to pay by installments. The poorer the family, the greater the number of installments, and the very poor could have it waived, provided the pupil was diligent and made good grades. Even if paid by installments, each installment consisted of half a sackful of bank notes because inflation was so bad. In many cases, money was weighed instead of counted because it would further depreciate by the time the counting was over as it depreciated with the tick of the clock.

Even as a child, unlike my siblings, I resented the circumstances under which I had to live. I felt that I deserved better, but there was nothing that I could do to improve my lot. There seemed to be 'someone' in me who longed to break out. My parents could never understand my contrariness, and why I would question what was taken for granted by my siblings. I had an identity crisis, and always felt that I was somebody else, and did not belong to the family. Perhaps I had been born at the wrong time, in the wrong place. I have often wondered if my mother's prenatal diet had anything to do with it (Isn't it typical for children to blame their problems on their parents?). There seemed to be someone helplessly trapped inside of me who longed to fly away.

The Civil War was going on in other parts of China, but for us in Shanghai, life was improving from what it had been during the Japanese occupation. Not only could I now go to school, I could also go to the movies, and sometimes skipped Sunday school for one. I believe I did not miss one single movie that came to Capitol Theater, mostly J. Arthur Rank productions, black and white adaptations from Dickensian novels.They were depressing because they were mostly tear-jerkers, but also enjoyable, because they were in English. One memorable movie was called *Stairway to Heaven* with David Niven and Kim Hunter. British and American movies were not dubbed as they are now. Those who did not understand English could pay what amounted to one-fourth the price of the ticket for a set of headphones to be plugged into the socket at the back of the seat in front, and get a simultaneous translation of the dialogue. I never had to spend that extra money. For tear-jerkers, I would borrow my father's big handkerchief because my own postage-stamp size one would be inadequate.

In all my childhood years, I did not have so much as a cold, even when I was made to sit outside selling boiled sweet potatoes from a bucket. More than once, I was soaked to the skin, and many a day I had to sit under the scorching sun, but I never had any physical discomforts. My father said, "the wind does not blow on a lowly blade of grass", the Chinese version of "God tempers the wind to the shorn lamb", and that was what I was. I remained the healthiest of the children in the family. My mother had had a good prenatal diet, perhaps?

One thing that clearly stands out in my mind now as I recall the old days is a hefty, somewhat tattered volume of the Montgomery Ward Catalogue that I used to pore over. It was my first English dictionary with pictures. Learning to read from it was a joy because of the visual reinforcement.

The day before May 27, 1949, the KMT troops staged a 'victory parade'. They marched down from Peking Road, passed us, on to the Bund and boarded ships and left the city altogether. The parade was a disguised get-away. Later that day, occupants of the rooms in our building which had verandahs facing either Peking Road or Sichuan Road, were told to hang quilts behind our windows, and that we were not to even peep out under any circumstances. We were also told not to sleep in our rooms, but out in the hallway. That night, we could hear the distant rumble of cannon, and uneasiness took hold of everyone. We had thought the war was over and done with after VJ-Day!! We woke up the next morning to find what laundry the residents had hung out overnight to dry on bamboo poles was gone, and ragged KMT army uniforms were lying all around instead. Worse still, the public drain was clogged. Someone went down to clean it, and discovered guns in the sewer, abandoned by the retreating KMT soldiers.

Families occupying rooms facing the street spent the night sleeping in the hallway as we had been told to do. Towards the end of the day, we found that a cannon had been placed at the intersection of Peking and Sichuan Road, aimed at the General Post Office on the other side of the Sichuan Road Bridge, which was one of the last strongholds of the KMT before they retreated. No one in our building was hurt in either the shelling and other military activities, but in the next building, a young man's curiosity got the better of him. He lived on the second floor, above what had been the China Sunday School Union and the Chinese Christian Bookstore and he peered out from behind the quilt hung in front of the window of his room, and he was shot at by sniper. The bullet lodged in his liver, but he could not be taken to the doctors because the fighting was still going on. Telephone calls were made and a foreign doctor, crawled his way across town, in one building and out the next, until he reached the building across from where the patient was, but could not get to him. As soon as the fighting was over, an ambulance came and took the young man away, but he died on his way to the hospital, from internal hemorrhage.

During the Japanese War, whenever enemy dignitaries visited Shanghai by plane, they would fly in, or out, through Kiangwan Airport, and the motorcade that took them to and from the city usually passed along Sichuan Road, and residents on both sides of the road would be warned ahead of time not to look out. There would be Japanese soldiers with fixed bayonets, standing with their backs to the street facing the buildings, ready to shoot at anyone who dared stick his neck out. After the Japanese surrendered, KMT and American dignitaries visiting Shanghai also came in and out of the city along that same road, but people were allowed to look as much as they wanted, though they were still warned not to hang out their laundry and to tidy up verandahs and windowsills for the occasion. VIPs like Chiang Kai-shek and General George C. Marshall and many others all passed by where we lived. In later years, Shanghai people were glad to have visiting dignitaries, including Nixon in 1973 and Queen Elizabeth in 1986, pass by where they lived because it meant the facade of their building might at least receive a coating of paint, of "vanishing cream", if only for appearance's sake.

2

The Shanghai Years After Liberation (1949-1956)

Life in Shanghai continued pretty much unchanged for some years even though people who were not Chinese were slowly leaving. We even went caroling, for the first time ever, in horse-drawn carts! I was by then 14, and could understand a lot in English, and could read quite a bit too, learning on my own. At church we played a card game called Lexicon, similar to Scrabble but with each word displayed horizontally. I liked the game, and my first win in a hand of ten cards was the word "industrial". I can't tell you how happy I was for days after that win.

If I remember correctly, I saw most of the J. Arthur Rank black-and-white movies at the Capitol Theater after 1949. American movies also continued to be shown after 1949, and I had an insatiable appetite for them. *The Search* with Montgomery Clift, was an unforgettable one. It was after seeing it that I realized that children elsewhere in the world had also suffered during the war, and that in comparison, I could consider myself very lucky because I had not been separated from my parents, none of the family was killed during the war, nor was our home bombed. Some years later when I read *The Diary of Anne Frank*, I was all the more convinced that what I had gone through was nothing, and I stopped feeling sorry for myself the way I previously had. So I took it for granted that life had to go on, that I was the eldest in the family and had to do my bit. Or rather, I was made to do my bit. Being forced to grow up in a hurry had its repercussions later on. I grew to be rebellious and contrary and very independent-minded, which was not always for my own good.

Until the early 1950s, there had been many foreign doctors in Shanghai. There were also internationally-trained Chinese doctors, many with American, British, French, German or Swiss wives. There was Dr Fu whose wife, Pearl, was a member of the Kwok family which owned the Wing On Department Store, and there were many well-known traditional Chinese doctors such as "Deaf Chang" who specialized in typhoid cases, and Shi Xiaoshan who specialized in bone-mending. The Chinese doctor our family went to was a Cantonese lady by the name of LGC. She enjoyed a very good reputation in the Cantonese communities on both sides of the Soochow Creek. It was said that this remarkable woman started her life as a maid in a rich Cantonese household. The playboy son of the master had gotten her pregnant, and his mother insisted that he marry her, which he reluctantly did. In time they had three or four daughters, but he took to smoking opium and squandered his family's wealth. She was desperate, and sought remedies to cure her husband's addiction. With the reduced circumstances of the family due to her husband's wasteful lifestyle, she could not afford medical care for her children and so took care of them herself, use old remedies she learned from older people. In time, this woman not only cured her husband of his addiction, but also a well-known doctor, while also providing a good education for her beautiful and clever daughters. She became the sole bread-winner of the family while her husband, now in good health, and no doubt grateful that she had cured him, took care of everything on the domestic front. She and her husband left for Hong Kong not long after 1949. They had a daughter who was newly-married and lived in a good apartment on Dixwell Road in Hongkew who committed suicide with her newly-wed husband by putting their heads in a gas oven during one of the early political movements.

Auntie Ellie had started taking me to the Endeavourers' Sunday School (ESS) just before 1949. That was when I earnestly began to learn to read and write English. My father had taught me to write the alphabet, simple sentences, and later longer sentences at the same time he was teaching me Chinese proverbs, but at Sunday School everything was in English. It was there, in the young people's group, that my English gradually improved through constant practice. I was good at mimicry, I guess. There was a room known as the library on the second floor of the church which had some books and obsolete issues of LIFE magazines that I used to pore over. There were other young people around my age in the same Sunday School class, and while few of them were Chinese-Chinese like me, that did not keep us from becoming friends. I started to read books they recommended, such as the Pollyanna books, and others that were not too difficult. The simplest book I read, was *Nibbles and Me*, written by Elizabeth Taylor, about a chipmunk. Elizabeth Taylor became one of my favorite movie stars until Audrey Hepburn appeared.

Auntie Ellie was my first Sunday School teacher. Everyone who knew Auntie Ellie agreed that 'to know her was to love her'. She was someone I could rely upon. After she left for Hong Kong, there were Auntie Annie (Mrs Hermann Wegener), and after she left, Auntie Daisy (Mrs Lawrence Klyhn), Chum, (Muriel Hoopes, the wife of Dr Y.C. Tu) and eventually Dutton. My reliance on these older women overlapped and there was no period in my life that I was without a pillar to lean on. In retrospect, I think Auntie Ellie began my life-long dependence on an older woman as a mother figure and that dependence on different women at the different stages even of my adulthood influenced my entire life.

I think it is the secret wish of every young person, especially a young girl, to have a fairy godmother, and I have been more than lucky because I have had my share of them in various periods of my life who have left their marks on me. I was not, and could not have been, born with the personality or values that I presently have; rather, I am a little of everyone whom I had been close to over the years, taking elements from them and melding them to form my own personality and values, and in the lifelong selection process, retaining some, discarding others, and improving on what is left, and hopefully developing into a more mature person. I see no end to the improvement process.

Life for me in those years was a monotonous round of home-school-church, and the highlights were sneaking in movies and reading. I was more interested in reading English novels than in doing my schoolwork. Being able to read in English opened up an entirely new world for me, and I lost myself in it. My mother could never understand why I would want to waste electricity and read far into the night, not knowing for herself the pleasure that a book can bring. So, instead of reading with the lights on I would sit and read on the verandah as the light from the street lamp outside was bright enough for me to do so. It was through reading whatever I could get my hands on that I accumulated my vocabulary and knowledge. In those days, there were no books around which I had access to that were bad. The first time I came across a book I felt I had to hide from my father was in 1973 on my visit home was a paperback copy of *The Godfather*. But by then I was already a mother of two children.

Early on, Auntie Ellie took me to visit the Talbot family, very good friends of hers. Old Mrs Talbot was a very kind and benign lady, and her daughter Cissy and husband John Wade lived in the same compound. Each member of the family had a house of their own, and there were many servants in the main household. I particularly remember a pretty housemaid called Lily. I only hope that her masters had the foresight to provide her with some education so she could take care of herself after they were gone. The family left Shanghai after old Mrs T died. Cissy and her husband John left in 1956 and were found with lots of greenbacks and jewels on them at the train station. Her brother left later than that because he could not bear to be away from his mistress. His wife Elsie left first. Their compound is now the pharmaceutical works of what grew from Kofa Drugs, once owned by a man named Li who had a German wife and two beautiful daughters, Mady and Eva, the latter of whom is now an artist living in Switzerland. The old Mr Talbot was Starr Talbot who made his money by preparing a cholera medicine called in Chinese "Ten Drops of Water" which was given out free on street corners to rickshaw coolies and other laborers in the summer. His picture was on every ampoule of the medicine, which contained opium, to treat cholera, diarrhea, dysentery or heat stroke, ailments common among those who survive by selling their muscle power.

Not long after Liberation, people with foreign passports were beginning to leave China, and the regulation at that time was that these people were allowed to leave with only a fixed amount of U.S. currency and household goods. Most of the Cantonese-speaking Eurasians who were leaving had never left China before and it just was not possible to take everything that many had accumulated for generations. Not all of them "ill-gotten gains" either, as was assumed by the authorities at the time. The majority of the people from the former Cantonese-speaking Eurasian community worked as office clerks or stenographers, and whatever they had was the fruit of their honest labor accumulated over the years for a rainy day, because many were single and had to think of their old age. There might have been a few who were wealthy because their parents or grandparents, or perhaps even themselves, had speculated and won in real estate. But I think they had to leave it behind without even an acknowledgment of receipt.

Since these people were only allowed to take out a certain amount of money, and that amount was only a fraction of all that they had, there remained the question of how to get the rest out, not including the property, of course. Whenever there is a demand there will be a supplier, especially in the business-wise city of Shanghai. There were people who took advantage of exactly the anxiety of those who were worried about how not to leave behind money or other things, or to leave behind as little as possible, and it was on these people that the racketeers preyed. Their prey were too decent to see through them. They baited the gullible and innocent by posing as middle-men reputed to have the right connections to people who were also leaving the country but who did not have enough money of their own so that their given quota of money was more than sufficient to cover their own needs and they had room to take care of more. They would take out money for anyone for a small commission, which sounded reasonable enough. Uncle Jimmy was one of those gullible people who swallowed that crap hook, line and sinker. The person to whom he entrusted his money and who had promised to deliver it once he arrived in England, disappeared altogether. He lost almost all his savings. I think that blow accounted for his early death.

Other people used whatever cash they were not allowed to take out to buy expensive items to ship as household goods. Business in mink coats, expensive rugs, and other valuables soared, if only for a short time. There were strict regulations on what, and how many, or how much of anything old and new which could be taken. There was a store that sold expensive Tientsin rugs on the corner of Nanking and Chengdu Road run by a very sharp businessman who helped customers make brand new carpets look like used ones by spraying dust and dirt on them. Once taken out of the country, the rugs could be vacuumed and sold as new, allowing some cash to be recouped. This businessman was clever enough to know that henceforth with few, if any, foreigners left in Shanghai, his store was likely to fold. There weren't going to be any local customers for what he was selling, that was for sure. There were also shops which sold expensive, carved, camphor or sandalwood trunks, some inlaid with seashells, and with double bottoms or hollowed-out corners, legs, or lids in which the owners could hide valuables. These items were in great demand. In those days, Customs did not have the scanners that are so commonly in use today.

Bicycle Tailor, a short and very untidy farmer, a native of Pootung, was so called because he went from house to house, with a hand-operated Singer sewing-machine strapped to the back of his bicycle. He made clothes for the different families in the Cantonese-speaking Eurasian community. He was good at his job and made silk, woolen, linen, or whatever material dresses and costumes his clients wanted. He would stay with one family, usually in the servants' quarters, with his meals provided, and make whatever clothes were needed. A family would usually call him over whenever there were several things to make, and he would be very patient and make alterations here and there until the work was completely to his customer's satisfaction. He was especially in demand prior to the departure of the folks of that community because many of the women bought silks and other expensive material with whatever money they could not take out and had the material made into dresses and other garments. After most of his former customers left for overseas, we never saw Bicycle Tailor again.

There was a very wealthy couple who had 'schemed' to take out more than the officially allowed amount. They were John Wade and his wife Cissy (nee Talbot), who is the eldest daughter of Starr Talbot, the man whose picture Was on every ampoule of 十滴水. She had a house in the Talbot compound on what was the Great Western Road. With the help of their servant, a woman who had served them since she was a young girl, U.S. dollars were sewn into the lining of their coats and jackets, and even in the bra that the mistress would be wearing on the day of departure. Precious stones and jewelry were hidden in shoulder pads or in the curls that were piled on top of her head in her usual hairdo. In other words, ways and means were contrived to take out as much of their riches as possible. At the farewell party they threw for themselves, they enlisted help from friends who were to be seeing them off the following day. They handed 'greenbacks' to their guests, and told them to take the money to the train station, and when they shook hands or embraced to bid farewell, they were discreetly press the money into their palms. Their guests were glad to be given a chance to show their friendship for them with this last gesture.

The couple had reputedly given their servants very handsome severance pay, and from all appearances, the servants were broken-hearted to see their masters leave. Especially the oldest servant, the housekeeper, the overseer of all the other servants, the one who had been with the family since she was a little girl, and who was now in her fifties if not sixties. She asked to borrow a sum of money from her masters to build a house in the countryside in Anhui, because it would take more than the severance pay to do it. Her masters angrily refused, deeming her request extortion. The master-servant relationship that had lasted the last half-century immediately soured.

The local residents' committee, had been educating the servants working in foreign households to report anything suspicious that they witnessed, and in this case, the education took effect. The servant went to them and confessed that she had been an accomplice in helping her masters hide away American dollars and jewelry in trunks, coat linings, shoulder pads and elsewhere. I doubt that the servant exposed her masters out of patriotism. If she had, she wouldn't have helped them in the first place. I think it was just anger that prompted her to do what she did. She knew they could spare what she was asking for, and that having been with them most of her life, they should know that she would stay true to her word of repaying the loan. After she squealed, she was promised a percentage of whatever that was to be recovered, but whether she eventually got it or not, no one knew.

On the day of the couple's departure, friends went to the train station to see them off as planned. It was an unusual send-off because there were reporters with cameras and flash-lights. The couple thought that the press was present because they were from a wealthy family and had a certain prestige in the Eurasian community of Shanghai, which could have been true. Someone in the crowd who had come to see them off noticed that the area was roped off, and immediately sensed that something was amiss. He went to the toilet and flushed away the money that he had been asked to return to them. Before long a few other men joined him and did the same. Those who were less observant were caught with 'illegal' money on them which they could not account for.

Before boarding the train, the couple was asked to declare their belongings again, and the regulations were read out to them once more. They answered positively that they had nothing illegal to declare. The Custom officers and police seemed to know exactly what was hidden where. The curls on top of her head were unrolled one by one and diamonds and other precious stones surfaced, the shoulder pads were cut open to reveal more gems, coat linings were ripped apart to reveal U.S. dollars, and the man's trouser legs were pushed up to expose wads of U.S. dollars wrapped around them. Except for the few who were still squatting in the men's room, the rest of the people who were there to see them off had their names and addresses taken down by the police and the 'illegal' money that they had brought to be returned to its owners was confiscated. When everything was recovered, the couple was allowed to board the train. They were a sight!

Photographs taken on that occasion accompanied a newspaper article I later read when I was in Hami. There was a big exhibition held at the Cultural Square (formerly the Canidrome) which displayed the pictures and also some of the things that had been confiscated.

In 1952 or 1953, there was a three-day "Youth for Christ" Rally at the Community Church (on today's Hengshan Rd) in which all English-speaking Christian young people participated. Among the main organizers were David Morken (of Lodi, California), Dick Hillis (of Modesto, California), Roy Robertson and Lois Raws. The words and music of the rally's theme song, "Jesus is a Wonderful Savior", were written by David. By chance, I met him again in Lodi in 1987, after nearly four decades. When I sang the chorus to him, he was very surprised!

Jesus is a wonderful Savior,
He will carry you through (repeat 3 times)
Until the battle's done, and the victory is won

My Lord will carry you through
Oh my precious brother, when the world's on fire,
You'll need my Jesus to be your Savior
He'll hide you ever, in the Rock of Ages,
In the Rock of Ages, just cleft for you.

David, who was still very active in his work when I met him again in 1997, had spoken at our church in Shanghai. His late wife, Helen, played the musical saw at the rally. His daughters, Andrea and Arlita, were around my age.

The International Refugee Organization of the United Nations (IRO) had its office on the Bund, and before it moved to Hong Kong, it was instrumental in helping many stateless people and Jews in Shanghai to resettle in other countries. In addition, it also helped many Russians, most of them were Pentecostals or Baptists from Xinjiang, to resettle in South America, Australia and elsewhere. These Russians from Xinjiang were marvelous singers. Like the Welsh, they sang without any musical accompaniment. Their voices blended so beautifully that it was sheer pleasure to hear them. Many of them spent a short time in Shanghai en route to other countries, and they attended our church to learn a few words of English. They spoke nothing but Russian and most had escaped from their own homeland when the October Revolution took place. They then settled in different pockets in Xinjiang, mostly in the three prefectures of Altai, Gulja, and Tarbagatay.

I was surprised to find some three decades later that the IRO had changed its name to the Christian Immigration Service after it moved to Hong Kong, and was headed by Pastor Stumpf, formerly of the German Lutheran Church of Shanghai, still helping the Russians, or people who claimed to have some

Russian blood, to emigrate from Xinjiang. I thought it would have been better to have the name changed from "Christian" to "Islamic" because it was mostly helping Muslim Tartars, to leave.

In the early 1980s, a half-Russian lady, a movie star of some fame who was the cousin of a half-Russian nurse in the dispensary of the Altai Prefectural Hospital, came to me with her IRO application forms and cried that she had been rejected, while many locals who applied later than she had already left. She claimed that her one drawback was that she had married a Han (Chinese) who did not have claim to any Russian blood, and her children had next to no Russian blood, and looked "very Chinese" and had a Chinese last name while others who did not "look" Chinese (Han) received their permits easily. However, that policy seems to have changed in the mid- to late-1980s when Chinese were accepted.

I studied at the Cantonese Baptist Mission Chung Tuk Girls' School which was directly across from the former Jewish School on Seymour Road. Our principal was Princeton Hsu. I visited him and his wife in San Francisco the summer of 1987 just before I returned to China after my first one-year visit to the U.S Principal Hsu was in his late eighties then, but still remembered the "old" days. He was a good friend of Auntie Ellie's and I had often asked her to remember me to him during the years we corresponded. Principal Hsu was stripped of his post when the school became the No. 7 Girls' School of Shanghai a couple of years after Liberation, and he and his wife left for Hong Kong after being "denounced" at an organized rally in the school. The older employees of the school were called upon to denounce him, among whom was the librarian, an elderly man called Mr Ou whose performance "disappointed" the leadership. The other main speaker was a senior class top student, a Cantonese girl who had enjoyed tuition waivers year after year because she was a good student from a poor family.

With the Liberation, new people began moving into our neighborhood. One day, a Cantonese couple moved into Room 12 on our floor. The woman looked much older than her husband, and one day, when several children were playing in Room 14, at Auntie Ellen's, they accidentally pushed onto the floor the revolving picture frame which held her wedding picture, and on the other side of the frame was another wedding picture and the bride was the new woman next door, but the groom was another man. My, did eyes pop and tongues wag! The new couple were store clerks at the Sun Company, the biggest department store in Shanghai, and this woman, Leung, had had at least six children with her first husband, then left him to marry this young man. Both were amateur Cantonese opera singers, and the Sun Company, with most of its employees being Cantonese, had a troupe of its own which performed on holidays, and the two took a liking to each other and married. She left her first husband, another store clerk working in the same department store as she, with the brood of children.

The young man's mother looked younger than her daughter in-law. She was a sweet and quiet person whose husband had left for the "Gold Mountain" (the United States) a few days after her marriage in Guangdong Province some three decades ago, and who was still away. She gave birth to her son after her husband had left and raised him in the countryside. When he was old enough to attend school, she took him to Shanghai where she worked as a domestic help to provide for his education. In the early fifties, with the help of the Red Cross, the son, now a young man, finally located his long-lost father. Overseas remittances started coming to them, and this daughter in-law, Leung, started to flaunt her lifestyle. She gave birth to three children, two boys and a girl in the three following years of her marriage, and each had a wet nurse from the countryside while her mother in-law waited on her hand and foot. One day, the mother in-law came in to chat with my mother, and told her that they were moving back to Guangdong Province to their native town because the 'old man' had sent money back to build a house so he could return after retirement, and he also requested that she get him a young 'concubine', not so much for himself, but to wait on her, his lawful, wedded wife, as he felt that he had owed her too much. This man had left China long before Liberation, and had little idea how things had changed since, and that rich people were no longer allowed to have concubines, and those who already had them had to release them if they wanted to leave.

Besides the original Cantonese families, people from other provinces started to move into the building. Actually, the native Shanghai people were those who lived across the Whangpoo River in Pudong (Pootung). They speak a dialect that is different to that spoken in the city. These folks were nearly all farmers and considered "country bumpkins" by the city slickers. They dressed differently, too. Most of their clothes were made from home-woven cloth of a narrow width and dyed blue. At one time in the mid- to late 1950s, the "16-pound" variety of home-woven blue cloth was very popular among young people. The material was not fast color and one had to be careful never to wear it in hot weather or with anything white inside. The Pudong ladies sold big brown eggs door to door while the men sold paper money to be burned to the dead.

Uncle Giles' eldest son, Frank Choi, had been schooled at St. Francis Xavier's and had become a Catholic. But he loved to sing hymns, and since there was no hymn-singing in Catholic churches in those days, he joined the choir of the Cantonese Baptist Mission Church which held its Sunday morning services in the chapel of our school. He would go to early mass so that would give him time to attend the ten o'clock Protestant morning service. Sometimes he would take me along. The older boys and girls of the choir, all Cantonese, were very nice people. Most of the girls were seniors (12th-graders) at our school. Often after morning services they would all go out for lunch, mostly Dutch treats, and then take in a movie. One which we saw at the Grand Theater was *I Wonder Who's Kissing Her Now*, a musical with Mark Stevens and June Haver. I still remember two songs from it to this day, including the theme song, "I wonder who's kissing her now, I wonder who's teaching her how…".

Another Cantonese family of three, the couple my parents' age, and the woman's mother, moved into Room 2 and 4 right next door to us. They claimed to be friends of Madame Sun, otherwise known as Soong Chingling, wife of the late Dr Sun Yat-sen. They had a framed inscription in Chinese calligraphy *Bo Ai* (meaning universal love) written by Dr Sun Yat-sen hanging in their room which they were very proud to point out to the neighbors who visited them. The story went that the old woman's husband had been a butcher who sold pork in Kiangwan, a suburb of Shanghai at the end of North Sichuan Road. One day at dusk, a man some plainclothesmen were stalking ran into the butcher shop and hid under the counter. The butcher was boarding up at closing time when the men barged in and inquired if he had seen anyone come into his shop. He said he hadn't, which was the truth. As all Shanghai old-timers know, butcher shops that sold pork then had a very high 'counter' which was a tree trunk with a part chopped off for the butcher to stand behind to chop his meat. After the butcher closed shop, the man who had been hiding behind the 'counter' came out and thanked the butcher, and asked for his name. The story was that when Dr Sun became president of the Republic of China, he sent for the butcher and his family and gave him a high position with the Hankow Railroad Bureau. The butcher became a big potato, took to drinking, opium-smoking and whoring with his new-found status, and eventually died of alcoholism and syphilis. But the family, including the son-in-law who lived next to us, still boasted of their "connection" with Dr Sun Yat-sen and Madame Sun! They were most pleased to learn that we were also named Sun, and that we were also from the same county as Dr Sun Yat-sen, the Father of the Republic. They thought we were related to him, which we wished we were, but when we admitted that we weren't, at least not to our knowledge, they cooled toward us. Their boasted connection did not seem to have provided any immunity when the son-in-law was denounced as a "rightist" in 1958. So it is only sometimes, not all the time, that it pays to know the right people.

In retrospect, what was remarkable about the actual process of the transition was that electric power was not cut, nor was water supply. Everything just went on as it always had, even telephone services functioning normally. The next day, May 28, 1949, was business as usual. The young people's group of our church even organized to go caroling in horse-drawn carriages that Christmas in 1949. Movie theaters were still showing the Hollywood or J. Arthur Rank films. In fact, American and British movies did not stop altogether until later when Soviet and East European movies started to come in. I think the Shanghai people made comparisons between the American and British movies which they had been enjoying before and after Liberation and the new Soviet and East European movies they saw in the years that followed. It was just before American and British films were altogether banned that I went to the movies most frequently. It would be more than a dozen years later before another Hollywood movie was shown, and that exclusively. It was a film based on a Mark Twain book, *The Million Pound Note* starring Gregory Peck. I think Chum got the tickets from either Margaret Scofield Wong, or from her own

71

school. What a treat it was! Another exclusively shown movie was *Salt of the Earth* which could in no way compare to the former one in entertainment value.

There was a British movie called *Black Narcissus* with Deborah Kerr and David Farrar which my Catholic classmates, some of whom were members of the Legion of Mary, were forbidden to see by their priests. It wasn't until years later that I realized why. Another movie with David Farrar and Mai Zetterling, *Frieda,* was unforgettable. We had hated the Japanese for what they had done to us, and the British people in the movie insulted Frieda because of what the Germans had done to them. People are the same all over the world. We have the same sentiments, and we usually transfer our anger for a few onto the innocent many.

A work team entered our school because it was a private one and connected to the Cantonese Baptist Mission. For singing lessons, we were now taught Russian, Polish, Yugoslavian, Albanian or North Korean songs. Young teachers (some of them were normal school undergraduates on practicum) took over the teaching of some subjects. One of the young male teachers, the one that taught geography, was given a hard time by our class because his face was covered with red pimples. Then there was a Physical Education teacher who was tall, dark and handsome with wavy hair. He was later put in jail in one of the early political movements for being an "anti-revolutionary". In 1965 when I visited former classmates and the former custodian of the school and asked her about the different teachers, I was sad to learn that some were jailed, others had committed suicide during the "anti-rightist" movement, and still others had left. There was only one lady teacher left. She was in her late thirties or early forties, always overly well-dressed and heavily made-up. I wonder about her fate in the Cultural Revolution.

Around 1951 or 1952, the China operations of Caltex (Texaco) where my father worked, were liquidated. The foreign staff left. An overseas Chinese by the name of Gordon Wong, and one or two locally employed stateless or Chinese staff with foreign names remained to wind up the work. My father, being a Chinese staff with a Chinese name, was registered with the union and later joined the China Petroleum Company, but not before being dragged over the coals. He was under suspicion for being a "spy" and a member of a "clique" which went around as a "library group" (!!!). He was isolated from the family and taken to a place in Kaochiao, Pootung, to write his thoughts and give an account of all that he had done to date, including the "spying". His having worked for the Germans at Siemens during World War II, and for the Americans at the Kiangwan Air Base, and Caltex after the war, were the "mortal sins" that nothing could wash away, and they remained to haunt him until several years after the Cultural Revolution officially ended.

While my father was kept confined or in isolation, undergoing "thought reform", people from his work unit would come to ransack our room, to look for "evidence." Of what, I don't know. They took away some old snapshots and pictures, among them ones of the Reverends Richard B. Gaffin and John Rhoads, and some letters written in English. After leaving Caltex, my father went through one political movement (*yundong*, which can also mean physical exercise, or athletic event) after another so that by the time the Cultural Revolution came along my father, and others like him, had become quite seasoned "athletes". There has been no evidence whatsoever to prove that he was guilty of any of the charges. But when he was finally left in peace, the "verdict" was not clean-cut nor conclusive. It was the typical "Grounds for suspicion exist, but no evidence found to date." In other words, the policy at the time was that such people cannot be totally left off the hook, and they still had to live with their tails between their legs, they still had to wait for the other shoe to drop, they still had to pass their days under the shadow of the guillotine. He lived for eighteen years beyond the formal end of the Cultural Revolution, but no apology was ever extended, oral or written, to him, or to others like him. But then, of the millions who had been politically harassed and those who had not survived the ordeal, how many, if any, had been offered apologies?

In later years, my father disclosed that he had been offered a job in Hong Kong with Caltex after it had liquidated its Shanghai office. He declined it because the condition was that he go alone. He could not think of leaving behind a wife and five children who depended on him for their livelihood. He did not tell my mother of the offer or I think she would not have agreed with him but would have instead upped and grabbed it. I think it was he who could not function without a wife to care for his food and clothing, and not the other way around. I wonder if he ever regretted his decision, especially when he was being endlessly harassed.

To my father's knowledge, and to the knowledge of almost everyone in China who had weathered the times, except for the few at the very top, none of the persecutors were ever punished for what they had done. Some were merely transferred to work units where no one knew of their past, while others stayed on, or were even promoted to higher positions. My father outlived those of his persecutors who were not transferred to other units, and many of his "cell-mates." He was never officially jailed because he had not committed any crime, but lynching and kangaroo courts can sometimes be worse than a formal jail sentence because there is no time limit to them, with no records kept. I doubt that the jails in China at that time would have had the capacity to hold all those who were in detention. Perhaps it was because he was never jailed that he merited no official apology.

What my father and millions of others like him had gone through for no obvious reason at all was, and still is, incomprehensible to me. In later years we had thought that an apology would be forthcoming. Whenever we hinted at it, we would often hear the advice of "an arm cannot out-twist a leg" (taking revenge is no use) and it is best to "*suan le*" (forget it). What we and millions of others wanted was not revenge. We are exactly the ones who know from first-hand experience that truly an arm cannot out-twist a leg, and nor was it safe "to dash an egg against a rock". All we wanted was a "*suan le*" for ourselves, a clean-cut apology, not a dangling tail that could be tugged at whenever another political movement took place. We wanted to be let off the hook, once and for all. Was that so much to ask for? It turned out that the "*suan le*" was only for the persecutors, and not for their victims. The result was that the persecuted were not given an apology, nor were persecutors brought to justice. In fact, the old 'guerrilla warfare' instinct still prevails even to this very day. "Never shoot shit in the same place twice." If you make a mess of matters in one place, get transferred to another so that nobody will know. Not only were persecutors not punished, some were even promoted when transferred to a different place. And how did the people react? We shook our heads, that is the most that we could do without asking for trouble. There was no system of justice to which anyone could appeal. So it boiled down to the fact that what a little shrimp like my father and other shrimps like him went through was considered as no big deal at all, because other influential people, people who had really mattered, were going through the same hell, possibly a hotter one. I thought we should all be taught to sing the popular song with the following words,

Let bygones be bygones forever,
We'll fall in love once again,
So let's tell the world of our new love divine,
Forever and ever you'll be mine.

There was no one to talk reason to. "Ask not what your country has done to you, but ask what you haven't confessed to your country" just about sums up the unwritten policy during those days. This all took place while I was in my late teens. The fear that I would have to go through the same ordeal as soon as I was old enough for the job market was enough to leave me cold. Yet there was no way out for someone of my age. The feeling of being trapped was intense, even though students were not bothered much by the prevailing political climate. It was true that we also had what were called political study classes, but I didn't have to believe in what was being taught. We were told how great the Soviet Union was, and were taken to see Soviet and other "progressive" movies, something which had never happened before. The first Soviet movie the school organized the students to see was *Cossacks of the Kuban*, about a collective farm. The Chinese subtitle was "The Happy Life". We were not at all impressed with the acting and singing, nor with the actors and actresses. The male actors were too coarse-looking and the women too dowdy and with figures like oil drums. But I was deeply impressed with how well they all spoke Mandarin. So there was some truth for all the bragging about 'Big Brother' after all. Little did I know that the movie was dubbed. Up till then, I had never seen a foreign film dubbed in Chinese. All the foreign movies were in English, and for those who did not understand the language, they could rent a set of earphones to plug in to the back of the seat in front and hear the simultaneous translation of the dialogue. Sometimes a tele-prompter-like screen would be by the screen with Chinese written on it. In all fairness, though, there were some very good Soviet movies in the years that followed. *Othello* and the ballet *Romeo and Juliet* were among the most outstanding Soviet films I have ever seen.

The Sino-Soviet Friendship Building was built on the grounds of the former Hardoon Gardens where our school had had most of its PT classes because our own grounds were too confining. The first exhibition after the building was completed was the Soviet Exhibition. Organized (compulsory) attendance was required. I can't remember enjoying it because it was full of huge, enormous machines and what looked like ball-bearings or gears which were as big as houses. The light industrial goods that were displayed could in no way compete with local Shanghai products, especially the printed fabrics. I think even the farm women from Pootung would consider the prints too country bumpkin. The candies, huge big pieces offered in only a couple of varieties, were worse than the cheapest candies made in Shanghai. Put one in your mouth and you become speechless because there was no room to move your tongue. As an assignment, we had to write a summary of what we saw. Those who spoke their minds were reprimanded. The second such organized exhibition visit our class was taken to was the Czechoslovakian Exhibition. It was great! What a huge difference it was from the first one. The cut glassware drew admiration from one and all, as did the leather goods. The image of "Big Brother" had shrunk in our eyes. Before 1949, there were several shoe stores by the name of *Bata*, pronounced 'batcha' in Shanghai, and they were said to be owned by a Czechoslovakian. One of them was near the Sun Ya Restaurant on Nanking Road, and another one was in Hongkew, near Henning Road. After the war, my parents had bought a pair of blue sandals for me from one of the stores which I was allowed to wear on special occasions.

Not having worked for Caltex for many years before it closed up shop, my father's severance pay was limited. Joining the China Petroleum Company also meant that he was only earning around one-fourth of his former salary. The children, five of us, were growing and our needs became greater. Our various aunties and uncles were leaving or had left the country because companies were closing down and they had to go where there were jobs. Those with British passports went to England, some were sponsored by their former employers for whom they had worked diligently for decades, many having known no other work since leaving school. Others settled elsewhere in the world. There were still a few American missionaries in Shanghai one or two years after 1949, some of them 'under suspicion.' Frank Price of the China Bible House on Hong Kong Road was one of them, or so I had heard. People like Dr Ralph Mortensen and others left soon after 1949. Dr Mortensen had a daughter around my age, also named Margaret, who was fondly called Peggy but 'Damsel in Distress' behind her back because she had a very stern-looking stepmother.

The Community Church still functioned for a number of years after 1949, and so did the Free Christian Church. There was the Summer Vacation Bible Class in the compound of the China Inland Mission conducted by Anna Swarr, Emma Sullivan and others. John Rhoads' 'revival' meeting was held around this time. He had unknowingly repeated the same mistakes of some of his predecessors — there is no way to convert people without an effort to understand their culture. Most missionaries had lived by themselves either in good houses or in compounds inhabited by their own kind, and with domestic help. In the eyes of most Chinese, there is no difference between a foreign missionary and a foreign somebody else. The soul has to be saved, but doesn't the body have to be nourished as well? And can it be done without proper food and clothing? How many will care about the "hereafter" when they have trouble coping with the "here and now?" My parents and the rest of the family attended those revival meetings, and they were "saved" and baptized. I had been baptized earlier than that.

I think John Rhoads was trying to do what Billy Graham was doing in the United States at about the same time, but his revival meeting did not turn out the way he had expected and he made some remarks to the church people which did not leave them too happy. Had he taken the circumstances into account, he would not have done so. First of all, even though Shanghai did have a small English-speaking community of Chinese people, many had left and others were preparing to do so. Of those that remained, many or most had never left China, where they were born and bred and had little idea of what their future would be once they left it. Foreign companies were closing down one by one, and nearly one everyone in the English-speaking community worked for one of them.

After all the foreign missionaries had left, with the exception of Helen Willis of the Christian Book Room on Yuanmingyuan Road, our church continued to function to a degree, with the senior members who were left taking turns in giving sermons on Sundays. The morning services had previously been held in the chapel of the Bubbling Well Cemetery, but that now ceased and all church activities were limited to the premises at 480 Chapoo Road. The last French diplomat in Shanghai, a Monsieur Monchantre, a Huguenot, attended our services with a Madame Pimor, formerly Madame Bao. Later on, they married. Madame P. was formerly married to a Chinese and had very handsome children.

With the departure of older members, new people arrived, but not sufficient in number to keep the church going. Among the newcomers were some who we suspected could be people from the government trying to find out what went on in the church three days a week (Wednesdays, Saturdays and Sundays). I doubt that anything incriminating was found because the doors were always open and anyone could come in at will. But if the people who came were sent by the authorities and knew no English, then he could suspect all sorts of things through lack of understanding as almost all civilities were conducted in English. If someone is sent to find out something, they cannot return empty-handed, and something would have to be cooked up. To feel insecure about things unknown is common to all of us, and that is why ignorance is such a bane. Much of the hostility in the world is generated from fear of the unknown, and yet have we sincerely and diligently tried to penetrate the unknown with tolerance? It seems that the saying "live and let live" is foreign to many of us.

With political movements following one after another, my father and all those who were left over from the "old society" and who did not belong to the "working class" were dragged through hell and high water again and again. We did not know which "class" we belonged to. In the "old society" even though my father worked for Siemens and Caltex, he was just an employee, an office clerk. Sure, he was a little better paid than an office boy, an elevator operator, or a watchman, but still, he was near the bottom of the office hierarchy. He performed better than some overseas-born Chinese, or local stateless Chinese, or Chinese with foreign names, but so what? He was still a Chinese-Chinese, and therefore allocated to the next-to-bottom rung of the social ladder. There was no one to whom we could go for justice. The political workers were mostly former PLA soldiers or cadres from other parts of China, mostly people who had never been in a city before. Their treatment of people like my father was "eyebrows and beard in one tuck." No differentiation was made.

One day, two people from my father's office came while he was again being isolated in Pootung to write his "materials", and my mother was away from home visiting a friend. They ransacked our room searching for something—what, I don't know. I bit one of them on the arm in an attempt to stop it because I was afraid my mother would give me "what-for" when she returned for turning the place into such a mess. For that, my father was detained a week longer in isolation and had to write apology after apology. It was only years later that he told me.

The political movement to eliminate and eradicate "counter-revolutionaries" continued. Numerous people were put in jail, some were detained in jail for questioning, others were actually sentenced. Among the former were Ann Chow, a very sweet young lady who spoke no English who was the girlfriend of Francis Carey of B.A.T.; Mildred Chen, because she hobnobbed with foreigners; Dennis Soong and his wife; his sister Greta Soong, and many others.

I was almost a daily visitor to Chum's on the sixth floor (penthouse) of 131 Museum Road (Huqiu Lu). The watchman knew who I was, but still I had to register at the desk on the fifth floor, take a sheet of paper which Chum had to sign, and which was handed back to the watchman when I left (although usually he wasn't around after office hours). I do not know the purpose of the visitors' registration. Was it to keep check of the visitors, or was it to keep check of the visited? Dr Tu would often stay up till very late in his office on the fifth floor, writing. He was a person of few words, and whenever Chum asked him anything, he would just grunt and keep on doing whatever he was doing, usually reading a newspaper or poring over thick books at his desk. He had taken to smoking a pipe. It was evident that something was wrong. He was then head of the China Youth Alliance, formerly the Chinese YMCA, and a professor of atomic physics at the Shanghai Normal Institute. He held also a "leading" post in the All-China Christian Three-Self Organization, and was a standing member of the Chinese People's Political Consultative Committee, going to Peking for conferences each year. I remember hearing him remark that Premier Zhou Enlai had personally greeted him on one occasion, saying he didn't recognize him in his Chinese gown. He would always return from the meetings with a suitcase full of papers. But in spite of his positions, he was not spared from the grueling trials that most intellectuals went through. On one occasion I remember clearly, he had been in his office for several days, staying late into the night, always accompanied by "someone." He came home one day, and went out to the verandah for a breath of fresh air. Chum followed him, and when he leaned out toward the ledge a little further than was necessary, Chum hit him on the head with a flowerpot, thinking that he was trying to jump off. Maybe he was. Many Chinese intellectuals would rather break than bend, as history showed. Suicides by jumping off tall buildings were not unusual in those days. I recall that Henry Choy once told me on the sly, in church, that "Dr Tu was a 'modernist'." I didn't know what that meant, but if a good person like Dr Tu was a 'modernist', then it was good enough for me.

Search without warrant, conviction without evidence, guilt by association, and sentence without jury were not inventions of the Cultural Revolution at all. They had been part and parcel of the Chinese culture since time immemorial, except for a few enlightened periods. The only difference is that in some periods of history they were more openly practiced, and in other relatively enlightened periods, less so. But they have always been there. Sometimes they are more potent when not openly used. In any period of history, there is always more than meets the eye. The casual observer sees only the appearance, whereas people actually living in that period sense the rapid undercurrents through personal experience. For foreigners who claim to be authorities on China, how many of them have lived in the country long enough to understand? How many have themselves gone through such grueling ordeals or have Chinese friends who have done so? Proficiency in the Chinese language can be mastered in an ivory tower, but the understanding of Chinese culture and its people requires the scholar to step out of his ivory tower and mingle with the people. China is such a big country that no one can claim to know all about it, whether a native son or otherwise. China has more regional languages and dialects than France has varieties of cheese.

The experience of each individual Chinese going through that same period in history was also different. What my father went through was hard to comprehend, in that he was near the bottom of the social ladder during the Japanese War, during the civil war that followed, and now again. He could not, and neither could many others like him, understand what was wrong with having worked for foreign firms, what was wrong in doing a job that paid better? After all, a man has a family to support. He was Chinese all along, adopted no foreign name, bought no foreign passport, and therefore had earned no foreign pay under false pretenses. But there was no way to prove his innocence, as he could not rip his heart out to show that there was no guilt there. His dilemma of being haunted by the past of having worked for 'foreigners', and not being able to undo it, was the same as that of countless other Chinese of similar backgrounds. In whatever period of history, some people get away with murder while others go through hell for nothing. For the latter, a theory was invented to counteract it: "No child should mind his mother for being ugly." Which was taken to mean that a child should not hold a grudge against his mother for having reprimanded him for his own good. Well, where to draw the line between "child abuse" and "reproof" or "abuse"? The long-suffering nature of the people has been exploited to the fullest. Patriotism should be stressed in the education of all regardless of time and circumstances. People should be taught to be proud of the fact that they are Chinese. But there is a big difference between the land and what happens in it. There is no great disappointment where there is no great love. Patriotism should be a two-way street. We, as Chinese, should love our country, but shouldn't our government love us as well? All give and no take does not last forever. Anyone who has the guts to defend his country from the abuse of its government is a patriot, and without patriots there would be no revolution, no new country. Would there have been a Liberation had the patriots not defended the country against the abuses of the KMT government? That a government, any government, can do no wrong is a fallacy. Otherwise we would still be at a very primitive stage of society. A government is also like an individual, it ought to see itself as others see it. There are things for the people to gripe about even in countries with the most enlightened of governments. Again, there is no great disappointment where there is no great love, and criticism of the government and its policies, should be viewed as such.

If my father, someone who was so timid that he was afraid even a falling leaf might crack his skull, was being suspected of being a "spy", then someone as outspoken as I would be in for a much worse fate. That thought was paralyzing. Because my father was in isolation almost six days a week, sometimes not even let home on Sundays, whatever overseas correspondence we had to do was left to me. Our aunties and uncles had left, and we always kept in touch with them. Letters to England were sent through Prague in those days, for some reason. Letters to the United States were enclosed in letters sent to Auntie Ellie in Hong Kong because there was no other way we could send them from Shanghai. Because I had learned to "think" in English, writing letters in English came as natural to me as breathing, and it helped to improve my spelling.

Even though I had Chinese schooling, I realized that I was not Chinese enough in that I had few Chinese-Chinese friends, except for one or two classmates with whom I was not very close. My world up to that point revolved around people in the church and the Tu family, especially around Chum whom I saw at least most days if not every day. It was through her that I had access to many books. She would recommend books to me which she had read and would question me on the books to make sure that I had read them. We had many discussions into the night on various subjects, and through them I gained much knowledge. Books by Edgar Snow, Agnes Smedley, articles by Anna Louise Strong, as well as novels by various writers were devoured with enthusiasm as they opened up new worlds for me. The difference in age, for Chum was at least a dozen years older than my own mother, was no barrier at all. My own mother was illiterate, and my father a man of few words much too busy either working or going through one period of isolation after another. Neither had much time to care for the education of the children. So long as we were in school, they were at ease. My father was on tenterhooks from one political movement to the next, and I was groping my way through adolescence and hung on to the first person who was there for me. In retrospect, I realized that there was a great need in me to 'leech' on to the first person with whom I could find a common language. There is a Chinese saying which says it well: *Tong jun yiye hua, sheng du zhinian shu*, literally meaning that "one can learn more from talking to a learned person in one evening than from studying in school for ten years". It was not so much that Chum was "learned" but that I was so "unlearned". Everything she had to say was new to me, and I soaked up her words like a sponge. She was like a mother to me, minus the nagging. She talked with me instead of at me, or to me. And I could argue with her, which was something I had seldom done with a grown-up before. Or if I had dared, I never came out the winner.

I think growing up the way I did, and under those circumstances, I just had no roots. There were no real relatives, no real aunties, uncles, or cousins, and no one on whom I could anchor myself, so I just clung on to the first woman who was kind to me. I have had the good fortune to have known a number of such women, even during my Altai years when I was a grown woman myself. I still had this inner need to either be close to, or to look up to, an older woman. But never a woman of my own kind, never a Han Chinese.

After the first few political movements in which my father was one of the targets and nothing concrete could be gotten out of him, he was taken along for the ride in other movements. In the "Three- and Five- Anti" movements (*san-fan, wu-fan*) he was also in isolation, and was also assigned to keep watch on a colleague (a 'tiger') who was under suspicion. The China Petroleum Company was then operating at the premises of the former American Club near Hamilton House on Foochow Road. One day, the colleague my father was assigned to watch over claimed he had a "bad tummy" and had to be constantly accompanied to the men's room. The last time he went in, he stayed longer than usual and my father became concerned. He called and there was no answer. He broke open the door and found the man on the window sill. My father was able to catch hold of one of the man's trouser legs for a second as he jumped to his death. It was a big shock for my father, and worse still, he had to account for his "oversight."

Not all those who committed suicide did so out of guilt, as people were made to believe. Some just went berserk, and were looking for an easy way out. The common Chinese folk saying, "*hao si bu ru lai huo*" literally means 'a difficult life is preferable to an easy death,' tells much about our will to survive under any circumstances. Anyone who commits suicide must be desperate and must see absolutely no other way out. We Cantonese have a saying, "even a beggar preserves his life for the day when he will become prosperous." (*hatyi laumeng dangfatchoy*).

One day I was waiting for the tram at the stop in front of the Bank of China (near Sassoon House, now the Peace Hotel building) to go to school when I heard a noise like a big pumpkin or watermelon being dashed to the ground with a big "plop." I looked behind me. Someone had jumped from the Bank building. That was the first time I had actually seen a suicide, but it wasn't going to be the last time. The experience was shattering not only emotionally, but also physically — my bladder gave way. Not long after that, I witnessed another suicide from Chum's, in the penthouse at 131 Huqiu Road where the Tu's stayed. Chum and I were talking outside on the porch, when we heard some commotion from the building across the road, then we saw a man jump down from the eighth floor.

I witnessed another suicide from Chum's penthouse. Chum and I were talking outside on the porch when we heard a commotion from the same building across the road, and we saw a man jump, again from the eighth floor. I suppose that was the office where people were interrogated.

At the recommendation of Auntie Mae Johnston who was working as a secretary at the British Consulate, my mother found a job there working for the Rameau family. She took care of their little girl, Jill, an angelic, blonde toddler around three years old. Mr Rameau, the second person in charge at the consulate, was an alcoholic and his wife was a very hard-to-please woman expecting a second baby. Their household had several servants, a cook, a house boy, a woman servant who took care of the washing and ironing, and my mother who took care of Jill. The person in charge of the British Consulate then was a Mr Gardner, who later became the British Ambassador to Cambodia. Mrs Gardner was a pleasant, generous and vivacious lady who had lived in Shanghai in her youth. But the job of taking care of Jill did not last long. One day, my mother was taken ill and I had to skip school to take her place. Then I understood why the servants complained so much of Mrs Rameau's arrogance, although I cannot imagine how an expectant mother with a toddler and an alcoholic husband could be happy, even though she was living a relatively comfortable life. She talked down to me like she would to any servant, and I talked back to her equally unceremoniously. She then gave my mother a lecture after she returned to work. The job lasted only a short time because Mrs R was going to give birth soon and her husband badly needed treatment for his drinking problem, so they returned to England.

There were still some other foreign families with children in Shanghai. One was the Norwegian Anvig family, another was a Belgian man with a Korean wife who claimed to be from an "aristocratic" Korean family even though everyone knew she had been a barmaid in one of the bars along the wharf down in Yangzepoo. He was a Catholic, and she had to move to Zikewei to be near the Catholic church so she could be tutored in catechism. They had a former Chinese Catholic nun who was fluent in French to take care of their children. Whenever there was a children's party, all the other children of the foreign families of that stratum in town would gather, and so would their servants, and when servants gathered they exchanged gossip about their employers. Many fascinating stories, with different degrees of truth or untruth, were exchanged. There was a half-Chinese little boy who was said to be the "adopted" son of a Norwegian gentleman. The boy was taken care of by a Chinese "servant" who was in fact his mother.

The British Consulate was by then the only place in town still showing American or British movies, which came in the diplomatic pouch, once a week. These movies were shown to a very exclusive audience. Among those who had access to the weekly movies were British subjects, other foreigners and a few rich Chinese who dared to hobnob with such people, among them Nien Cheng, author of *Life and Death in Shanghai*. I was never invited, of course, And why should I have been? Chum would tell me about the movies she saw, but among the many, I only remember *Moulin Rouge*, It was the first time I heard the name Toulouse Lautrec. Queen Elizabeth's coronation in 1953 involved a big event among the remaining foreigners in Shanghai. So many had already left that all the stateless people who had previously never been included in big events when the Somebodies were in charge of the various big companies, were invited to the event as well, creating quite a hubbub and new spurt of business at Logaifok, the Silk Store on the ground floor of the former Hardoon Building right next door to the former offices of Siemens. I think that was the last big 'do' for foreigners after 1949.

The Hongkong & Shanghai Bank was still functioning, though not at its former premises or in its former capacity. A Mr Buchan, head of the bank at the time, let the choir of the Holy Trinity Cathedral use his residence for weekly practices.

Shanghai in those days had many churches belonging to as many Protestant denominations. Ours was interdenominational, or non-denominational. There were many Catholic churches and chapels as well, and a Greek Orthodox church, a Lutheran church, and also a Christian Scientist church. Our church had its Sunday morning service in the chapel of the Bubbling Well Cemetery where many local foreigners and Eurasians were buried. After the missionaries left, the senior members each took turns in speaking at the weekly meetings. As members became fewer, the church stopped functioning, but it was still in operation when I left town in 1956.

I had almost no Chinese-Chinese friends my own age. The only two girls with whom I was on friendlier terms were from primary school days. They were the eighth and ninth children of a Cantonese family by the name of Ho. Their father and uncle were twin brothers who worked as cooks on an American ship and when the Pearl Harbor attack occurred, they were at sea, so could not return to China. That separation from their families lasted until the mid-sixties when the men were retired. The U.S. government policy threatened to cut off their pensions if they returned to the mainland, so they had no choice but to settle in Hong Kong, and for the wives to join them there. These two girls volunteered to serve in Xinjiang right after they finished school in 1954 because their having a father in the United States created difficulties for job assignments in Shanghai. It is not uncommon throughout Chinese history to find wives spending their lifetimes waiting for their spouses who were sometimes off at war or banished to faraway places on job assignments or serving sentences. That no chaste woman married twice was the accepted moral standard in feudal times, and continued to be for some time.

Up until 1956, I had little or no idea of what the rest of China was like. I had never been out of the city limits of Shanghai except to Kaochiao for picnics once or twice, and another picnic to the Lunghwa Airport very early on. Shanghai was a city of extremes. There were some very poor people in Nantao and also in a place near Jessfield Park where Miss Helen Willis lived. The people there lived in shacks, and nearly every family had a crippled, or deformed, child, usually from polio. It was unbelievable. I realized more than ever that the world I was in was not only unreal, it was also coming apart with the departure of more and more foreigners. I come from a poor family myself, but the people whom I was with most of the time were not poor, and neither were they Chinese-conscious like Chum was. I began to think seriously about my own future. My grades were not so good that I could ever contemplate the possibility of a college education, and with that, there would be the eventual *tongyi fenpei* or "unified allocation" of students that was feared by people my age. Leaving Shanghai was the last thing that anyone wanted to do. After all, there was only one Shanghai in China. The fear of the unknown prevailed among those who knew next to nothing about their own country. I was one of them.

There were young people who had already finished college, or were about to, who dropped out of school in fear of the unified allocation which meant that they would be sent away from Shanghai. Some 're-entered' college disguising themselves as high school graduates in the hope that by the time they finished their four-year college education the 'tide' would 'turn'. History disappointed them.

The Cultural Club was a place where top members of the academic world, the literati and scientists could gather. It was at the former French Club diagonally across from the Cathay Theater in Frenchtown, on Maoming Road, and I was able to get in to see movies there. I particularly remember *Miracle on 34ᵗʰ Street*, with John Payne, Maureen O'Hara, and Natalie Wood and *The Perfect Marriage* with David Niven and Loretta Young. Dr Tu was a member of the National People's Political Consultative Committee (NPPCC) and a noted physicist, and it was through him that I had access. I once met a Czechoslovakian expert there, by the name of Zdanyk Kostlivy who spoke some English. He talked about the ills of the "planned economy" and said that at one time, his country had no safety pins because they had been overlooked in the government plans. When I became a mother some years later, I realized how important safety pins were.

The Russian community in Shanghai boasted several ballet masters. The best-known school was across from the Lyceum Theater, run by the Skolskys. They helped train China's first ballerina, Wu Yongyong, labeled China's Shirley Temple. Another of their students was Blossom Lawlor Shek, whose mother worked for The Imperial Chemical Industry (ICI), BLS later danced with the Sadler Wells Company. The Gao family had a daughter who was a ballerina, but she was denied the role of dancing "The White-haired Girl" because she looked 'too foreign'. Her mother was English. The residence of H.H. Kung, former Minister of Finance of the KMT Government, became the Soviet Club after 1949. All the Russians of Shanghai were encouraged to register for Soviet passports, and some openly admitted that they were "radishes" (red on the outside, but white inside). Some became "Soviet experts" overnight and taught Russian in colleges and universities, while others, with the help of the IRO, left for Western countries. Those who stayed with Soviet passports mostly went back to the Soviet Union after the break in Sino-Soviet relations. Where they went decided their fates in later life.

In 1956, my feeble attempt to get a job at the Indian Consulate failed. I did not know shorthand, which was required. There were two British ladies giving shorthand lessons in Shanghai, but the fee was high and there was no way my parents could afford it. As for typing, I learned that quite early on at home when my father bought an old typewriter at a second-hand store in the Central Arcade. It weighed a ton, and was in very poor condition. Press the wrong key and the whole machine would fly apart, as it were. My father used very thin wire to hinge all the keys, and finally got it to work. I taught myself to type from a tattered manual that came with it. Coming from a poor family had many disadvantages. I have always enjoyed music, but my parents could not afford piano lessons. I envied people who could ride bicycles, but I never had one to learn on. I never learned how to dance, to play cards, except Lexicon, the card-form of Scrabble, to smoke, or to drink. In other words, I was not able to be a sociable person because my interests were very limited. I had an inferiority complex.

I made up my mind to start my life over again. I realized that I could not go on living the former cycle of school, home and church. I was more and more disenchanted with how things were developing and was also scared that soon I would be in my father's situation. Politically speaking, I was very "backward" because no one had enlightened me, and I had too many questions that were unanswered. I would have to leave school one day, and home … well, what is home when father was always in fear of the next detention? My brothers and sisters seemed content, but I was not. There was "someone" inside of me longing to break out, and the older I grew, the more frustrated I became. As for our church, I knew it was bound to close down sooner than later since the people were leaving one by one.

The lane people knew more about us than we did about ourselves, which was troubling. The lane committee definitely knew of the suspicions that my father was under, and sooner or later his offspring would have to pay too. So I decided to look for work elsewhere in the country, the further away from Shanghai the better. I wanted to run away from the kind of trouble my father was in and I decided on going to one of the three most remote places I could think of in China – Tibet, Inner Mongolia and Xinjiang. My two former classmates, the Ho girls, were already in Xinjiang, but I had not heard from them since they left so I had no idea what their life there was like. Perhaps if we had kept in touch and they had let me know something about how they were getting on, I would not have made the move that I did.

My reason for deciding what I did was that since young people had to accept "unified allocation" on finishing school, why not take the initiative and volunteer to go to a remote place to work? At least that would be a plus in my file, and after having been to the furthest and remotest place, one would not be afraid of being sent anywhere else. That was my very simple reasoning. I had no one to consult with, except Chum, and what advice she had to offer was limited. The place to go, I decided, was Xinjiang because by coincidence, there were people just then recruiting young people in Shanghai to go to Xinjiang. I attended a meeting to find out what it was all about. We were told that Xinjiang was literally a land of milk and honey, and that people dressed in woolen material instead of cloth. The terms stated at the meeting were more or less acceptable. We were to work in offices at least at the company level, paid according to our degree of education, which would be 50-70 yuan for junior high school students, and 70-90 yuan for senior high school students, with increases later on according to merit. We were promised that no one would be assigned to work as salespersons, a job that was looked down upon by many. We were also promised that we could have home leave once every two years before we married, and once every ten years after we did. And a string of other promises. Chum encouraged me to go, and I met with no resistance from my own parents. I couldn't be living on them forever, and because of my father, I would probably be soon sent to heaven-knew-where anyway, so I decided I might as well sign up, little realizing that by doing so I was forfeiting any future right of residence in Shanghai. Perhaps I was chasing after the dream of starting life anew, unaccompanied by the poverty I had known and by the kind of political harassment my father was going through. Unknowingly, however, I was being chased by precisely that which I was running away from.

Now, more than six decades later, after much heartbreak and sorrow, I can say that all things worked out for the best (touch wood!).

3

VOLUNTARY EXILE (1956-1960)

THE DEPARTURE DATE for Urumqi, Xinjiang was set for September 29, 1956. I was with a group of around thirty people my own age and some older, none of whom I knew. I had been to the North Station only once or twice prior to leaving Shanghai. We had been told that we would be traveling by hard sleeper all the way to the rail terminus, which at the time was a small town called Zhangye. The railroad tracks had only been laid a little way past Lanzhou at that point. But instead of traveling hard sleeper as promised, we had to sit all the way. It seemed to take forever to reach our first stop which was the city of Xi'an. The Nanking Bridge had not been built then, so the train cars had to be ferried across the river a few at a time, then re-hitched before we could continue the journey.

We arrived in Xi'an in the morning of October 1 and were told to leave the train and rest for a day before continuing on the next leg of the journey. We were herded into the waiting room of the train station because a National Day Parade was taking place in the city and traffic was at a halt. The waiting room smelled so terribly bad, and was filled with such dirty-looking people speaking such a strange-sounding, unheard of, dialect that I felt as though I had been plucked from one planet and transplanted onto a totally unknown one. I am sure many others in the group felt the same.

I was not the only girl who started to cry. If one or two day's distance from Shanghai was this abominable place, where would several days' journey land us? The public toilet was a line of big square trunk-like containers with no seat but only planks across them, and we didn't know how to use them. The girls had no choice but to go to an isolated corner in the courtyard and took turns squatting there to relieve ourselves one by one while the others stood in a half circle with their backs toward the 'squatter', shielding her while she did what had to be done. Many in the group realized then and there that things were not going to be as we expected.

When the parade finally ended, we were taken to a courtyard of the local government and shown into two big rooms, one for the females, another for the males. We had to unpack our bedding, and spent the night sleeping on the floor. We had to take care of our own meals, and some in the group went into town to look for a place to eat. They returned shaking their heads because the local diet was very different from the Shanghai one, and all the food had a muttony smell. I just munched on the cookies I had brought along.

The courtyard we were in had a dining hall for government workers. I noticed that the portions of food from the dining hall were extraordinarily big, and that the people did not sit at the square tables which had a bench on each side, but that they rather stepped on the benches and squatted to eat, while others took their food out to the courtyard and squatted by a wall holding a piece of steamed bread with one hand, a pair of chopsticks in another, and their bowl of vegetables or meat placed almost directly under their crotches. I could not believe what I was seeing. Traveling surely opened one's eyes!

We left Xi'an by train after a day's rest stop and continued on to Lanzhou. The further west we traveled, the more desolate the landscape became, and the more ragged the people appeared to be. Having grown up in Shanghai, I had seen my share of beggars, but these village people by the railroad tracks who begged for food whenever the train stopped were more pitiful than any beggars I had ever laid eyes on. As the train climbed in altitude, the temperature dropped, and we had to put on more clothes. Because we were traveling on hard seat and not hard sleeper as we had been promised, by the second night many had to crawl under the seats to find a place to stretch out. Someone from the group went to the hard sleeper section and found the recruiter and demanded that he find sleeper slots for everyone as he had promised, but he was told that they were all occupied. All he had from the recruiter was a promise that he would make up to everyone the difference in money between a hard seat and a hard sleeper, but that promise was never carried out. No other promises ever were either.

We finally arrived in Lanzhou. It was worse than Xi'an. The drinking water was muddy, the climate was dry, and some in the group immediately developed sore throats and aching ears. I was one of them. We saw people sitting by the street at food stands and eating from bowls the size of wash basins which they held in their hands. We had thought food portions in Xi'an were big. Here, they were huge.

Almost four days on the trip and I hadn't been able to make a single friend. I talked to nobody, and nobody talked to me. I had brought along a book to read, I have forgotten the name of it. But it wasn't my Bible because that was packed in my bedding. In Lanzhou, we were allowed one and a half days to rest. We had known that a big clothing store from Shanghai, the Xin Da Xiang, (or was it the Yeh Da Xiang?), had moved here lock, stock and barrel, and everyone was eager to find where it was so that they could talk to some Shanghai people in Shanghai dialect. I found that the dialect spoken in Lanzhou did not sound any better than the one we had heard in Xi'an. Several people in the group asked if I wanted to go with them, the first time anyone had talked to me, and I tagged along.

I never have considered myself a Shanghainese but always a Cantonese, even though I was born in Shanghai and had spent my life up until then in Shanghai. We were always registered as Cantonese because we are Cantonese. This is also one of my betwixt and between "misfit" aspects, as the real Cantonese who are born and bred in Guangdong Province or in the city of Guangzhou do not consider Cantonese-speaking people born in Shanghai, or elsewhere outside of Guangdong Province as genuine Cantonese, while the Shanghai people call us Cantonese even if some Shanghai-born Cantonese people considered themselves Shanghainese because they spoke little or no Cantonese. I attended a Cantonese-speaking school, and the few Shanghai girls that were there soon had to learn to speak Cantonese in order to be accepted by the majority. In a way, we bullied them, and when they asked us to teach them Cantonese, we would always teach them the wrong words so that when they practiced it on other Cantonese girls they'd be called names. All people who are not in their native land tend to band together even if they have their differences. I have always remembered being bullied by a couple of Swatownese boys when we were children. No doubt they felt intimidated in our neighborhood of Tengfenglay where the majority were Cantonese-speaking people.

From Lanzhou we boarded the train again, this time to Zhangye which was as far west as the railroad tracks were laid at that time. Zhangye, a tiny town in the Hexi Corridor in Gansu Province, was one of the poorest places in China. It was unbelievably dirty, and the people were literally grime-covered and in rags. The inn where we stayed had no electricity. The one outhouse was a hole in the ground circled by bundles of dried reeds. The only restaurant in town had a suspended "orange" from the ceiling which was called an "electric light bulb". We had a meal in a tiny hole-in-the-wall 'restaurant' there the second night we were in town, and I was more than surprised to find the lady who served us had on a "black satin jacket" and I remarked to the person sitting next to me (whom I married five years later) that it seemed "out of place" to wear "satin" in such a dump. He explained that the sheen was from grease, and not from the luster of satin.

The inn we stayed had several small rooms which were identical. Each had doors made from two very crude narrow boards, not of the same length, which opened inward, and the rooms had no windows. The space between the courtyard and the bare mud platform (*kang*) on which we slept, was just long enough for a pair of shoes, measuring from heel to toe. A person with a longer stride would step right onto the *kang* upon pushing open the doors. We stayed there for more than two nights, awaiting transportation further westward.

Zhangye was a poverty-stricken little town like most of the other small towns of Gansu Province. There were no paved roads, dirt tracks which floated inch-deep dust on dry days, and became muddy quagmires on rainy ones. There were people squatting on street corners selling a brown-skinned variety of pears little bigger than ping-pong balls. Others sold dirty looking hard-boiled eggs. The breakfast vendors carried shoulder poles with a charcoal stove and a pot of boiling water sitting on one end, and a hand-operated bellows on the other, with a basket of fresh eggs and a clay container of *laozhao*, known in Shanghai dialect as *jiuniang*, which is fermented rice and rice wine, and a stack of chipped rice bowls and a few spoons, and another rusty can with water for rinsing the used bowls and spoons. The rinsing did not seem to affect the 'half-moon' marks left on the edges of the bowls by different customers. But we hardly noticed how dirty the bowls were because our eyes were blurred with tears at downing a breakfast which reminded us so much of home, now so far behind us. Another locally-sold breakfast item was deep-fried rice cakes. These were very familiar to people from Shanghai and everyone from our group gorged themselves on them. It was the only real meal that we had enjoyed since leaving Shanghai on September 29.

The trucks — not buses — that would take us to Urumqi arrived. Each of us was given a pair of goggles, for what, we didn't know. The four-ton *Jiefang* trucks were covered with tarpaulins and we were told to line our luggage consisting of just a bedding roll and a suitcase on the sides of the truck and in the center. We then sat in four rows, with those sitting in the middle rows back-to-back facing the people sitting on either side. The ride to Urumqi lasted an entire week. We stopped every night at a village inn, but some of us, including me, found it much too bothersome to unroll our bedding because packing it back up was so arduous. The bedding, which is naturally soft, had to be packed tightly so that it would not sag when sat on. I just slept leaning against it. If the inn at Zhangye was crude, then the others we visited on our way to Urumqi were not much better. Some were worse.

We passed Yumen, near Jiayuguan, Yumen — literally, the Jade Gate. Khotan, at the foot of the Kunlun Mountains, is a great producer of jade. It has always been a much sought-after stone, not only by the imperial court but by people from all parts of the country, so there was a thriving trade in it. All jade coming out of Xinjiang and down to the Central Plains had to pass through Yumen, and a tax was levied on it. Hence the name.

Jiayuguan is the westernmost end of the Great Wall. Further

west was what amounted to many people as the Siberia of China. Countless stories from both feudal times and modern times tell of patriots, warriors and criminals who have been exiled from the Central Plains when they lost favor with their rulers, or when their noble causes had been defeated, or when they had committed heinous crimes warranting life sentences, passed through this place. Also young girls sent by the imperial court as concubines to tribal rulers as tokens of peace-offerings also traveled this same road, so much so that that there are lines from Tang Dynasty poems such as "The winds of spring do not reach the Yumen Pass" and "Upon leaving Yumen Pass, tears do not dry", which are familiar to all Chinese. Mine was a "voluntary exile," but that didn't prevent an ominous feeling from taking hold of me. I kept repeating the 23rd and 27th Psalms, and sang the hymn *God Will Take Care of You* to myself over and over again.

God will take care of you, be not afraid
He is your safeguard through sunshine and shade
He will take care of you when time is past
Safe to His kingdom will bring you at last.

And He has taken care of me. I wonder what comfort others sought as I could not have been the only person who was scared. Passages from the Bible and hymns and choruses that I had learned in Sunday School and Church were the only source of comfort that I could fall back on then, and in the difficult years that were to follow.

The roads were unusually bad, and the ride was bone-rattling. We bumped along each day in the dust. So that was what the goggles were for! Sometimes we would be on the road from morning till night without encountering a single human being. There was nothing but gobi (gravel), mountains and sky.

Even though we had been warned not to drink too much water, the driver still had to stop several times during the day's journey, with the males to one side of the truck and the females to the other. First, we had to tell the direction of the wind in order to decide our position or we would wet a leg of our pants or even our own faces if there happened to be a whirlwind, a small dust devil. At the end of each day we were all so dust-covered that the sight of our reflection on another's goggles would send us roaring with laughter because we all looked as though we had been rolled in gray cement powder.

When we finally reached Hami (Qumol, or Komul in the local tongue), we were able to rest one whole day before continuing on. We stayed at a place called *da ying fang* (the big camp) which was the headquarters of the 5th Agricultural Division of the Xinjiang Production and Construction Corps. It was a pleasant surprise for everyone to find a place such as Hami after the last few days on the road where we saw nothing but gobi. The town of Hami was nice and cool in the shade of the straight rows of white poplar, and ditches by the sidewalks where clear water flowed that was used to spray the streets to lower the temperature and put down the dust. The local honeydew melons (Hami melons), several varieties of them, were sweet and fragrant and very reasonably priced. Most of us had only heard of, or read of, the melons sent as tributes to the imperial court in Peking from local princes, and now we were actually enjoying them ourselves! We were a bit reluctant to leave when we had to continue on our way to Urumqi, our final destination. I did not know then that I would be returning to Hami in less than two weeks.

We reached Turpan at night, and it was not as hot as we had been told it would be. The roads in the tiny town were covered in powder-light dust, our steps echoed with a "wuff wuff" noise like a big powder puff pressing into a huge can of talcum. The street was a haze and the dust choked us and penetrated our clothes. When we got up the next morning to continue on our way and the temperature began to rise. By late morning, it was unbearably hot, not the humid heat we had all been used to in Shanghai, but a dry, searing heat which left everyone "scorched". We did not stay to sample the famous grapes and melons that Turpan was known for. We had read stories of the Monkey King and how he had extinguished the fire from the Flaming Mountain with the fan from the Iron Fan Princess. Well, the fire might have been put out then, but judging by the heat we were experiencing, it must have reignited after the Monkey King left.

We arrived in Urumqi in mid-October. I will never forget how surprised I was when we were taken to the regional Bureau of Commerce, which had been responsible in recruiting the group, and saw a white woman (Russian) on her hands and knees scrubbing the staircase. I had seen more than my share of white women in Shanghai, but never one on hands and knees doing menial work. All the menial work that had needed to be done was done by Chinese when there were white people in China, especially in Shanghai. How different things here were, I thought.

I had looked forward to arriving in Urumqi because there was someone there I could look up. Before I left Shanghai, Chum's friend, Juanita Byrd Huang of Shanghai University, had given me a package of *ruosong* (wok-dried shredded meat) to take to her sister in-law, Delia Huang, at the Xinjiang Medical College. (Delia was a classmate of Chum's eldest daughter Anna and her husband, Eddie). Juanita told me that Delia and her husband, Julian Wang, would befriend me. They were from the No.1 Medical College in Shanghai and had been sent along with some of their colleagues, to start the Medical College in Xinjiang. I asked around and was told that the Medical College was at the other end of town, near the city limits. I took a bus there and delivered what Juanita had entrusted to me. My new-found friends were a very kind and pleasant couple. They were the first people I made friends with after leaving Shanghai. Delia headed the Obstetrics Department and Julian was a teacher.

Most of the buildings in Urumqi seemed to have been built from the same blueprint, and people seemed to be from many different ethnic groups. After we were all rested, we were summoned to attend a meeting and were told just who would be allocated where to work. Even though in Shanghai we had been specifically promised that everyone would be working in the city of Urumqi, allocations to other parts of Xinjiang were announced. The majority was assigned to companies in Urumqi, but others were assigned to Ili (Gulja), Turpan and Hami. The "bolder" people who were assigned to places other than Urumqi flatly refused to leave because they felt they had been short-changed the minute they left Shanghai, and that enough was enough. The more timid ones just accepted their fate. I belonged to the latter group.

When I arrived in Hami in late-October of 1956, I was sent to work in the state-owned Produce Company store selling groceries and locally-grown farm produce. I came to realize that not one single promise that had been made to us in Shanghai was ever kept. We were told that we would traveling hard sleeper, and that if they were 'unavailable', the difference would be made up to us in cash. We were told that our jobs would be in Urumqi, but some had to work elsewhere. We were told that we would all be working in offices, but more than a few were sent to work as shop assistants. As for our pay, it was not what had been promised, either. I began to suspect that the road ahead would be still rougher because these few initial steps had been already so bumpy. What was I to do? No one had forced me to come, and there was no shoulder around for me to cry on, so whatever tears

there were had to be swallowed or shed quietly at night, in bed. I
suppose wetting my pillow is better than wetting my bed.

I was assigned to live in a room in the courtyard of the Hami
Produce Company on Jiefang Road. The room was only big
enough to hold three single beds and a suitcase or two. I shared
the room with two other older girls from Shanghai. One had
come a few months earlier than I and the second, WWY, was a
young woman from our group who was assigned to the same
company as I was. There was no electricity, no running water,
and an out-house that was unmarked. The only telephone in the
company had to be cranked and cranked some more to get it to
work. I was sent to work in the company's store on Zhongshan
Road, across from the local Post Office.

Each day of the six-day week began with political study before
breakfast, under a gas lamp that had to be pumped. A typical
session was one with the manager reading an article, usually an
editorial, from a newspaper which was at least a week to ten
days old, or a local government directive. The people just sat
and listened or huddled in a corner to continue their disrupted
sleep. After that was breakfast. Those with homes went home
for it, while single people just grabbed a bite of whatever was
available. Then it was time to open shop. In the evenings, there
would be political studies once or twice a week, but once a day
whenever a political movement was in progress. More often than
not, one was.

The produce sold in our shop was all locally grown from
the agricultural cooperatives in the nearby countryside. The
year 1956 was before the age of 'communes'. Our store had a
contract with a certain cooperative and we bought wholesale
whatever they produced. The farmers, mostly Han Chinese,
were descendants of people who had moved from other parts
of China such as Shantung Province, generations ago. The local

soil was rich and water was plentiful. The farm produce grown was superior to what we had in Shanghai. Everything was big. Carrots, turnips, radish, cucumbers, onions, eggplants, squash, tomatoes, potatoes, beets, chives and garlic were at least twice the size of those in Shanghai, and of a much superior quality. Greens were also plentiful, with the exception of lettuce, broccoli and Brussels sprouts which were then unheard of in Xinjiang. Hami was especially well-known for a kind of cabbage that seemed to be a hybrid of cabbage and what is known in Shanghai as Tientsin cabbage and *huangyacai*, but more like Napa cabbage except that it was longer and much bigger. Fruit and melons were sold by the local *kahperaht* (cooperative) and not by our *kerk dookan* (Green Grocer).

Every morning as we opened shop, the big horse cart would come laden with produce that had to be weighed separately according to variety, haggled over, written down and signed for. I was new and could only observe, or do whatever I was told to while trying to learn the ropes. The bargaining back and forth was at its worse whenever *dahtsoong* (big green Chinese onions) were delivered. Big green Chinese onions are bought for their white stalks, so their quality was judged according to how long and thick the white stalks were. The women in charge of the store would complain that the onions had too much dried mud stuck to the roots, or the roots were too long, or not enough of the green leaves were trimmed, and she would shake out the mud bundle by bundle before laying them on the scale, and the farmer who accompanied the horse cart would prevent her from doing so, claiming that it was the age-old custom that one *jin* (equivalent to 500 grams, in those days divided into sixteen *liang*, or ounces, instead of 10 *liang* to a *jin* now) of *"da cong"* is made up of four *liang* each of mud, whiskers (roots), leaves, and stalk. Tomatoes and cucumbers were wholesale priced by weight or piece, whichever was to the farmers' advantage. When sold by weight, they would let the cucumbers grow to the size of baseball bats. Sold by piece, they would be the size of cigars, at most. The farmers may have been illiterate, but they were certainly not stupid. They knew how to get a good bargain for themselves.

Urumqi had already been using the metric system years before we arrived, but Hami, closer to the rest of China by two days' journey on the highway, was still using the old Chinese system. Salespersons had to learn and memorize the *jinliangfa* by rote, which is a conversion table breaking down the sixteen *liang* (Chinese 'ounce') into decimals, by reciting the following table when we used the abacus to calculate the price of a commodity:

1=0625, 2=125, 3=1875, 4=25, 5 =3125, 6=375, 7=4325, 8=5, 9= 5625, 10=625, 11=6875, 12=75, 13=8125, 14=875, 15=9375, 16=1

We were also required to know how to use the abacus. Fortunately, when I was very young my father had taught me how to use it and also to recite the conversion table before I started school. I found that my colleagues, with the exception of one or two from somewhere near Hangzhou who had arrived several months earlier than we did, had had some high school education. The rest, local Han, or Han from Gansu Province, and the local Uyghurs, had only minimal schooling. The vice manager, a People's Liberation Army soldier from Shantung, was illiterate, and the man in charge of personnel, another PLA soldier who had served in the Korean War, was also illiterate beyond being able to write his own name, something the vice manager could not do. The principal person in charge was a man of the Hui ethnic group who was a local. He was also head of what would amount to a local Chamber of Commerce, and a member of the local People's Political Consultative Committee. He name was Zhang Wenrui, a man in his early fifties. He was much respected in Hami, and known by all the local business people.

In Hami, there were over a dozen or more young people from Shanghai working in the different companies and stores in town, and when I got to know them better, I found out that nearly every one of them had been short-changed as we had been. Like most people of those days, we had no choice but to bow to fate, except for two young men in our company. They had stiff necks and they made their discontent known. But how can an individual win against the establishment? Can an arm really out-twist a leg? They were as vulnerable as 'eggs' and were expelled after the anti-rightist movement and returned to Shanghai. In truth, they were voicing the sentiments of many who were in that same boat, but they could not get the others to join them in their demand for what they termed 'justice'. Before they were expelled, they were 'dragged over the coals' by being 'denounced' in mass meetings with one accusation after another thrown at them by Youth League members, all 'active elements' and one more radical than the next.

In spite of the painful ordeal that they had to endure, they were still considered lucky because now they could return to where they had come from – Shanghai. A few other youths even regretted that they had not join them in "kicking up a ruckus" so that they could also be sent back to the city that they came from. The rest of us knew that even if these two young men were returned to Shanghai, they would certainly not be allowed to stay there for long. First of all, the lane residents' committee would be notified of their reason for returning, and they would surely be assigned to somewhere else because of what was written in their personnel files. It was this fear that sealed the mouths of others. To volunteer for work in a remote place is one thing, but to be sent to another remote place as a form of punishment was something else altogether. Maybe these two young men and many others like them thought that any place could not be more remote or worse than Xinjiang, and maybe they were right.

Geographically speaking, Xinjiang was not a bad place. The only drawback was its distance from home, and its harsh climate and environment. But today, that distance can be covered in three or four hours now that air travel is so widespread. The Lanzhou-Xinjiang Railroad has now been laid past Urumqi, all the way to Kashgar, bordering Pakistan, and construction on the double tracks are also being completed. Buses now reach every nook and cranny of the region, and the mileage of paved roads is now many times more than what it was when we first came to the region half a century ago.

Hami was the first unbelievably green oasis upon entrance into Xinjiang proper. When I first arrived, there were still Soviet experts working in the town. Somehow, I think, because of its proximity to the Soviet Union, the Russians were more aware of the potential of the area than the Chinese government had been in the past. First of all, the latter did not have what it needed to tap the local underground resources in this relatively remote region, and the Russians did. Near Hami was the Sandaoling Open-cut Coal Mine – the biggest open-cut coal mine in Xinjiang – the Yiwu Military Horse-breeding Farm, and the Yamansu (Bad Water) Copper Mine, which was the principal copper mine in Xinjiang. Xinjiang is also known for its abundance of other resources such as gold, salt, mirabilite, oil, lumber, and many others. Hami was primarily known for its various varieties of honeydew melons, its apricots, mulberries, pears, apples, strawberries and other fruits, and also for its rare wildlife. In a word, it was a treasure trove, as are so many other places in Xinjiang.

Between late 1957 and the following year, all private business had to 'marry' into the government and become 'public-private jointly operated'. The double happiness character, *shuangxi*, generally used at weddings, was used to announce a merger ('marriage'). Our company, the one and only state-owned one selling farm produce, had the responsibility of having the half a dozen existing privately-owned produce stores merge into it. The first step was to have the owners of these stores attend meetings, have the value of their shops assessed, assets declared, their inventories checked, and then have these 'capitalists' sit in political study sessions. As the double happiness character indicated the movement to be a 'marriage', I think the bride was the private business sector because it had the 'trousseau' whereas the groom was penniless. She married, taking with her the last penny of the family.

Many shop owners were barely scratching out a living even though one and all were labeled 'capitalist'. One of them was an opium addict, and the thought of 'marrying' into a state-owned company meant that he would become a future state employee with a fixed pay, and most likely he would not have what it would take to indulge in his habit, which had anyway been declared illegal after 1949. He was the most stubborn of all the shop owners while the rest were glad to merge because they could not compete with a state-owned store. This opium addict was later self-cured of his habit. If he needed a perker-upper during a political study session, he would ask for permission to go out into the courtyard. There he would climb a tree and swing from one of the branches like a monkey. He would swing hard and long until he was totally exhausted and fell to the sand-covered ground in a dead swoon. After a while he would wake and pick himself up, dust off his clothes, and sheepishly return to his seat at the meeting. He was quite a spectacle.

Among my colleagues were several Uyghurs. The men

were named Hajji, Yimit, and Yunus; later on, Tahiyr, joined the company. The two teenage girls were Ayimhan and Ursnehan. Our manager, ZWR, spoke Uyghur, but none of the other Han people did. All the Uygur employees could speak some Chinese and we met each other half-way with the help of smiles and body language. I felt very uncomfortable not knowing the language and decided to learn with the help of my Uyghur colleagues. I had trouble at first, but improved with time and practice. I did make some embarrassing mistakes more than once by pronouncing certain words incorrectly, but all in all, I got along while none of my Shanghai colleagues felt that there was any need for them to learn the local tongue, since most of our Uygur colleagues could speak some Chinese. Our interests differed, that was all.

I became friends with Ayimhan and got on well with Patam (Fatima) who worked in the Post Office across from our store. Another girl, Amerahan, at the Kaparaht (Cooperative), also became my friend. Ursnehan, labeled *tartook* because she had a big scar below one eye, was often the butt of good-natured jokes because of her rumored 'free' lifestyle. With these Uygur colleagues around me, I would strain my ears whenever I heard them speak, and in the process, picked up a little of the language here and there, until I could make my simple needs known to them in their language.

Aside from writing home regularly, I kept up a correspondence with Chum in Shanghai and Auntie Ellie in Hong Kong, and through her with other friends. I wrote most of my letters in English and received letters from them regularly. I noticed that some of my colleagues, especially the woman, ZYZ, who worked as group-leader of the store, would peer over my shoulder whenever I was reading a letter in English, or whenever I was writing a letter in English when there was no business in the store. She reported all she had seen, none of which she understood. She was in her mid-thirties, at least, but was still a member of the Youth League (!). She was childless and married to a man who had been a low-ranking officer in the Kuomintang (KMT) Army at the time Xinjiang was peacefully liberated. She had been a prostitute in a small town in Gansu Province, and probably became a camp-follower and later married someone she had followed. She was the most radical woman I had ever come across. Hami had a number of her former customers who later 'exposed' her past in a political movement. I wonder if that cured her radicalism.

Most of the people living in Gansu Province were very poor, and some of its female population became prostitutes out of necessity. In those days it was well-known that girls in Wuwei, Zhangye, and other counties which were equally poor, could not even afford to buy cloth to make pants. They walked around the village in long jackets, and whenever they saw someone approaching them that they didn't recognize, they would crouch there until the person passed. Few, if any, outsiders ventured into those villages because, literally, there was nothing there except stark-naked poverty. Any man with a suit of the cheapest clothes, or even just a pair of pants, could get a wife from any one of those counties. Many truck drivers in Hami had gotten their wives from that area for exactly that, and they raised families and lived happily ever after, fully-clothed.

At about this time, there was a nationwide campaign for sales people to improve their service. Something equivalent to "Service with a Smile." The slogan was *Bai na bu yan, bai wen bu fan* which literally means that if a customer asks one hundred times to be shown a product, the sales person should not be tired of showing it to her, and if a customer asks a hundred questions, the sales person should give the answers willingly. How times had changed! In later years, when demands were high and supply was next to none, a customer could consider himself lucky if he didn't get "service with a snarl" in state-owned stores.

The following year (1957), the two older girls who shared my dorm married on May 1, Labor Day. One of them, YMH, in her late twenties, married a short man her own age from Shaanxi province, someone by the name of Liu Yujie. He was the company statistician. YMH had had a boyfriend in Shanghai, but "distant waters cannot quench a nearby fire", and since she was out of his sight, she was soon out of his mind, and she made do with another man. The other girl WWY (who turned out to be a divorcee) married a fellow Shanghai guy WHB who had left Shanghai a few months later than we did. Both were later expelled because of financial problems. There was no way, unless one had strings to pull, that anyone sent back to Shanghai as a punishment could regain his permanent residential permit to live there. That punishment would be on his file to haunt him for the rest of his life, and perhaps his children too.

There were some Swatownese and Hakka-speaking young people who could understand some Cantonese who were working in the different companies in Hami. We had our meals in the same dining-hall. These young people were mostly from the countryside of Guangdong Province and I could not relate to them at all; and neither could they to me because I was considered 'so different'. In comparison, I related better to the Shanghainese-speaking people, even though not well. At least with those from Guangdong, we had a common dialect. Until I left Shanghai, I had never really spoken Mandarin (Putonghua) because the need had never risen except in school when we were called up to read an essay or a passage from a book. Communication with classmates was either in Cantonese or in Shanghainese, and if we had used Mandarin, we would be ridiculed of putting on 'official airs' (*da guan qiang*). Anything that wasn't Shanghainese was considered "foreign" and made fun of. Cantonese was only spoken among fellow-Cantonese.

The "marriage" between the state-owned and the privately-owned stores was not a smooth one in that before everything was officially signed and sealed, a lot of "toothpaste squeezing" went on. The private business people were accused of refusing to declare their assets honestly. Since notes had to be taken during such sessions, I was one of those called upon to do the job. It was unpleasant. I witnessed at first-hand how people were coerced into "admitting" certain things. I know exactly how hard it is to start a business from scratch, and these people had earned what they had by the sweat of their brow, no doubt about it. They may have been resigned to their eventual fate, but I could sense their resentment. I hope they were not brought to account in ensuing political movements.

Mergers like this took place all over China. In Shanghai, the most successful was the 'merging' of the Wing On Department Store and the flour mills owned by the Rong family. I doubt it could be called a 'merger' because there was no state-owned store to merge with. It was more a 'take-over' because nothing changed except the nature of the company, from privately-owned to so-called 'public-private jointly owned'. The proprietor of Wing On was a Cantonese by the name of Kwok Lum Song who was an 'enlightened capitalist'. Another similarly 'enlightened capitalist' was Rong Yiren. Once when Chum and I were at Tchakalian's for a meal, his sister, Rong Suren, a very well-dressed lady at the next table, came over to exchange greetings with Chum. The Rongs had studied at St. John's University where Dr Tu had been president. These two "capitalists", Kwok and Rong, were about the best-known of Shanghai entrepreneurs of that generation. But their prestige, reputation, and most important of all, their cooperation with the new government, didn't save them from the scourge of the Cultural Revolution ten years later. Both suffered greatly during that period.

As for the businessmen of Hami, I would suppose they were not put through a similar ordeal during those abominable years. It is unbelievable the amount of unnecessary suffering the system inflicted on its people. There is not a people on the face of this earth who are as long-suffering as the Chinese of our parents' and my generation, and we are sure that we are 'the last of the Mohicans'. People of those generations have become an endangered species, and there is no organization equivalent to the World Wildlife Fund to help protect us. Ironically, our children do not inherit our values and long-suffering mentality, which they consider to be obsolete. They cannot relate to what we have to say to them, and they draw their own conclusions. Many have become so cynical that it is frightening. And yet, are they to be blamed? Who is responsible for the disparity between what is preached and what is actually practiced by the preachers? It is incomprehensible to many of my generation to find that those who benefited the most from the system have appreciated it the least, while those most indispensable to the country have been persecuted the most.

The political movements that I witnessed in Hami after 1956 where I was working did not involve the non-Han people at all. But they were certainly aware of the Han's 窝里斗 (in-fighting), and wondered why we were so eager about it while they could see nothing wrong at all with the targets of the 'wrath'. I think their non-involvement was largely due to their lack of language proficiency, but goodwill among people is never hindered by a language barrier, I know that for myself. Things changed in later years.

Each spring, Hami had raging sandstorms, called *kara boran* in the local language, meaning black storm. The first one I experienced almost scared me to death. It blew around the clock, and high noon was as dark as night because of the blanketing sand. The howling of the winds was beyond description, blasting sand against the walls, windows, doors and through their cracks. Our room, like the other rooms on the compound, needed maintenance badly, and wind and sand entered through the cracks creating a minor *kara boran* indoors in sync with the major one outside. There was nothing to do but to huddle in a corner of the room with a kerchief over my head and a surgical mask over my mouth, and close my eyes and pray for the wind to stop. I should have covered my mouth with a wet towel instead, but no one had warned me ahead of time.

The only place that one could avoid the storm was in an underground cellar which we did not have, but that could be dangerous as well; the entrance to the cellar could be buried by the sand and cause suffocation to those hiding in it. As long as the storm raged, there was nothing one could do for food or drink. There was nowhere we could go because the wind was too strong. To step outside one would be to risk being hurled away by the sheer force of the wind.

Man is so helpless when Nature is in a rage that I felt any physical punishment would be more endurable than this interminable howling, black storm. The air raids and bombings during the Japanese War were a ball in comparison to this, I thought, because they were not so drawn-out. For those caught outdoors during such a sand storm, death is almost certain; it is even worse than a tornado because the latter is fleeting while this goes on, and on, and on. When it finally died down, our room was covered with several inches thick of sand. I took my bedcover by the four corners and with someone's help, carried the load of sand out to the yard to dump. As for us, we were all thickly coated with sand, and even our ears were full. We were all parched in the extreme and very, very hungry. For the following week or so there was sand in every mouthful of food we swallowed. But I gave thanks for surviving the experience, and it provided me with something to write about in my correspondence.

Summer in Hami was long, and very hot during the day. But as is true elsewhere in Xinjiang, no matter how hot the day is, the mornings and evenings are always cool, if not actually cold, which accounts for the popular saying, *zao chuan pi ao, wu chuan sha, huai bao huolu chi xigua* which literally means "wear fur coats in the morning, dress in organdy (or voile) at noon, hug the stove and eat watermelons". The temperature range within the day is usually 12 to 15 degrees Celsius, if not more. Before the honeydew melons *kawhoon*, watermelons *tawooz* and grapes *uzium* are ripe there is a season of apricots *urook* and mulberries *sahngze*. The latter is sold in small willow-twig woven baskets lined with mulberry leaves, for next to nothing. The former is sold by number. If eaten immediately, the price is calculated according to the number of pits the customer spits out. After the pits are counted and paid for, the customer usually takes them home and cracks them up for the nut (a small almond) inside. It is a delicacy, and is used in traditional Chinese medicine, and there are merchants who buy the pits for the nut which is then ground and pressed for its oil – a hair beautifier used by all local females. Fresh apricots that are not sold are dried and later sold to the Kaperaht (Cooperative).

It was in about early 1958 that I saw a letter in an issue of the *China Youth Daily* written by a young boy (Lennart Anderson from Oscar-Fredricksburg, Sweden) looking for a pen-pal his own age, which was about 12. Just for fun, I wrote back and our correspondence continued on and off for about three years. I have no idea where he is now because I have not written him in for several decades. I did not know at that time that my writing and reading in English would be a source of suspicion against me in later years.

I bought my very first English-Chinese dictionary in Hami. The two people who worked in the Xinhua Bookstore were from Suzhou (Soochow) and had been in Hami since 1954. The lady was very surprised that I wanted to buy the one and only English-Chinese dictionary, which had been in the store for longer than she had been. After that, I visited the bookstore quite often in the hope of finding something in English, but I never once found anything. Instead, I bought Chinese books and started to read Lu Xun, Wen Yiduo and others. They were people that I had read about when I was in school, and excerpts from their works had appeared in our textbooks, but I had never once read a novel, long or short, in Chinese until then. I found that I preferred reading in English than in Chinese because with the former I didn't have to keep telling myself what it meant whereas with the latter I had to. I apparently did not have enough background information to fully understand what the books were about.

After my two roommates married, I had the room to myself. There was much speculation as to when I would get married. Our manager, ZWR, was a fatherly figure. He had a grown daughter and he constantly worried that she would not be able to find 'in-laws', meaning a husband. The Hui people marry very young and if she waited another year or two it would be doubtful if she would ever find a mother in-law in Hami. It turned out that he just didn't know that his daughter had a boyfriend and they were planning to marry as soon as the boy's father was in better health. ZWR often asked why I didn't marry. I told him that I had not come to Hami to marry, I had come to work. I also said that we southerners (as people from the coastal areas were called) did not marry that early, and that my parents had also married late.

ZWR told me about his marriage. He lived right across from the store where I worked, and I visited his home often. I took a liking to his baby son who was about five years' old. His wife, at least six or seven years his senior, was a sickly woman who seemed to have a permanent case of jaundice, and she looked bloated. She hardly ever left her *kang*, a mud platform which was heated throughout the year, and she could not take a step without panting and puffing, and holding on to the wall for support. Their eldest child, a son, was already in his early thirties then.

ZWR was the only son of a local Hui family and his parents found him his wife when he was only about eleven years old. A wife in such a case is an 'old gray mare,' seamstress, scrubwoman, cook and bedmate all rolled into one. His parents needed a servant, and this homely but healthy girl from a poor family who could not afford a dowry was given to this family. ZWR recounted the many beatings and ear-twistings he had had from his wife after their first child was born. He asked me to look at him squarely in the face and check if one of his ears was longer than the other. This wife had her in-laws to care for, a not yet teen-age husband, and now a newborn baby plus all the work in the home and on the land. With little or no time for rest after the birth, she was on her feet again. She strapped the baby to her husband's back and sent him out to play, as that was all that he could do. She told him to return after two or three hours for the baby's nursing, but boys will be boys, and he would wander off, baby or no baby on his back, with his play-mates and not return for hours. By the time, the baby would be so exhausted from crying that it would be asleep, and could not be awakened to be nursed. And all the time his wife, a young mother in her prime, would stand on the hilltop outside the village, her hands supporting her swollen breasts, yelling out for him.

Once in summer when it was too hot to have the baby on his back, ZWR let it lie down under the shade of a tree and went on playing, sometimes swimming in the muddy pond, sometimes playing hide and seek with other children, and after a while when he heard his wife yelling for him, he panicked, and scurried home because he was afraid of yet another spanking, or ear-twisting. In his hurry, he had clean forgotten about the baby he had left under a tree. But which tree? Both of them went out and looked and looked, searching high and low with his wife chasing after him with a branch and threatening to skin him alive if the baby was not found safe. Fortunately, the baby was still under the tree, sleeping, or ZWR would not have lived to tell the story.

Unlike most other Hui men his generation who were male chauvinists, ZWR was considered a modernist. He often expressed gratitude for his wife – not to her face, of course – for caring for his parents and him, and later their family. He said that without her as the pillar of the home, he would not have accomplished anything. When their last child was born, she developed heart trouble and was confined permanently to her bed, and was not able to care for the child at all. Her daughter, someone old enough to be her baby brother's mother, took over her mother's chores. To nurse the newborn baby, they bought a nanny goat which had just kidded. They shaved the hair around her udder and put her on the *kang* at feeding time, taught her to lie on her side and put one hind leg up on a support when the baby sucked at her, through a nipple attached to the teat (a goat's teat is too long for a baby). After several months, the baby was strong enough for regular food and the "nanny" was retired.

My former roommate, YMH, was expecting a baby, and wanted to return to Shanghai for the birth and had planned to leave the child behind to be cared for by her mother. Momentum was gaining for what would eventually be the anti-rightist movement. Since I was not a Party member or even a Youth League member, I was not supposed to be in the know. But someone who worked in the same store with me, a young man, HCD, who was a Youth League member from Zhejiang Province, purposely or accidentally leaked that 'some people' were to be in "trouble". I doubted him. All of us were working very hard, and to my knowledge, no one was courting "trouble". It wasn't until history further unfolded that it was known that each company had to produce a certain number of "rightists", and that students were the last to be considered unless they were truly out of bounds.

In our company, at least five Shanghai people were expelled as a result of that movement. Two, because they could not swallow the fact that no apology was extended or explanation given for the promises made to them in Shanghai not being carried out. But I think what finally got one of them was the fact that he kept rubbing it in that since an illiterate person could be the vice manager of a company, his own ten years of schooling should have merited him the position of town mayor. Nobody took him seriously, and we knew he was just letting off steam. Wasn't our illiterate vice manager risking his life for cause of the liberation while that twerp was still in open-crotch pants? Another guy from Shanghai, divorced and carefree, was considered a "womanizer" just because he visually appreciated the female form and expressed it. This guy had also said a lot of things in jest which had been taken down by some radicals. Two others had messed with company funds.

Looking back, I think because all five of them had come from working class families, they had had no experience as I had of what it was to witness a family member as a target of an ongoing political movement. They were all from the 'working class', and had thought themselves invulnerable. After all, the working class had been the exploited class, and therefore were now the leading class. I knew better. My father's advice of "pray not for merit, but only that there will be no fault found" (*buqiu yougong, dan qiu wu guo*) was useful at a time when people were "looking for bones in eggs." There is an old Chinese saying which literally means that if you want to condemn someone, never fear that an excuse cannot be found to justify the action. Witch hunts were not the exclusive preserve of Salem. Perhaps the early Americans pirated the idea from China.

There was a Protestant church in Henan Xiang (Henan Lane) which was just a few steps away from the store where I worked. I was sorely tempted to attend one of their services, even though I had no Chinese Bible and had never read one. But each Sunday that I made up my mind that I would attend a service there, I would freeze at the door when I heard the loud moans and groans coming from behind them. The noise was sometimes so loud that it sounded like thunder rumbling, amidst shouts of hallelujah. I never bucked up enough courage to enter the premises. I was scared because it was so different from any church that I had ever been to. To this day, I still do not know what all those moans, groans and rumblings were about. When I later told Chum about it, she said they could be "Holy Rollers". I didn't know any such thing existed, and had taken for granted that all churches would be the same as the one I had attended in Shanghai.

I was surprised to find that the church was still there in the summer of 1990 when the UNESCO Silk Road Survey Group (Desert Route) that I was with passed through Hami. We stayed for one day at the local government guesthouse located at what was formerly known as the East Riverbank (Dong Heba). One evening, I took a walk with a Professor Stamp of Oakland University in Michigan, to where I had worked from 1956 to 1959, in the hope of finding one or two familiar faces. I did not, and neither did I recognize Hami anymore, not having been back for thirty-odd years. The store that I had worked in was boarded up, the post office was no longer at its old location, and even the sand dune at Beishawo was gone. Instead, in its place was a wide, paved street lined with buildings at least four or five stories tall. We walked to Henan Xiang and I asked a Uyghur lady where the former church was, and she pointed it out to me. She wanted to know how I knew there was a church, as she could see that we were strangers in town by our dress and by Professor Stamp being a foreigner. I told her that I used to work in the store, and asked if she knew what had happened to it. She told me that it had moved further into the Huicheng (the Hui City). I mentioned several names but she had no idea who they were. Just for fun, I asked her if she remembered a fat girl (meaning myself) working in that same store, and she could not recall. Well, I had been gone and now forgotten.

A tragedy occurred in a workshop across from the company. Hami is known for its local vinegar, which is as indispensable as soy sauce in its local cooking. There were many ma-and-pa shops which made vinegar, flying a ragged cloth flag with the word *tsoo*, meaning vinegar, written on it. One young couple had a toddler son who wore an anklet with a small bell on it so his parents could hear him as he toddled along in the house. As long as they heard the bell, they knew where he was. One day, when they were out in their courtyard, they heard the frantic ringing of the bell, and went indoor to look for their son. The poor child had plunged headlong into the shallow pool that was dug in one of the rooms in which vinegar was ageing. He choked and was beyond help.

I gained a lot of weight the first two years I was in Hami. I was very lonely and I stuck out like a sore thumb. I felt out of place there and could not find a single soul to whom I could talk, in the real sense of the word. Food was my consolation. The local Uyghur staple of *nan*, a kind of bread sometimes made with pieces of lamb and keptirgan kaimak sold by the Kazakh shepherds who came down from the pastures of Barkol, and any amount of fruit and melons agreed with me one hundred percent, and before long I was known as *simiz* (fatso) by my Uyghur friends. Many Shanghai girls complained that I had a "smell" from my diet of yogurt, cream, nan and lamb as most of them did not eat lamb at all, nor touch any dairy products.

However smelly, fat, and ungainly, I was still a Shanghai girl to many local males, and a Shanghai girl is a Shanghai girl is a Shanghai girl. I was very much a loner who did not mix easily with people my own age. I was not coy or coquettish like some other girls were, and neither was I out to catch anyone. I would not give any of the males, colleague or otherwise, a second look. The only person who merited a second look from me was the local commissar of the Youth League, a half-Russian who with quite some imagination on my part resembled Tyrone Power. But then he did not give me a glance. There were several northerners who had asked to be introduced, or who were bold enough to approach me themselves, but I had nothing in common with them.

There was news that Zhu De, the army general, was visiting Hami. Before I came to Xinjiang, I had read Agnes Smedley's *The Great Road*, which is a biography of Zhu De, Edgar Snow's *Red Star Over China* and several other books and articles by Anna Louise Strong and other Westerners who were sympathetic to the Communist cause, and I felt that I knew about Zhu De, Chairman Mao and other top leaders a lot better than any of my colleagues. because none of them had ever read those books since they were written in English. Prior to reading *The Great Road,* all I knew about Zhu De was from a lesson in one of our Chinese textbooks, called *Mother,* which was supposedly written by him. Imagine how excited I was to learn that he was coming to Hami! I looked forward to seeing him in person, as he would be the most important person that I would ever have seen, actually, face to face. I had seen some dignitaries from our verandah years earlier, but never at close quarters. I asked the manager if I could be one in the crowd that would be lined up to welcome him at Da Ying Fang when he flew in, and added that I had read about him, and gave some details of what I had read. The answer was a definite "NO".

The composition of the crowd was hand-picked, and I was not among the 'anointed'. I had made the fatal mistake of telling people that I had read that book which no one had even heard of. Worst still, I had expressed interest in seeing Zhu De, which really raised some eyebrows. Perhaps it was because I was not a member of the Youth League, or that I had shown too much interest in him. Could it be that I was suspected of having an ulterior motive, to assassinate him??! That was the first and the last time that I showed any interest in any visiting dignitary, regardless of their rank, and created in me a life-long aversion to people of "position", with the exception of Premier Zhou Enlai, and a couple of decades later, Burhan Shahidi and his wife, Rashide.

Gong (pronounced gung, as in gung-ho) Wen Bin, a young man in our group to whom I had spoken a few words when we were both staying in that dirty little inn in Zhangye, was about the only person I felt I could talk to. He was assigned to Gulja upon arrival in Urumqi, and had the guts to refuse the job, claiming that he would only work in Urumqi as he and the rest of the group had been promised. When I left for Hami, he was already assigned to the Hardware and Chemicals Company in Urumqi. We carried on a haphazard correspondence, writing mostly about the work that we were each doing.

On the same bus that took me from Urumqi to Hami was someone in his early or mid-thirties who claimed that I looked "familiar" and struck up a one-way 'conversation' with me He told me he was a Hui and had studied in Fudan University, and blah, blah, blah. When we reached Hami, he took me to the company where I was to report for work, and settled me down. He told me that he often came to town and that he would look me up the next time he came. He seemed like a gentleman and told me that he was working with a certain company in Urumqi and made frequent business trips to Hami. He gave me his name and address, which some time later I passed on in a letter to GWB, and asked him to find out if that certain company did have someone by that name. He wrote back to confirm that there was such a person, and that he was married with a twelve year-old son. I didn't know whether to be disappointed or relieved. I put all the letters he had written me, and a photograph he had sent of himself in mortarboard and robe, in an envelope and mailed it back to his office. Later I was told he was denounced as a rightist. Probably because he had been to university.

The 8502 Railroad Building Corps of the People's Liberation Army were doing the preparatory work for laying the railroad tracks which were eventually to reach Urumqi. They bought all their food supplies at our store, and the logistics officer, with four stars on his shoulders, was a nice and clean-shaven man from Shantung province. He liked to sit and chat with us in the store. He was woman-shy even though he was married to a salesperson in one of the biggest department stores in Harbin. I did not razz him for being bashful like the other married women, and so he preferred talking to me. That raised some eyebrows. It seems that in Hami, a single female, however old or young, comely or homely, is always gossiped about, much of it unfounded. Some people judge others by their own standards - measuring the bowel cavity of the gentleman according to the chest cavity of the villain (以小人之心度君子之腹). It was sad for me to see how some people spent time gossiping and smearing other people's reputations when that time could have been spent in bettering themselves. It seemed that many of them were totally unaware of how terribly inadequate they were in every way. Some were literally smug that they were illiterate as that proved they were truly a member of the exploited class. What a mentality! They just seemed to wallow in the bliss of their ignorance. Some even claimed that knowledge only brought worries, and that is why those who had it aged faster. It rang a bell. Hadn't I read somewhere before that "If ignorance is bliss, then 't'is folly to be wise"? I wasn't so far from home, after all!

The accountant of the Cooperative was a bashful, fair-skinned, tall man in his late twenties or early thirties, with very small eyes. He was a college student from the Northeast and had been assigned to Hami after graduation in 1952 because he had come from an 'exploiting class' family. Our company and his work unit had political studies together and we were nodding acquaintances. One day, out of the blue, he came and told me that his widowed mother was calling him home, probably to get married. He asked if I would marry him so he wouldn't have to leave. I was too confounded to respond. Was that a proposal? Is that how men proposed? I told him it was out of the question since we were almost total strangers. He left according to plan and returned a month later with a wife, someone from the disaster (flood) area of Lungkou. They had a baby in due course and he was named a rightist in the political movement that took place sometime after. Not that he had done anything wrong or had said anything that he should not have; he was just the most likely target because he had more years of education than any of his colleagues at his work place. Remember, each work place was given a quota of "rightists" and they had to come up with the required number.

YMH's husband, LYJ, was one of the targets in our company, in fact the first man in our company to be accused of being a "rightist". His wife, YMH, was in Shanghai having their first child. Their room was plastered with "big character posters". People in the Party and Youth League who were "in the know" were the ones who ran the show. They accused LYJ of calling all the Youth League Members *tewu* (secret agents), and other unheard of things that they claimed he had said and done in the past. How long a past could a 28–year–old man have? He was born in the countryside of somewhere near Yenan, and from a poor family or he would not have been selected to attend vocational school where he learned statistics. Some well-meaning colleague secretly wrote to his wife to tell her what was happening, and advised her to return as soon as possible to be by his side. Liu was very indignant that he, someone from an area known as "cradle of the revolution", should be the target. The more indignant he became, the more vehement his language, and the deeper he sank into "trouble".

The most active elements who had schemed to "give him the hat", have him condemned, were all Youth League members and Party members. The former displayed radicalism because they wanted one day to be the latter, and no one is ever punished for leaning to the 'left'. The latter wanted to curry favor for future promotions. Imagine what a backlash there would be in having Liu back, Why, their prestige would reach rock-bottom and that would set off a chain reaction throughout other companies who had the same problem. The first man who proposed to me suffered the same fate, but he was lucky in that he opted to go back to the Northeast.

Yao Meihua returned with a daughter, half of the baby's face covered with a maroon birthmark. By the end of the campaign, the five Shanghai people had been expelled, but Liu Yujie was not as lucky. He and the person who had asked me to marry him were both made rightists and sent to fell trees in the mountain forests somewhere near Barkol.

I was soon told to move to a dorm with several other girls in another company – my room was needed for an office. That meant that I had to cross what was called the *Beishawo* (Northern Sand Dune) to and from work each day, and during the summer it would mean four trips a day because of the long siesta, and I had nowhere to go to rest except back to my dorm. The distance was not so far, about a kilometer, but it was exhausting to climb the dune. The more I strained, the deeper I sank and the less progress I made. There were no nylon socks in those days, only cotton ones, and I wore out a pair each day, it seemed. I also had to wear hiking boots because shoes would just get lost in the sand. Sometimes even hiking boots were no use. Instead of having to worry about what to do during the week-ends, they were now spent darning socks and nursing sore feet because the sand had rubbed the flesh raw between my toes.

I petitioned to move out of the dorm because the trips across the sand dune were getting to be too expensive with all the socks I wore out. I spent a lot of time nursing my feet to keep them from being infected. My plea was finally listened to, and I found a room in a courtyard near the East Gate where I could have my meals with a neighboring family. The man was a political commissar with the Transportation Section of the 5th Agricultural Division of the Xinjiang Production and Construction Corps, and the woman was a housewife with seven children, four of whom were from her first husband, a KMT officer who died of TB, and the other three from her first husband's messenger boy whom she later married. The woman, YXY, was a native of Zhangye and was married to this officer because her parents could not afford to keep her. She was considerably younger than the first man she married, who was from Mei County of Guangdong Province. Her second husband, an honest, quiet and hardworking man, was good to all the children, and after she married him, the four older children changed their last name to their step-father's. I had my meals with that family, and took the little children for baths in the brook near the East Gate on my days off in the summer. Both YXY and her husband have since passed away, but my friendship with their eldest child has carried on to this day, more than half a century after my first encounter with them.

One day years later, in Urumqi in 1993, I heard a knock on my door and someone calling my name. I looked through the "magic eye" and saw a weather-beaten old lady standing there with a young woman wearing a headscarf almost totally concealing her face. I did not know who they were until I opened the door and the old woman announced herself to be Yao Meihua. What a surprise! The last time I had seen her was when her baby was about a year old. With her was her eldest child, the one who had the maroon birthmark on one side of her face, now in her thirties. The birthmark seemed to have darkened and thickened with time, covering half her face. There was a lot to catch up with because more than three decades had passed since we had worked in the same company, she in the office and me behind a counter. I had wished then to be doing her job because it was so much cleaner in the office than in the store. We had never developed a friendship even though we had shared the same dorm for several months.

Out of politeness, I inquired about Liu Yujie, her husband. She said that he had passed away. After he was made a rightist and went through the usual rigmarole of admitting his wrong in public, he and other rightists of Hami were sent to the lumber area up in the mountains, given home leave once a month or so even though he was only a three-hour bus ride away from home. Before he was eventually "rehabilitated", they had had six children. When most of the 'rightists' were rehabilitated, their former places of employment did not want them back, and many had no choice but to stay on to work in the lumber area, under slightly better conditions because their "status" had changed. Liu was in that situation. A few short years later, he died in an explosion, leaving his poor wife with all the kids. The eldest daughter had a hard time finding a husband, but eventually found one. The other five children in the family were just getting by, and Yao Meihua was retired. I asked her about other former colleagues and people whom we mutually knew, and was relieved to find that many were still in Hami, though retired. ZYZ, the radical woman who had always been watching me, was now dead from cancer. Others who had been persecutors during the Cultural Revolution were now in different leading posts, while others were not as "fortunate."

I sensed some resentment when she asked me what was I doing in the Foreign Language Department of Xinjiang University (of all places!). It seemed that while she was in town she had come to verify what she had heard about me through someone who was a close relative of an administrator of the University whose relatives happened to be one of her neighbors in Barkol, where she lived. She also mentioned that a few former colleagues were anxious that I keep in touch with them. I had neither the time nor the wish to rekindle what had not been a friendship. Many people knew my address, and if they wanted to write to me they would. I was not going to take the initiative. Wasn't I looked down upon because I was different? Didn't some of them say I was a "spy" and that I was writing "coded" messages to my "superiors"? Why the sudden wish to get in touch? Wasn't my leaving them considered good riddance of bad rubbish?

It was easier for me to make friends with older men than with men around my own age. One of the older men with whom I became acquainted was a 60 year-old gent who ran a small stall next door to our shop which sold, among other things, big sweet peaches from trees in his own backyard. I was one of his regular customers. He told me that as a young man he had traveled between Tianjin (Tientsin), Hangzhou (Hangchow) and other parts of China doing business. He had brought back several young peach trees from his trips, someone had helped graft them, and they yielded the best peaches in town. He also had a lot of fascinating tales of his travels in the inland regions in the early part of the century. To me, it was safest to be friends with elderly men because no one would gossip that I had designs on them, or they on me.

Each of the older people I became friends with was a history book and their accounts of past events absolutely enthralled me. Moreover, they made me realize how little I knew. How brave these men must have been in their heyday! They had to travel on foot, on camelback or horseback, or on horse carts as there were no railroads and very few paved roads then. These men considered themselves much more sophisticated than those of their generation who had never had the courage to venture out of Hami. He was certainly one of the people who had seen "the world". Men like him each had a story worthy of print. They had tales of how the bandits looted the local people, discriminately, depending on what ethnic group the bandits belonged to, and which ethnic group had the upper hand, and how the tides changed with each transfer of power, whether from one ethnic group to another, or from one individual to another. One thing never changed; every time, the ones who bore the brunt were the people. An African leader once said, "When elephants fight, the grass suffers." How true, even to this day!

I remember the first time, but not the last time, that I saw how some locals in Hami did their laundry. They took bed-sheets, pillowcases and other things, after they were washed and ready to be hung up and dried, soak them in a thin starch, then smooth them on the floorboards. Most old houses had wooden floorboards, or if there is a *kang*, the top was usually of boards. Because of the climate, the laundry dried fast, was peeled off the floor and folded. The dirt accumulated from use was on the thin veneer of starch instead of eating into the cloth itself, which both made washing easy and protected the cloth. In later years, I saw the same practice in other parts of Xinjiang in old houses with wooden floorboards scrubbed squeaky clean, especially in households where the mistress was a Russian or half-Russian.

There had been a grossly overweight Kazakh up in the mountains of Barkol who was one of the very first Chinese People's Political Consultative Committee (CPPCC) members of Xinjiang. He was to have been taken to Beijing to meet Chairman Mao, if only there had been a car with a door wide enough for him to enter so he could be driven down to Hami, to fly him to Beijing, if there was also a plane with a door big enough and a seat wide enough to hold him. This Kazakh was a man of very humble origin. He had been an indentured servant, or slave, to a wealthy cattle owner, and had served not only as the builder of his master's houses, but also made the sun-dried bricks and did the carpentry work for the window and door frames. He served as contractor, laborer and carpenter, and had three sawed-off fingers to prove it. One day when he was digging the ground for mud to make the bricks, he came across some treasures, and the deeper he dug, the more treasure surfaced. They were artifacts of gold and gems and jade. He gathered his find and went down to Hami with them, sold some of them and with the money went back up to Barkol and bought out his master on very generous terms. His master retired to Hami with the money. This once indentured servant now owned what had been his master's property and flocks of animals.

When Xinjiang was peacefully liberated, there were still bandits in Hami, and especially up in Barkol. This Kazahk was in favor of the new government and the PLA because he had heard that they were there to liberate the poor, and he had been one of their number until recently. He donated food and clothing to the soldiers who were in the mountains fighting the bandits and made a name for himself doing so. The Central Government got to know of him and made him a CPPCC member. By then he had gained so much weight that he could not travel. Whenever he was visited by government cadres, he always showed them his left hand minus three fingers to prove he was not from the "exploiting class" but a lowly laborer and carpenter.

In feudal times, princes of the different principalities, (and Hami had been a principality) and khans of the different khanates in Xinjiang had sent annual tributes to the Imperial Court in Peking. These tributes consisted of treasure such as gold, silver, jade, precious stones, local medicinal herbs, melons and other kinds of fruit. These would be carried by a caravan made up of a dozen or more camels, but not all the tributes reached Peking because some caravans would meet with a *kara boran* on their way and the whole caravan, with the drivers, camels, and accompanying officials would disappear, never to be heard of again. The treasures from such caravans were buried by the sand, no doubt. Some would surface later as archaeological finds, while others may be lost forever. What this Kazakh came across could have been part of an annual tribute meant for the Imperial Court in Peking. How fitting that he, of all people, should discover it. From the people, to the people, for the people.

Most camel drivers are good knitters, but only with a single needle, usually made of bone. It's not a crochet hook as it does not have the hook. When winter is over, the road from Barkol to Hami would be opened to traffic, and camels were used to carry supplies up to the alpine pastures where the Kazakh shepherds lived. The journey from Barkol to Hami would take two days, sometimes longer, if met with a snowstorm or sandstorm. The camels in a caravan are linked one to another by a rope attached to the rod pierced through their nostrils, so the driver needs only to lead the head camel and the rest follow. The life of the camel driver is a very lonely one. He spends his life on the go between two places, sometimes not seeing a single soul on the entire journey. The camel, known as a "ship of the desert ", is a benign creature. It can carry an enormous amount and asks for little in return. The camel driver sits on the head camel and goes on his way, and if he gets sleepy with the regular bobbing up and down as the camel crosses the sand dunes, he will dismount, and to kill time, take out a spindle and a bone needle. He tears hair off the camel, spins it and knits, usually socks or gloves. It is unusual to find a seasoned camel driver who does not know how to knit with one needle.

We had been promised a home leave trip every two years as long as we stayed single. My two years was up, but my application for leave was not approved because we were in the middle of a political movement. I started to imagine the worst. I imagined that the reason for detaining me was that I would be the next target. I had seen with my very own eyes how before a meeting to accuse a target, certain people would gather to plan the whole thing out, who would say what and when. I came to realize that a hit target could be anybody at all, depending on the company's Party leadership. Our hit targets were not people who had worked for foreign companies like my father had. In fact, someone like Liu had never even laid eyes on a foreigner, let alone worked for one. Yet this man, the son of a poor peasant from an area that was called the Cradle of the Revolution, was labeled a 'rightist'. As for the others, well, they all came from working-class families. Actually, I would have been a more reasonable target considering the way my brain operated and my background, and worse still, the "coded" messages that I had been sending. I had begun correspondence with my Swedish pen pal, Lennart Anderson, but luckily I could cite where I had gotten his address, and why I was writing him. Surely, the *China Youth Daily*, an official paper, would not mislead me to correspond with a "young spy"? Another thing I could fall back on was the fact that Dr Y. C. Tu was a member of the standing committee of the CPPCC, and unless the government were blind, he couldn't have been a spy either. It was true I was corresponding with his wife, an American, but she had given up her citizenship for a Chinese one. Almost all of the targets were men, and after some questioning I was left alone. But I was still not granted permission to go on leave.

Hami is a well-known oasis. I remember as a child, Uncle Jimmy (James Pomeroy Hawes) gave us a pile of *National Geographic* magazines, and in one issue there was an article on exactly this place. It was called Qumol, or Kumul, or Kumol. It was an expedition led by foreigners, perhaps Owen Lattimore or someone of that caliber.

The Hami region was well-forested. Xiheba (West River Bank) was a pleasant park and tree-filled. In the summer, when it was blazing hot in town, one needed to take along a sweater to put on if going to Xiheba. Stepping within the confines of Xiheba was like stepping into a freezer. It was colder than any air-conditioned theater that I had ever been to in Shanghai. Dongheba (East River Bank) was not as big in area, but it was equally cool. The two riverbanks were the only two places which could be called parks. Further into the Huicheng (the Hui City) was a big mosque and the mausoleum where former princes of the Hami Principality were buried. Looking back over the last fifty years that I have been in Xinjiang, I have come to the conclusion that the people of Hami were much more "enlightened" than the people in the south or southwest of Xinjiang. I think its proximity to the rest of the country accounted for this.

Life in Hami also had its lighter side. Even though it was an altogether new place to me, it had "familiar" features that were endearing. Didn't someone say that the sweetest sound on earth was one's own name? In this case, it was not my name so much as other names, names of things and places that reminded me dearly of the past. Our store was on Zhongshan Road, named after Dr Sun Yat-sen. To the Chinese he is known as Sun Zhongshan, after the name of the county of his birthplace, which is the county I register as my ancestral home. And I have the same family name, Sun. Another thing was that there were two courtyards in Hami named Jinyun, pronounced "gum wun" in Cantonese, written exactly like my name. Our manager, ZWR, teased that I clearly had a *yuanfen* (fate or destiny) to be in Hami. Whether having that family name or ancestral home ever helped me, I would say the answer is negative.

Standing outside the store where I worked and looking toward the right, I could see the Tianshan mountain range. Zhongshan Road ran perpendicular to the run of that mountain range. In the winter, the mountains are snow-covered, but in the summer, the highest peak resembles a big chocolate sundae topped with whipped cream on which I could gaze to quench my thirst and to reminisce on the first sundae that I had in my life. I did have a *yuanfen* with Hami after all. Who would have thought that I would see a 'sundae' in Hami, of all places! The sight brought back such memories that tears would flow uncontrollably and my colleagues would ask me what was wrong. Would they understand if I told them? Would sharing my thoughts of Shanghai sundaes get me into trouble later on? I decided to clamp up instead, because silence was the best policy. For a natural chatterbox like me, keeping quiet was a difficult thing to do. I had to keep reminding myself to "shut up".

Our compound had a well which was our only source of water. I had never taken water out of a well before. This well had a cover, and a big wooden wheel with a thick rope around it and a hook at the end of the rope. To get water, the handle of the bucket was clasped onto the hook, the handle of the wheel turned in the reverse to let the bucket into the well, then turned back when the bucket was full. The very first time I tried to get water from the well, a man out of nowhere appeared and he offered to do it for me. I thought to myself, how chivalrous! All the more chivalrous because this was not Shanghai. I mentioned this to ZWR and he laughed. The compound belonged to a Hui (Muslim), and the family took water from the same well. It was considered unclean for them to have an infidel like me near the well, much less draw water from it, and that was why the man was helping me with my bucket. But in Hami, Xinjiang, I was an "infidel" in a "Muslim" land.

The employees of Hami were each given a quota of how many *jin* of animal manure to collect to 'contribute towards agriculture.' Having grown up in the city of Shanghai where animals were hardly seen in the city except for stray cats and dogs on streets or in homes as house pets, collecting droppings was something new to me. I was given a burlap sack and told to collect on my days off and hand in my pickings to be weighed and registered. Being a greenhorn and reluctant to admit it, I naturally went where there were the most animals. In this case, it was to the other end of town to the yard where the caravans gathered to load supplies to take up to Barkol and other places where trucks did not go. The yard was full of camels.

The first time I had heard of camels was from a nursery rhyme my mother had taught me, "The camel's hump, is an ugly lump......". I had never been near a live camel before Hami. Camels were indispensable for transportation of daily necessities and farm implements to remote places of high altitude such as Barkol where most inhabitants are Kazakh shepherds, and for moving the shepherds from summer pasture to winter pasture where roads were limited.

The camel drivers were feeding their animals with huge tubs full of a thickish, yellowish, soupy gruel that was to be their last food before they reached their destination two or three days later. The camels were mostly Bactrian, not dromedary. I was told that their humps were indicators of whether they were in good condition for a trip. After returning from an arduous journey the humps would almost always sag, or even be collapsed, dangling listlessly, all fagged out, as it were. After the animals were relieved of their burdens and rested and fed, the humps were once more proudly erect, as though standing to attention for an inspection before going on the road again. It was to this big herd of camels that I repaired with my sack over my shoulders. I was disappointed to find how few droppings there were on the ground. Well, something was better than nothing and I didn't want to return empty-handed. I cleaned up what was on the ground, and kept my eye on those places where more would be forthcoming. Often there would only be "thunder" but no "rain".

At the end of the day I trudged back with the fruit of my labor to be weighed and registered only to find that camel droppings were not acceptable because they were too alkaline to be good for the soil. So instead of lamenting, "A whole day's wages trod in the mud...." as Eliza Doolittle did in *My Fair Lady*, mine was a whole day's pickings thrown back to the mud. Well, one has to live and learn, and learn, I did. The next time I teamed up with Yimit, my Uygur colleague. We borrowed a two-wheel push cart with a big box and two burlap sacks and he led the way. Being a native, he knew where we could find what we wanted. This time, our findings made up for my previous futile trip.

Local Uygur weddings were open-house parties. Whenever any of my colleagues had a friend who was getting married I would be taken along. There were a lot of folk dancing and merry-making. I never felt comfortable at such weddings because the girls who married were barely out of their mid-teens, and knew next to nothing about what marriage involved. I felt sorry for them. But at the same time, they were feeling sorry for me as I was considered by their standards to be an "old-maid". What? Over twenty years old and still haven't found a mother in-law?! Something has to be wrong with her. I guess something was "wrong". I felt complimented. Had everything been "right," I would not be putting all this down on paper.

One wedding stirred the town. It was between a Han girl, someone who had a bit role in the movie *No.5 of the Women's Basketball Team* and a Uygur basketball player by the name of Nizam. The two of them met at a tournament in Lanzhou and even though there was a language barrier, it was love at first sight. All their correspondence prior to their marriage was done through a translator at the local bank.

Not all marriages in Hami were first marriages. The local people were much more "enlightened" about marriages than

I had thought. Divorces were not uncommon. In fact, a native male was likely to exaggerate how many times his wife had previously been married just to show how much she had been "sought after" and how "lucky" he was to have competed in winning her hand. One local woman who was considered the pick of the crop worked in the local bank. She had long braids that reached to her heels and was a very good dancer. She was also married a record number of times, I forget how many, but whatever it was, it was exaggerated.

Local females took great care of their hair and eyebrows. For the former, they combed their hair only once or twice a week, at most. They used a kind of hair-setting mousse-like concoction which they call *yilim*, composed of water in which leaves from the Russian olive tree have been soaked, creating a gluey substance somewhat like present-day hair mousse. That liquid kept each hair in place, but it also bred hair lice. So it was not unusual to see shiny black hair peppered with the eggs of lice. It also created an unhealthy smell, but all local females believed that that glue worked wonders for their hair. The hair oil they used was extracted from the seed in apricot pits. As for their eyebrows, they used a kind of vegetable dye called *osma*. Juice is extracted from the green leaves of the plant whenever the leaves are available, usually in the spring. The leaves are first left on cool ash so excess moisture is removed, then the juice is squeezed onto an overturned rice bowl, and applied across the brows with the help of a match stick. Mothers use *osma* on their children's brows from infancy onwards. It is believed to make the eyebrows grow dark. Some even apply it on their skin at the position where a beauty spot would be, and the juice of the *osma* darkens it permanently. The girls and ladies dye their finger nails and palms by wrapping their hands in *henna*, a vegetable dye.

In the mid-fifties, the most expensive materials for a woman's dress were *crepe de chine* and *chiffon*, the latter locally known as *shipong*. The former is pronounced the same as in both French and English while the latter is pronounced the local way for the word 'chiffon' whether in French or English. There are few foreign words in the local language of Uygur which begin with an "f" or "v" sound. These sounds are usually replaced with a "p" sound, such as the word "chauffeur" in French and English is pronounced *shopir*, meaning the same word, and the word "*chiffon*" becomes *shipong*.

Ladies spent much money on dress. A new dress is worn to death, and only then another is made. It was not unusual to see a female in an expensive chiffon dress squatting by the street, resting and wiping her nose with the inside hem of her expensive dress. One big difference between how the native Uygur and the Han treated their children was that the former never beat their kids whereas the latter did.

Male children of Moslem families are circumcised at age seven instead of at birth. I never heard of any female circumcisions. Births, circumcisions, weddings, deaths and the first week after the death, equivalent to the Chinese "first-seventh", and the fortieth-day anniversary, equivalent to the Chinese "seventh-seventh", and the first-year anniversary were commemorated by inviting guests for a meal in the home. The first anniversary of the death is always commemorated before the actual year is up for fear that the dead will think that their relatives have forgotten them. On the whole, the Uyghurs seemed to have more occasions for social gatherings than the Han who were very much isolated from each other in that there were few, if any, occasions where everyone got together for a celebration or commemoration, since all the Han came from different provinces in China, and spoke many different dialects, some mutually unintelligible.

The ethnic people lived in houses built of sun-dried bricks, and during the summer people slept on their roofs in spite of the cool, if not cold, nights. For an early riser and a newcomer like myself, it was quite unusual to see all the roofs of nearby houses colorfully decorated with covers of various shades of the rainbow, and literally shocking to see a couple, or a family under each cover. The flat roofs of adobes are very useful for sun-drying fruits and vegetables. Due to the lack of precipitation, there is no fear of being caught in a downpour in the middle of the night. Or in a *kara boran*, as they only occur in the spring.

After the 8502 Troops, the railroad-building division of the People's Liberation Army, moved out and the building of the railroad was taken over by the Railroad Bureau. There were a lot of new people in town, mostly staff of the RB who had been sent to Hami to take over from the military. One day a group of about eight middle-aged men came to our store, and they were talking in Cantonese! I was overjoyed. I had not met a real Cantonese since arriving in Hami, and immediately struck up a conversation with them. The first question they asked me was why I was in Hami. When I told them I had volunteered, they all agreed I had been stupid to have come.

These men were engineers of the RB which was in charge of the various projects involved in railroad construction in Xinjiang. After that, they visited me each Sunday. I think they could sense how lonely I was. I looked forward to their coming all week, and realized how isolated I had been without people to talk to in Cantonese. Their families were all in Lanzhou and would not be moving to Xinjiang until housing was available. These people had never been to Xinjiang before, and were delighted at the abundance of fruit in Hami. Each Sunday they would come into town and we would go out for an evening meal after I got off work, and then all go to my dorm for dessert, since it was full of melons. The men just helped themselves to whichever variety they liked best. My association with these men raised some eyebrows. What?! A single girl with a roomful of men?!

A few of them made business trips that took them to Shanghai, and I gave them my parents' address and they visited them, and brought them melons for me. I realized that a common language – in this case, the Cantonese dialect – was such a bond. I could not imagine how I would have reacted had I had the good fortune of meeting someone who could speak English. I guess I would have just clung to them for dear life and perhaps smothered them with affection. And if it had been a "he", I can't imagine how many eyeballs would have popped out of sockets. I would have been the talk of the town. That no such person ever surfaced in Hami was a blessing in disguise. The frustration of not being able to speak English when I thought in English was very hard on the nerves. I did not know then that many, many years of not being able to speak to anyone in English were still in store for me.

By early 1959, the anti-rightist movement had died down, in the sense that people who had been secretly targeted to be rightists were already decided upon, named, dealt with and sent to wherever they were to go for their punishment. The Great Leap Forward movement had also lost its steam, and the first signs of the famine that was to last for at least three years and claim many lives were beginning to take hold. By this time, January of 1959, the railroad tracks had been laid to Liuyuan, a place several hours' truck ride from Hami. I asked again for home leave. After all, we had been promised a home leave after two years if we remained single. To make sure that I would be granted permission to leave this time, I made up a story about going to Guangdong Province to get married, when in fact I did not even have a boyfriend, least of all one in Guangdong, a place I had never been to.

4

Unsuccessful Attempt To End Voluntary Exile (1959-1960)

IT WAS GOOD to be back in civilization again, to be among people with whom I was familiar, with whom I was comfortable, and most important of all, where I could speak English. I felt as though I had been serving time and was now released. I wondered how I had passed the two and a half years of "isolation" in Hami, the number of tears I had shed, and the bouts of depression that had engulfed me. I had felt that I was doomed to spend the rest of my days there. And now, I was back in familiar surroundings again!

After I arrived home and told Chum what I had experienced while I was in Xinjiang, she suggested that perhaps I should try to stay in Shanghai, now that I had 'served' there for over two years. I was hopeful at first. I wrote to the manager ZWR to have my leave extended, giving him a flimsy excuse, and then I wrote a letter to Madame Soong Chingling (wife of the late Dr Sun Yat-sen), care of Jerry Tannenbaum, an American who lived in Georgia Apartments and was her secretary, and with whom Chum was acquainted. The purpose of my writing was to tell her my story and ask if there was a chance I could remain in Shanghai. I was naïve to think that she would have the time to do anything for someone whom she didn't even know, but I had once heard of her doing something for a family whose wife was rumored to be one of her god-daughters, the daughter of an old Shandong magician by the name of Long Tack Sam married to a rich Chinese known as the "cement king" of Shanghai. With Madam Sun's help, this family left Shanghai in the early fifties when few Chinese were able to leave.

While in Shanghai I went to several secondary schools to inquire if they needed anyone to teach English, but in each case I was turned down when I told them I did not have a college degree. In addition, Russian had to a great extent replaced English as the foreign language taught in junior and senior high schools, and foreign language study had been done away with altogether in elementary schools.

Several well-meaning friends-of-friends even went so far as to introduce me to young men in the hope that a marriage would materialize so that I could remain in Shanghai. One was a young doctor from the No.1 Medical College of Shanghai who had been denounced and labeled a rightist, and another a man at least twice my age, a chemist, who had involuntarily returned to China.

This involuntary returnee, ZGZ, had gone to the U.S. for his doctoral degree in chemistry some years before and had stayed on, and had stopped corresponding with his mother after 1949. When the Chinese-American Ambassadorial Talks began in Warsaw, first with Wu Xiuquan, then later replaced by Wang Bingnan, representing China, ZGZ's younger brother had given his name to the Chinese Ambassador, claiming that nothing had been heard from him since the Liberation, and that something had to be wrong because he was to have returned to the country, and that the American government could have detained him, and a lot of other imagined reasons. In fact, at that time this chemist was already working in the U.S. and living with an American woman. It was said that one day he was approached by some US government people, probably FBI agents, then questioned, put in detention and later told to leave. All that he had was confiscated, and there was nowhere to go but back to his homeland. He returned to China and was assigned a job suited to his profession.

Chum and I later introduced a very fashionable Chinese lady to him, someone nearer his own age. Whether anything came of that meeting, I don't know. But I doubt that someone like him would have been spared during the Cultural Revolution, especially if word got out that he had not returned of his own free will since even those who had returned voluntarily were in hot water at that time.

While in Shanghai, I met Chum's eldest daughter, Anna (1925-1986) and her family for the first time. They had returned from the U.S. at the end of 1956, answering the call of the late Premier Zhou Enlai in his report concerning intellectuals. Both Chum and Dr Tu thought that China needed them more than the U.S. did. Anna was a wonderful person, genuine, warm, and caring. Anna and her husband and four children who were born in Elizabeth, New Jersey, returned and settled in Shanghai. Anna was a tumor pathologist and Eddie was a surgeon and both were very well known in their professions. They were a very handsome couple, and their children were lovely.

Nothing worked out for me from the several people to whom I was introduced. Whenever I was introduced to someone I either got the creeps or actual nausea, depending on how he affected my visual sense. There was just no chemistry at all. The thought of marrying someone with the ulterior motive of being able to remain in Shanghai was too much. And what was more, who can guarantee that that someone wouldn't be sent out of Shanghai later on? The fate of the individual was not in his own hands, people went wherever they were sent, and who had ever heard of anyone disobeying an order and not being punished for it later on? If I married someone with my eyes closed, wouldn't I be asking for trouble?

In retrospect, I think what prevented me from staying put in Shanghai was "fear". First of all, I no longer had a residential permit to stay in the city where I was born and grew up because I had left it, voluntarily, in 1956. Secondly, I had no one to fall back on who could protect me from being forcefully evicted. And lastly, even if I did stay on, I would be spending the rest of my life waiting for the other shoe to drop. It was a "no win" case. Who had ever won against the establishment? I was too scared to be the one to even try. Another thing that made my staying difficult in Shanghai was the famine. People with no local residential permits did not have food ration stamps, and non-rationed food was very expensive.

GWB, the Shanghai boy in Urumqi with whom I was still in correspondence on a very platonic basis, and who had visited Hami once in the over two years that I had been there, was someone my own age, and with whom I could feel at ease, and he was also someone who had no designs on me. I had written him telling him I was going to Shanghai and gave him my Shanghai address. When I did not return to Xinjiang at the time I had said that I would, he began to write, and I told him of all that had happened in the meantime, and admitted that I would not return to Xinjiang if I could possibly help it. His letters became more frequent. He asked me to return if there was no better way out. After several months I realized that I had no choice but to return to Xinjiang with my tail between my legs.

While I had been away in Xinjiang, my father's situation had not improved. He was still under suspicion, and even though there was no way to prove himself innocent, he could also not be proven guilty. But he was still waiting for the axe. All my siblings were still in Shanghai, except for child No. 3, Charles

Jr., always called Junior, who completed a five-year course at the Wuhan National Academy of Survey and Mapping, and was later assigned to the National Bureau of Survey and Mapping in Xi'an. It is not unusual for each Shanghai family to have at least one member assigned to work elsewhere in the country and regardless of where you go in China, even to the remotest parts, it is quite possible to find someone from Shanghai there, probably playing a key role. That there had been no move to tap the intellectual resources of Shanghai youth to develop Pudong (Pootung) and the nearby countryside at that time was a sad oversight of those in power, and should be painfully regretted by the decision makers. Countless people suffered as a result of it.

Young people were shipped out by the trainload, and even factories were moved out of the city, lock, stock and barrel, but this did not result in a decrease in the city's population; quite the contrary. As for all the heartbreak, sorrow and loss suffered by families who had members assigned elsewhere in the country, there are no statistics to reflect this. Matters of the heart cannot be expressed in figures.

Times have changed. There are no longer any Chinese youths who are as "stupid" as those of my generation. Unless they are looking for greener pastures, they stay put in Shanghai come hell or high water.

In retrospect, I think Shanghai people are much less inhibited than people in the north. In spite of the many political movements they had weathered, they were still very outspoken, and would say things that others didn't even dare think of. At that special time in history, most people were 'schizophrenic', in the sense that they had two sets of vocabulary, one for use in public and the other for use in private and among like-minded people.

I recall my father's reaction to the big billboards with slogans such as 'A warm welcome to our Japanese friends'. 'What??!!

We spent over a decade and paid such a high price to get them out of the country, and now we want to welcome them back?? I won't miss them if I never again see a Japanese in my life!' It's nothing unusual for the laymen, literate or illiterate, to think of a people as the system they represent. During the Japanese War, boycotting Japanese goods was a sign of patriotism, and most Chinese practiced it fervently. Now, it's just the other way around, where electrical appliances are concerned, if it isn't Japanese, it doesn't sell well. During the war, the Chinese term for 'shoddy goods' was 'East Ocean (Japanese) products.'

The reaction to other political billboards on the streets of that city, such as 'We have friends all over the world' was somewhat different. One day in Shanghai standing in front of such a billboard with my three-year old son, pointing out the people who represented different races of the world, I heard a man beside me remark, 'Yeah, the more friends we have the less we have to eat. Why do we want to make friends with countries who want to be friends with us just for what we can give them? Aren't we ourselves poor enough? These are not friends, they are leeches!' And so on. The Shanghai people's reaction to the Cambodian prince seeking refuge in China was even more straightforward. They called him a 'high-class beggar', and 'dead crab' because the first two syllables of his name sound exactly like 'dead crab' in the Shanghai dialect. Even today, the phrase 'dead crab' is still used in Shanghai dialect, to mean 'helpless' or 'done for'.

One day as Chum and I stood talking outside our entrance on Peking Road, she met a blonde lady with glasses and they exchanged greetings. I had seen her before when she visited Bill Burgess, a former American soldier, when he was living next door to us above the Chinese Christian Bookstore and had assumed she was a Russian. She turned out to be Anna von Kliest, former wife of the Chinese statesman, Wang Bingnan, who had taken over from

Wu Xiuquan in the Sino-U.S. Ambassadorial Talks in Warsaw. It seemed that she had returned from overseas to visit her son who was in a military academy in the northeast. I reprimanded myself for thinking that she was just another Russian woman, when in fact she was Prussian. Well, I missed by only one letter.

Not all those who were labeled "rightists" received the same punishment. The "Ultra Rightists" were punished most severely with jail sentences. Lesser ones were banished to the countryside to live among the peasants. It was not until twenty years later that some were exonerated, and many did not live to see that day. Others had already married local peasant girls, raised families, and were stuck living among people with whom they shared almost no common interests.

Some of the 'labeled' who were married or divorced, and some of the divorces were only on paper, in consideration of the children. There would not be much chance for offspring of "rightists" to enter university regardless of how clever they were, and some of the parents "divorced" so their children would not be deprived of further education. Such couples had to wait almost two decades, if not longer, to be reunited. Other couples each went their own way, forced by circumstances. Several decades later, some university students found it strange to see some professors with wives doing janitorial work because the younger generation is ignorant of all that had taken place since 1949. There has been little or no effort made to acquaint the young of the recent past. The Cultural Revolution is almost as remote to them as the War of the Roses.

There are no statistics to record just how many deserved, or undeserved deaths and life sentences were meted out to people in all the political movements that had taken place since 1949. It would take volumes and volumes to record each individual case. No one had the foresight that the "anti-rightist" movement would herald the worse persecution for intellectuals that was to follow.

The fact that people allowed themselves to be so manipulated is evidence of both ignorance and of fear of retaliation. The average education level of the population was, and still is, in certain places, pitifully low, and given the cultural and historical background of the people, it is not the usual inclination to question power. That the government can do no wrong was an accepted "truth". But history has since taught us otherwise. Down through history, it has always been the ones with the gray matter or guts who start revolutions. The reason that intellectuals suffered so much in the past is that they were usually the ones who knew enough, sometimes too much, and they questioned authority, so they had to be silenced. And they were. If heavy lies the head that wears a crown, then heavier laid the hearts of those who saw what was happening to the country and yet had no choice but to be swept up in the crowds when they stampeded toward the precipice.

The policeman who had charge of our area knew that I had overstayed, and visited us at least twice a week to see if I had left. That was pressure enough on my father for, no doubt, the people in the residents' committee would be passing the information on to his company. Even though my father had no "hat" and was never officially labeled anything that would permanently stick, my parents no doubt wished that I would leave. As to where, it was up to me. Going to one strange place was a bad enough experience, I did not want to go to yet another even stranger place. I had no choice but to return to Xinjiang, but first I paid a visit to Guangzhou.

I was appalled to find how backward that city was. The men and women on the streets were fluent in Birdese, "fowl" (foul) language. They did not open their mouths without using the most graphic and obscene words. It was shocking. For the first time in my life, I was ashamed to be a Cantonese. The city buses were so rickety that they could have been salvaged from a Shanghai junk yard. Even during the Japanese War, our buses were in better condition than those running on the streets of that city. The bus conductors wore no uniforms or shoes. They were dressed in a Chinese jacket unbuttoned and pants with no front or back, hitched up at the waist with a long piece of cloth. Their feet, bare, were in wooden clogs. How a city could be that close to the colony of Hong Kong and yet be so backward was absolutely beyond my comprehension. I came back to Shanghai after a few short days, absolutely disgusted with what I had seen.

Chum invited me to visit Beijing with her when she visited Mary, her second daughter and younger sister of Anna, to take Monkey-Dee, Mary's three-year-old son, back to her. Monkey-Dee had returned with Dr Tu after he attended a CPPCC meeting there in March. I had never been to Beijing before. We visited Bob Winter at Peking University (formerly Yenjing University) and looked up Anna Louise Strong at the Peking Hotel, but I can't recall if we visited Rewi Alley even though that visit was on our itinerary. We had a reunion with Dorothy Fisher and her family, and went on to visit Tianjin as house guests of Betty Chandler Chang, an American friend of Chum's who was the wife of a thoracic surgeon in that city. After returning to Shanghai, we visited Hangchow. The trip was my last "fling", as it were.

The famine was already spreading, and food was a problem. An extra mouth to feed meant less food for everyone else. Except for those who could afford high-priced, non-ration food, the common people had a hard time fending for three decent meals a day. I grew very sensitive to any subtle remark about food, and felt most uncomfortable at home knowing that I was not welcome. That alone was enough to discourage me from staying, even though I dreaded returning to Xinjiang. I had no choice but to go back to where I had come from.

5

BACK TO THE BOONDOCKS (1960-1962)

WHEN I LEFT Shanghai to return to Xinjiang, it was already mid-1960. I had overstayed and my home leave, which had been extended more than once, was over. I knew that if I returned to my former place of work, trouble would be waiting for me because I could be accused of being absent without permission. So I decided to go and work in the same place that GWB did, and when I passed Hami, I stopped only to pick up my things. I left to the company the Chinese books I had bought because I had no place for them. I had bought too many. I went to work in the mill that GWB had been transferred to after the Big Leap Forward, the Dongfeng Caimao Gangtie Chang (East Wind xxx Iron and Steel Mill), situated in what was then the outskirts of the city of Urumqi. It was a direct product of that period in history, the Big Leap Forward.

Many young men from the commercial sector of Urumqi had been sent to Motosala, a mining area high up in the mountains of Balguntay in Hejing County, the Bayingol Mongolian Autonomous Prefecture. They were sent to dig for iron ore, with picks and shovels and not one piece of machinery. The air was thin, and each move was an effort. Food was always half-cooked because of the altitude and there were no stoves but just a hole dug in the ground fed with whatever firewood that could be found. These young men worked shoulder to shoulder with criminals who had been sent from various provinces to serve time in Xinjiang, and no doubt there were some local criminals as well. The casualty rate of the young men working on the upper levels was not as high as for the criminals working at the lower levels. Oftentimes it was too late to warn those below of rocks that had been pried loose and were rolling down. The dead were taken to a flat piece of ground and casually buried. No records were kept, and no tombstone erected because, weren't they "class enemies"? There was no timely care for the injured, and the young men on the upper levels, mostly assigned from various companies in Urumqi, dawdled as much as they could in their work because that was the only way to avoid death or injury to themselves.

Who knows how many of them actually deserved their sentences? There was a lot of hidden mutual sympathy in the hearts of some of these men. Some older criminals asked, on the sly, why the young men were there digging with them, and from where they had been sent, and for what reason. The young men also wanted to know why they had to work with these criminals, and were curious to find out as much as they could about them. Just how much ore was dug at the price of how many lives, no one, including the authorities, knows. How the dead were accounted for, if at all, to their family members, is again, anybody's guess. The lives of these criminals were as cheap as flies, and many died as such.

At the Dong Feng Steel Mill, I was assigned to work in the accounts department to do bookkeeping. For the first time since 1956, I was working in an "office". My pay was 42.84 yuan per month as I was not officially transferred but rather had resigned from my former job, thus canceling the over two years of work I had done in Hami. I began as a new employee from the very bottom, so earned the lowest pay.

Married people with families lived in houses on one side of the hill while the office and workshops were on the other side. The dormitories for single men and women were on either end of the U-shaped, one-story office building. From my desk I could see the hill, and one day when a windstorm was brewing, people from the office shouted for me to look outside, and I watched as empty oil drums were blown up the hill on their own. Before long what seemed like a gray *boran* (storm), instead of a *kara boran* (black storm) began to take force. It blew strongly but did not last more than an hour. What was in the air was not dust but cement from the open pool of the Cement Works on the adjacent lot. A school-age child was hurled into it by the wind and asphyxiated.

I was assigned to a dorm room big enough for four double-decker bunks, with seven other females, five of them girls from the countryside of Guangdong. Four of them spoke Cantonese even though none of them were from Guangzhou (Cantonese in Guangdong Province was the common language like Mandarin was in the rest of China). One woman lived in town and went home on the weekends. That seems to have been the rule because the mill was out in the suburbs and there were no buses to take them to and from work during the week. Their children either boarded in nurseries or schools, or were cared for by their husbands who worked in town.

I was assigned the upper bunk above PSJ, a young women with the worst case of B.O. I have ever encountered in my life. Why didn't she use deodorant? But of course China did not have it in those days. The rest of the girls complained to the housing department that they wanted to change dorms or have her assigned to another one, but she had already made the rounds of the other dorms and ours was her final destination. PSJ was a tomboy by nature and was actually a nice person. She was an orphan raised by her grandmother and she had the habit of gnashing her teeth at night, and had frequent nightmares in which she would break out in heart-rending sobs. But she had a boyfriend who did not mind her smell at all. The way he sniffed deliciously at the steam from the hot water in the bucket of laundry he did for her in our dorm every Sunday proved it. No one was surprised when they later married. If beauty is said to be in the eye of the beholder, in this case it moved to the nostrils.

When news got out in the Mill that I was the girlfriend of GWB, his colleagues, all bachelors, came to evaluate me. Some were polite and said nothing. One of them, an anemic shrimp, reluctantly gave me a passing mark of "60", I was later told. That was more than I would have given him.

GWB was in a dorm at the other end of the hall which he shared with several other young men from Guangdong Province, and all except one of them spoke Cantonese. There were many Cantonese-speaking people at the mill but not one was from Canton city. I was interested to find that they did not swear like troupers in the way the Cantonese did in the city.

The mill operated at a loss, like most of the mills that sprouted up during The Great Leap Forward in 1958. Famine was sweeping the country and Xinjiang was not spared. Food in the dining-hall went from bad to worse. The steamed buns which had been made from wheat flour were soon replaced by ones that were half flour and half mashed potatoes in their skin, and the finished product was gray in color and soggy and flat, as though they had been purposely stepped on. Later they were replaced by slabs of steamed bread (*fagao*) made from either rough corn flour or bean flour mixed, again, with unpeeled mashed potatoes. The latter was most unappetizing in appearance, greenish-gray, and even less appetizing in taste. Rice disappeared soon after wheat flour did, and then corn flour and bean flour were replaced by red sorghum flour. With next to no meat or oil, not even grease, and precious few vegetables, hence no roughage, everyone suffered from constipation. The men said that they now knew what having a baby felt like. Three times a day, every day, people were faced with the dilemma of "To eat, or not to eat, that is the question. Whether 'tis nobler in the mind to suffer the pangs of hunger or to steel one's nerves against the agonies of constipation..." And yet, no one had the courage to oppose it or to end it either, by dying. It seemed that we were more likely to live suffering than die starving. The human instinct is to survive, under all circumstances.

Around this time, China was flooded with Iraqi dates. Popsicles, instead of being made with traditional red bean soup, was made with Iraqi dates; steamed buns, instead of having traditional mashed red bean stuffing, were filled with Iraqi dates again. Every direction we turned, we were confronted with Iraqi dates! Another thing was Cuban brown sugar. It was rationed, but that was the only kind of sugar we saw for a long time. The third thing was canned Moroccan sardines. They were not rationed, but were expensive, and few could afford them. but canned sardines did not fit swell with the Chinese diet.

To make up for the lack of natural fiber (roughage) in our diet, we were sent out to the countryside right after the surrounding farms had finished harvesting their cabbage. We worked in pairs with *taibahzi*, a stretcher-like thing with two roughly cut branches on each side and fresh twigs woven zigzagged across. We collected whatever discarded cabbage leaves could be found and brought them back. The cabbage leaves were dumped in a vacant concrete pool. One layer of leaves, and one layer of salt were sprinkled on them, and the stronger men wearing high rubber boots would stamp on them until they changed color, and another layer of leaves and salt were added, and the process repeated until all the leaves were firmly packed in the pool and weighted down with pieces of rock or slabs of concrete so that the leaves were under salt water so they would not get moldy. That was to be our source of natural fiber for the coming winter and early spring.

We seemed to be always hungry. As soon as office hours began, we would be looking forward to noon when we could have lunch. Before the afternoon work began we were hungry again. Those who had the means could afford to buy cookies or other eatables, but GWB and I were not among them. One pay day we decided to have a "good" meal in town. We went to a restaurant and ordered four small meat patties, a fish, and two bowls of rice. The check amounted to half a month's pay for the two of us. The four meat patties were equivalent to the size of one hamburger. It was like eating banknotes! Those who had money spent it all on food, the price of which was exorbitant.

Even before the famine, the steel mill had affiliated farms where "undesirables" were sent to grow grain and vegetables. Now that the famine was all over the country, more "farms" were set up in other places and more people were sent to open up more land to grow more grain and vegetables. The new farmland was bleached with alkali (salt), the ground hardened and cracked almost as soon as it was watered. GWB and I were sent to a farm on the outskirts of the city, Ulanbo, reputed to be in the wind gap (*fengkou*) of Urumqi. The winds howled there at least three hundred days out of the year. There was no housing for single people because all those who had been sent there had families. There was no choice for us but to get married even though we had not yet planned to do so. This was March, 1961.

We went through the usual procedure of obtaining written permission from the Steel Mill Personnel Department before having health check ups, then we went to the local government to register. With the marriage license, a couple was allowed to buy a quilt cover (*beimian*) and an aluminum cooking pot. We had money for neither. GWB was in debt to his office because he had been sent to different places on several business missions and he had overspent the allotted amount on his three meals a day. Food was very expensive, and he had a healthy appetite. The only alternative was to clear the debt by installments every pay day. We were thankful that neither of us had anyone to support besides our own selves. Some young people had dependents at home to whom they had to send money on high days and holidays, if not every month. GWB's pay was 46.62 yuan and mine was no higher. So we just put our scant belongings together which consisted of our two rolls of bedding and two modest suitcases with our clothes. We were given an army tent as our first home because the few simple adobe brick houses were already occupied by existing families. The very fact that we were sent to the farm labeled us as "undesirables". Why, we never knew.

GWB was a native of Pudong but grew up in the city. The youngest of five children, his parents died one after another when he was a mere infant. His eldest sister had married and given birth to a girl before he was born, so this uncle was younger than his niece. As a result he was known as the "sesame seed of an uncle" and his niece was the "bean niece". His parents were ordinary farmers and when they both died, the family just broke up with the eldest daughter already given away in marriage. There remained the second child, a son, two younger daughters, and this infant. Their poor relatives, already with too many mouths of their own to feed, were not in a position to adopt any of the remaining four children, and so the two daughters were given away as child-brides. The elder son, not knowing what his fate would be, ran away to the city across the river, and became an apprentice to a shop owner for three meals a day and a place to stretch out at night. The infant was passed from one relative to the next. No family could be found for him even though he was a male child, as all families had their own male children. Finally, an uncle on his mother's side, took him in. His wife was childless, but she preferred taking in a child from her side of the family to one from her husband's. But a woman had very little say in those days so GWB stayed on in this family to finish high school. After his uncle died in the early 1950s, his aunt took up with another man, so there was no room, or feelings, for him anymore.

The one lucky thing about it was that GWB had not lost touch with his three sisters and brother. Even though none of them were able to give him a hand, the feeling that they were there made all the difference, I assume. When the Korean War broke out, the husband of his youngest elder sister volunteered for the army to serve in North Korea and he was encouraged to do the same, but he did not pass the vision test. His brother in-law survived the war and remained in the army until his retirement. And the fact that GWB was not from an "exploiting class" family was a plus because of the prevailing political climate.

GWB was tall, and very dark for a Chinese. In some ways he was very much like my father in temperament. A man of few words who was better at concealing his feelings than at revealing them, and with a stubborn streak. The things we had in common were that both of us were from Shanghai, both spoke Shanghainese, and were of the same age. Other than that we were almost strangers, in spite of the fact that we had met nearly five years previously, and had been corresponding on and off all along. I was 26 and if I stayed single much longer there would bound to be talk. If I married at all, I would naturally prefer it to be someone who could speak English so that at least we would have a common interest to share, but out here in the boondocks, to my knowledge, no such person existed. The saying of "marry in haste and repent in leisure" came to mind and I was undecided even though GWB, as I had mentioned earlier, was the only person of the opposite sex with whom I felt safe and comfortable. If we got married in haste, then we got acquainted in leisure, in the fifty years that followed.

There was nothing resembling romance prior to, or even after marriage, at least not the kind that we see in movies, or have fantasies about. First of all, before we got married, we were not in the same town. We did get to know each other better through correspondence, and the only time that he passed through Hami on his way further east to Xiadong was on a work day, which meant that I could not be free until after work, and we went to a movie together, and he had to leave after the movie to go back to the hostel where he was staying because the truck that was taking him to Xiadong the next day was leaving very early in the morning. He had no girlfriend although there was a girl in the group that he liked, but unfortunately, he did not earn the kind of pay that she would like. I had no attractions, good pay or otherwise. But we enjoyed being in each other's company, probably because we did not know people whom we would like better, under those circumstances. Few Shanghai males considered marrying non-Shanghai girls. The few that did marry non-Shanghai girls had first been turned down by their own kind because they did not earn "enough." As for Shanghai girls, many married non-Shanghai men older than themselves and mostly because they earned better pay than Shanghai men their own age. At that time, and perhaps even now, seniority meant higher pay.

In Ulanbo, where we had been sent, there was a chicken farm nearby. It had recently been hit by fowl epidemic and the chickens died in heaps. Plague or no plague, when anything is cooked to pulp, it is safe to eat. One man's loss is another man's gain. During the famine when grain was tightly rationed, it was wiser to eat in a public dining-hall than to do one's own cooking. Many families found that they used up their month's ration in less than ten to fifteen days no matter how they scrimped on the portions. There was no way it could be avoided, except not to have any grain at home. So people entrusted their grain tickets to the dining-halls and had their meals there. This way they could be sure that their ration lasted the time it was meant to, as meals were prepared exactly to ration, and no one could eat more than what he was allowed per meal. If he wanted to eat more than his share, then he would have to go hungry later for eating his ration in advance. There were couples who divorced because of the endless fighting over food.

We married, but had no wedding. Our marriage license, stamped with the date of March 14, 1961, was shown to the man in charge to make it legal for us to move into the tent that we were assigned to. It turned out that someone in the Personnel Department of the Mill who was responsible for dispatching people to different places had made a mistake and thought that we were already married and that was why we were both sent to the same place. On the second day that we settled down in Ulanbo, the person in charge, MYK, sent GWB to Changji, to a Dianba Commune where another farm was. He was gone for a week. It was not anything urgent at all, and if this man had had a little of the compassion we take for granted that all human beings should have, he could have at least waited a few days before sending GWB off. But there are some creatures who delight in the misery of others. That is one way of making their weight felt. But ours was not to question why, but to do as we were told. Tears were swallowed behind backs like they had been since I cast the die. I was left on my own in that big tent which swayed with the winds that howled throughout the night. The tent had no door but just a flap at the entrance that was tied down by a piece of string.

There was no direct transportation to Changji, so GWB had to go by bike which was a seven-hour uphill ride. Then he had to ride a horse for several hours to where the Dianba Commune was. A week later he returned, with a badly blistered seat, and had to waddle around for days, like someone with a gigantic hernia, before the sores finally healed.

The second person in charge at Ulanbo was someone called Yin Weimin. He had had a college education and could read English, I think. His being sent to Ulanbo was due to having a father in Taiwan. He had gone there with the KMT army in which he was serving. Yin was married with a wife in Urumqi, but we never met her. He was very circumspect toward us because he did not want to "make trouble" for us, but because he was the first person I had met (after Delia and Julian, the doctors in Urumqi) who could read English, I was thrilled. Chum had given me some paperbacks when I left and they had been read and reread. One day when he saw me reading, he asked to borrow one. I lent him the whole stack. A week later he discretely returned them to me with no comment. So I never found out if he had enjoyed them, or even if his English allowed him to understand them.

After six months at Ulanbo we were sent to the farm near Dianba Commune in Changji which was more than a day's horse cart ride away. We were given a room in a courtyard which had several rooms and a stall (barn). All the rooms seemed to have been made of pie crust because the walls were so flaky that they just crumbled when poked at. The one we were given was black with soot because it had been a kitchen, and now it was next door to it. The walls were black, covered with flies because it was still September. The roof had holes, and so at night lying in bed we could see the stars. Like Ulanbo, this place had neither electricity nor running water, not even a well. Our water, for drinking and for washing, came from what is called a *laoba* - a water-logged hole in the ground. The water tasted puckish and was rusty brown in color. I was to stay in this place till March, 1962, and my husband another two months longer. I had just discovered that I was going to be a mother.

Not long after we arrived at this new destination, a Kazakh shepherd family pitched their *keygiz ue* (yurt) on the grounds outside our courtyard. Their belongings were carried by two oxen. The frame of the yurt was collapsible. The family was headed by an elderly father, a weather-beaten man in his late sixties who spoke very good Chinese, his name was Nurseyt. He had been a local *xiangzhang* (village head) in pre-Liberation days. In his time he had seen one local war after another and he had lost two families in succession. His present family was comprised of a young wife, a very quiet and sweet woman whose name I never heard called, and five children. The eldest was a daughter called Kapan, afflicted with serious rheumatism, then four sons. Kajan was about thirteen and old enough to help his father tend their flock of nanny goats that belonged to the commune but entrusted to their care. After Kajan, there were Smyil who was around eight, then came Slembek who was about five, and the baby, Tangkai, who was just under two, and Joldyak, their family dog, who helped its master care for the herd of expectant nanny goats.

The famine continued. It was blamed partly on the Soviets. In every movement, there is a scapegoat or scapegoats. This time it was the Soviets, and the weather. Anything that could be called food was rationed. The farmers in the communes were a little better off because they had their own postage-stamp private plots on which they could grow something. The shepherds had no private plots because they were nomadic. Their rations were next to nonexistent. The commune gave each family a milk cow or two, even if it was understood that cows don't give milk when their stomachs are empty or when they are carrying a calf. Nurseyt, a model shepherd with many *seeluk* (citations) hung in his yurt to prove it, had in his care a flock of almost 200 *yeshke* (nanny goats) which had to be taken out to pasture in the early morning and herded back at sunset. The lambing, or in this case, the kidding season, began around March 15 and lasted for a month or so. The surrounding countryside was barren and the flock had to be herded to quite a distance to forage.

Here is a typical day for this family. It begins with the wife getting up very early to milk the *seer* (cow), brew tea for her family, get the children up for breakfast, and then pack what little food there was for her husband and son, Kajan, to take along for the day when they would be away – usually nothing more than a handful of dried *krude* (curds) and a piece of stale bread. Then the nanny goats are let out of the pen and counted. Joldyak is chained to Nurseyt's saddle because he was very reluctant to leave each day. The flock sets out, with her husband on horseback guiding the head billy goat who led the way each day, and Kajan, on another horse rounding up the stragglers. Nanny goats heavy with kids and a half-empty stomach, are slow on the move. She tidies up the bowls (wooden) and breakfast things, and her daughter, Kapan, badly crippled with rheumatism, helps with whatever she can, such as dressing her two youngest brothers. She takes the goat and sheepskins that they sleep on at night, to be thoroughly shaken and beaten on the ground, fur-side down, to rid it of any tiny little creatures that are lodged there. After breakfast, the two younger boys, Smyil and Slembek are sent out to pick firewood, and she tidies up the pens and collects all the goat droppings from overnight and heaps them up for fuel. The fresh cow droppings are either left to dry or mixed with goat droppings to be made into cakes and also left to dry for fuel. Then she makes trips to the nearest waterlogged hole, which is usually quite a distance away, with a bucket to carry water for the day. After the children come back with the firewood - twigs and branches - she boils the milk from the morning's milking. In their case, one cow did not give milk because she would be calving in a few weeks. So there wasn't much milk to boil. Then she sits down to have her breakfast of whatever is left after the family has finished, usually just scraps. The children contribute by spending their day picking kindling and cow chips, but their chores are viewed more as play than burden. Kapan had gone to school when they were near where a school was, but as her rheumatism worsened, she had to stay home. Smyil went to school when there was one nearby. Nurseyt was illiterate both in Kazakh and Chinese, but spoke both fluently.

At sunset the flock returns. Again it is counted as they enter the pen. The family cow is milked again, and tea is ready for her husband and eldest son. Then she prepares supper, usually a big cauldron of rice or wheat gruel. Both the rice and wheat were usually "finds" in vole lairs. After supper, everyone goes to sleep. Their "bed" is the hard ground with a layer of *keygiz* (rough, home-made, felt) and *tare* (sheep or goat skins). The two youngest boys sleep naked, snuggled against their parents for warmth. Little boys hardly ever wet their 'beds' as the mother would usually give their bottom a whack when she thinks they need to relieve themselves, and they get up and stand at the doorway of the yurt to do their job, regardless of the weather. When they are babies they are tied into their *besuk* (cradle).

Years later I discovered from my students from the Medical College that the country's highest incidence of cancer of the esophagus, and cancer of the stomach were found in the Altai area, among the male Kazakh belonging to a certain tribe, and especially among the shepherds. Their lifestyle probably contributed toward it. The bowls and bowls of piping hot tea that they drink several times a day, the full meal (when the famine was over) consumed just prior to lying down to sleep because supposedly a full stomach protects them against the cold, and the streptopolin, a bacteria produced in the fermentation and drying process of milk curds which is reputed to be a carcinogen, combined to create that high rate of cancer patients. The affliction of having difficulty in swallowing food, commonly known in Kazakh as *kiltamak* (thorny throat), was known down through the ages, It wasn't until modern medicine was developed that it was given the name of cancer of the esophagus. It is said that the highest incidence of cancer in Xinjiang are cancer of the esophagus among the Kazakh men of northern Xinjiang, and cancer of the uterus among Uygur women of southern Xinjiang. For the child-bearing age woman of the Kazakh shepherd population, there is no such thing as "sitting the month" after birth like Han women do. After childbirth she is up and on the go again. If she is unlucky to give birth at the time when the family and flock are moving to a new pasture, she would have to be on horseback right after birth. There is no such thing as Kotex for them, or for the rest of the female population of China until very recently. Talk about liberation for women!! She stops her discharge with either a piece of rough home-made felt or a bag of cold ashes from the fire. Prolapse of the uterus, or metrotopsis, is not unknown or uncommon among the older generation of the nomadic female population which are far from cities or towns where even minimal medical care is unavailable. The Uygur custom of having the daughter give birth to her first child at her mother's home and stay for a month, must also have grown out of painful experience, too.

At this time, meat was scarce. Whatever Nurseyt could

trap, sometimes a hare, sometimes a fox, and once he trapped
a badger, was not for food because Kazakh, being Muslim, ate
only lamb, mutton, beef or horseflesh. Neither do they eat any
meat that has not been bled. So whatever was caught was flayed
and the skin sold and carcass given to the dog, or sold to a Han
who would eat anything. Nurseyt was experienced in finding
vole lairs where unhusked rice and wheat had been squirreled
away by the animals. The voles in Changji were big with stiff
tails, measuring at least 30 centimeters from head to tail, if not
longer. These animals were pests in crop-growing areas. One
hole would yield at least half a *jin (500 grams)* of either *gureursh*
(rice) or *beedai* (wheat) kernels and Nurseyt would put every last
grain of his find into his bag and take home to his wife when the
flock returned at the end of the day. She would husk the grain by
pounding it in a wooden mortar carved out of a tree trunk and a
wooden pestle, and then winnow it. The cleaned rice would then
be boiled in a cauldron of water to make a *kurzhur* (gruel), then
laced with *suizbe* (salted cottage cheese), which is *ayran* (yogurt)
poured into a muslin bag and hung up to drain over a container
to catch the whey to be used later as either a bleach or softener
for sheepskins or goatskins which would be used later either as
mattress or to be sewn into coats. After the whey is thoroughly
drained from the yogurt, salt is mixed into it, and stuffed into a
cleaned cow or sheep *karin* (stomach), tied up and suspended in
the breeze to dry. What is inside the *karin* would keep for a year,
if not longer. The cauldron of rice gruel would be the evening
meal for the whole family, plus some milk tea. If there were some
suer (smoke-dried lamb, beef, or horseflesh) left over from the
previous year, it would be boiled in the cauldron with rice or
pounded wheat to make the gruel.

The Kazakh shepherds had only one meal a day, just before
he lay down to sleep. The rest of the time they drank piping hot

salted, milk tea with either roasted *tarr* (millet) or *baosak* (fried square pieces of dough). But during the famine, they just made do with whatever they had. They drank hot tea several times a day if they had the leisure time. Nurseyt, being a goatherd who took his flock out early in the morning and did not return until after sunset, could only have milk tea twice a day. But since he took the flock out with his son Kajan, and the family dog, Joldyak, he would often leave the flock to the two of them and wander around on horseback looking for vole holes. If he came within a short distance of the family yurt, his wife would brew him a kettle of tea. The Kazakhs use a variety of *taschai* (brick tea made from ground tea leaves that have been pounded brick-hard), and it is brewed in an aluminum kettle. Salt is added and, if milk is plentiful like after the nanny goats or cows have calved, then the tea will be drunk with the skimmed-off *kaimak* (cream) that is taken from the top of a cauldron of boiled *soot* (milk). A cow is milked early in the morning and again after sunset. Each milking yields about half a pail if the cow has recently calved, then the milk is strained with a piece of muslin and poured into a cauldron to be brought to a boil. (Where muslin is not available, a horsetail is used as a strainer!) But just before the milk comes to a boil, the bigger pieces of firewood are withdrawn from under the cauldron so that the milk is left to simmer while it is being *sapripp*-ed - ladled and poured back again and again, supposedly forcing the cream to the surface. That is done until the fire dies down. This way of boiling the milk thickens the layer of *kaimak* (cream) on top.

When I was in Hami, the Kazakh shepherds from the Barkol pastures would come down to town to sell stacks of *keptirgan kaimak*, which were pancake-like layers of cream taken from cooled boiled milk. After a cauldron of milk cools down, the layer of cream on top hardens because it is very thick and it is peeled off and turned over on a reed mat to dry. Then the milk is boiled in the same manner again, and another layer is peeled off, until there is little cream left. This *keptirgan kaimak* was part of the Barkol Kazakh shepherds' form of cash. They would come down to Hami to shop with a stack of these cream pancakes and did their modest shopping with what they got from selling them in town. I guess I gained most of my weight in Hami from overly enjoying those pancakes even though my Han colleagues, especially the Shanghai ones, wouldn't touch them with a ten-foot pole, and smirked at how "dirty" they were. And undoubtedly, it wasn't always "clean".

Nurseyt's children had never known anything such as cookies, candies, or other goodies. Their only treat was a piece or two of *krude* (dried milk curds), or if they were lucky, an occasional piece of *irimchik* - milk boiled dry with a piece of the bitter sheep intestine to make it curdle. Nurseyt's children were timid and very well-behaved. Neither Nurseyt's wife nor any of his children spoke Chinese. I wanted to get to know them badly, but language was a barrier. My ration of grain was more or less left untouched because of morning sickness, and there was no medicine such as thalidomide those days (Thank goodness!!!) so we could share some of it with the children. We became friends. The children had lice, and I spent my free time looking for them one by one on Tangkai, the youngest child, who was also the cutest. He was roly-poly and not one bit shy like his sister and brothers were. We collected scraps from the kitchen next door to give to Joldyak, their dog. As time went on, he had to be literally dragged to Nurseyt's horse to be chained to his saddle every morning as they set out because he refused to leave but instead wanted to wait at our doorstep for scraps. The poor creature was hungry most of the time, but then so were the wolves and foxes. Joldyak was needed to chase them away from the nanny goats who were getting clumsier everyday, and could not run away fast enough when attacked. We felt very guilty about it, and Nurseyt wasn't happy with us either.

The little Uygur I had learned while in Hami and in Urumqi might as well have been Greek to Nurseyt's wife and children. I exhausted my limited Uygur vocabulary but not one word got through. That didn't keep us from being friends though. I think we could have developed a much better relationship had there been some verbal communication other than just smiles, grins and gestures. This friendship of sorts, brought home many Sunday School lessons. That deeds were more important than words was one, the shepherd and his flock was another, the lost sheep, and many others. Nurseyt and his family were good shepherds. Their devotion to their flock way surpassed the quality of feelings that some humans had for each other at that time. That these honest-to-goodness folks brought home Biblical teachings to me really got me thinking about certain things. One need not profess to be anything, one's deeds told all. These people who had so little, and wanted so little, and yet gave so much in return. I have not met anyone like the Nurseyt family since.

I spent time with Nurseyt's children hoping to learn a few words of Kazakh. Their mother was busy all the time. She had to make winter coats for the whole family from goat and sheep skins, and also to make *keygiz* (rough felt) which was used for mattresses and coverings for the tent, among other things. The way the Kazakh women hold sewing needles, and the way they sew, are identical to the way Eskimo women sew. The Han women sew holding the needle width-wise across the cloth from right to left, while the Kazakh women hold the needle vertically, length-wise up and down the cloth and sews toward herself, from top to bottom. Even the tools used for scraping and dressing the sheepskins are identical to those that the Eskimos use. Cloth, at that time, was also rationed, and shirts for her family were hand sewn. I gave her daughter what clothes I had "grown" out of and would probably not grow back into ever again.

Keygiz is indispensable to any Kazakh shepherd family. It is made from *koyjun* (sheep wool) which is not good enough or the fibers long enough to be spun into yarn for knitting. To make *keygiz*, the inferior quality sheep wool is first fluffed to rid it of dirt and then evenly placed on a reed mattress. Boiling hot water is poured onto it to make it shrink and mat, then soap is rubbed on it, and it is tightly rolled with the reed mattress. Very much like how a baker would use a rolling pin to roll a lump of dough into a flat cake, only in making *keygiz*, the Kazakh women use the back of their arms to roll the reed mattress (with the layer of sheep wool inside), on the ground. So, most Kazak women, wives of shepherds, have very red, coarse and blistered lower arms. The process is repeated until the *keygiz* is of the required thickness and density. Then it is unrolled and left to dry. Sheep wool that is long enough to make yarn is fluffed to rid it of the dirt and sand, then handspun on an *urrchoke* (spindle) and the yarn is used for socks, gloves, and sweaters.

I was picking up a little of the language, and was eager to practice whatever new word I had learned to see if my pronunciation was understandable, and in the process made a fool of myself many times over. Actually, my worst experience was in learning Uygur in Hami. When someone asked me where so-and-so's wife was, I told them that she was selling honeydew melon on the street corner, but instead of the word *korhoon*, I stressed on the wrong syllable and it sounded like she was selling her 'fanny' instead. The two words sounded the same to a new learner like me. One day, Nurseyt's wife came to me for what sounded like *beedai* (wheat kernel). I was so glad that I knew the word. I told her that I didn't have it, but that I did have *oon* (flour), and handed it to her. She pinched a little of it with her finger and thumb, and sniffed at it, and then shook her head. I was puzzled. I repeated *beedai* (wheat kernel) and made the gesture of grinding with my arms. She shook her head helplessly again and again and left. She came back with a piece of goatskin that was one of the many goatskins laid on top of the *keygiz* that the family used as mattresses to sleep on, parted the hair on it to reveal some little creatures that were scurrying around, and made the gesture of sprinkling something on it. It suddenly dawned on me that she was asking me for *beetdare* (lice medicine), a disinfectant for killing lice! I was sorry to tell her that we didn't have any, but I was happy that I had added another word to my vocabulary. A few days later, I went into their yurt to borrow a shovel. Ours were too big and heavy, and they had one that was just the right size for me to use. The family was in the middle of a meal, and I said, "*kewrook berap truche*". They all choked on their food. What I had said sounded to them like "Please lend me your bottoms (asses)". I should have said *krerk* (shovel, or spade) instead of "*kewrook*" (tail). It was not until I practiced on them each word that I had learned that I was sure the words were pronounced correctly. Later on, my Kazakh vocabulary grew and my pronunciation improved during my sixteen-year stay (1962-1978) in the Kazak-speaking prefecture of Altai.

The kidding season had arrived. Animal husbandry in Xinjiang is very much at the mercy of the elements, and the shepherds have to work extra hard during that special season to ensure the smooth delivery and the survival of the new members of their flock. The majority of Nurseyt's nanny goats had twins, some even triplets. I realized that the awards pinned up on the wall of his yurt had not been easily earned. The kidding season drags on for almost a month, from mid-March. Some nanny goats give birth on the way to the pastures and Nurseyt and his son, Kajan, would then have to scoop up the *lahk* (kid) after its mother had licked it dry and warm it inside their *tohn* (sheepskin coat). March is early spring, and the temperature can be way below zero. The young kids are dripping wet at birth, and if the nanny goats do not lick them dry right away, they freeze, encased in a shell of ice, and many just die from that initial cold. Due to lack of forage, some nanny goats were already quite weak at the time of giving birth, especially those who had twins or triplets, and would die soon after kidding, without the strength to lick their offspring dry. So, orphans who managed to survive are left in the care of the shepherds.

When the first kids arrive, they are kept in the yurt at night with the family because it is too cold out in the open. The nanny goats are fenced in at night, and the ones that had kidded were separately fenced in another pen. Goats, when not heavy with kid, are very playful, they frolic and butt each other. If the ones that are now light are fenced in with the expectant mothers, it would not be safe. The newborn kids are separated from their mothers at night because too much sucking supposedly brings on diarrhea, which can also be fatal. Kids with bad tummies have a red string tied to their tail to mark them out so that the shepherd can take them away from their mothers after their feeding instead of leaving them alone to enjoy more "quality time" of bonding with their mothers like other kids with healthy tummies are allowed to. In the middle of the kidding season when most nanny goats have kidded, the young are now strong enough to be left out in the cold in a separate pen from their mothers. The orphans are still kept in the tent at night. Some kids develop sores on their tender gums, and refuse to nurse, then Nurseyt and his family, except for the two youngest children, would open each kid's mouth for inspection, and any one with a sore was administered a little salt rubbed on as a disinfectant, then cleaned by applying some mutton fat as a salve to cover and soothe it. To Nurseyt and his wife and children, the flock was an extension of the family, and each member of the flock was treated as such.

Whatever milk that could be gotten from these nanny goats after their kids had had their fill would be given to the orphans. Nanny goats don't usually allow kids other than their own to suck. A nanny goat wet nurse has to be gotten by the horns and tightly held between the legs while another person brings the orphan for a feed. Usually goats that have had a single kid are selected to nurse an orphan or to nurse the odd kid of a set of triplets. Whatever can be gotten from the milking after the kids have had their fill will be Nurseyt's family's food until the next kidding season. If he had been herding cows instead of nanny goats, he would be much busier.

Calves have their nostrils pierced with a pencil-like piece of wood at a very young age. The purpose is to hang a flap of wood no bigger than the size of a poker card from it to prevent them from sucking when they are old enough to be taken out to pasture to forage with their mothers. The flap does not prevent the calf from grazing, but it does prevent it from sucking because once they lift their heads to suck, the flap covers their lips. They are allowed to suck only before and after the morning and evening milking. What milk can be gotten from cows is made into *sarmai* (butter), and what is left after the butter is skimmed off, is *irkit* (butter milk), for the children to drink as much as they want. What cannot be finished is then poured into a muslin bag to drip-dry, with the whey kept for bleaching and softening sheepskins. What is in the bag is taken out and hand pressed into small pieces to make *krude* (dried milk curds) and left outdoors to dry. When they are thoroughly dried, they are kept in bags to serve as snack, food, and thirst quencher, to last until the next season. Most shepherd families have sacks and sacks of it, depending on the size of the flock in their care.

One would think that living so close to nature, the fresh air, the healthy diet of milk and meat, would be ideal for the growth of children. And I think it would be had it not been for the sore lack of veterinarians. Cows afflicted with tuberculosis often pass it on to the people, especially to the young, considering the Kazakhs' closeness to animals. Another malady was from consumption of the innards of sick sheep, especially when the liver is afflicted with cysticercosis. The liver of the human is then the breeding ground for cysticercus, and it is mostly fatal. However, both would have been avoidable maladies had circumstances been more favorable.

Each day, as soon as it was a little light, the kids would begin their loud "meh-mehing" for their mothers, and their mothers would respond with even louder "meh-mehing" for their kids. After a nanny goat has kidded, it is milked twice a day, like cows are. It is much easier to milk a cow than a nanny goat as the latter does not give milk unless one literally socks hard at her udder. Have you ever seen how a kid sucks? Sometimes the mother is knocked off balance by the force the kid exerts just to beg for a drink. The kid feeds kneeling to show how grateful it is for his food. This has been cited by people, along with young crows bringing in food for their old parents, as lessons of gratitude that humans can learn from the animal world. The Chinese proverb *Yang you guai ru zi en, ya you fan pu zi yi* is an example.

When a nanny goat has had triplets the shepherd makes a mark on the odd one because a goat has only two teats. Odd man out, this kid is immediately taken to another nanny goat who has had only one kid, or whose kid has died, to be thoroughly sniffed at. If that odd kid is accepted, it is allowed to nurse, but sometimes it is rejected, and the nanny goat will butt it so hard that it would send the poor thing hurtling. If all attempts at finding that kid a wet nurse fail, the family has no choice but to bottle-feed it until it is weaned. Kids fed in this manner usually turn out scrawny.

The more nanny goats kidded, the busier Nurseyt's wife became. Sometimes she had a friend or two to help her with the twice-daily milking. The meh-mehing of the nanny goats, mothers and kids in unison, can be deafening. First thing in the morning the pen where the nanny goats were was opened and they were counted and let out. Then immediately the kids' pens was opened because if they were not opened in time the mothers would stampede toward it, each eager to get at her baby or babies. Each set of mother and kid or kids have their own special meh-mehing that is identifiable by them alone. The seeming frenzy as the loud meh-mehing kids rush towards their even louder meh-mehing mothers is fleeting as each finds its mother, or vice versa, in next to no time. The few kids that are slower are soon found by their mothers. Others who try to sneak in a drink or two from an aunt, are sent flying.

For a city girl like myself, I felt that two eyes just weren't enough to take in all that was happening right outside my doorstep. I am truly grateful for all that I witnessed. A few years later, when I read James Herriot's trilogy (*All Creatures Big and Small, All Things Bright and Beautiful, and All Things Wise and Wonderful*), I wept. Had I not had the experience of being Nurseyt's neighbor, I would not have been so touched by the books. They brought back so many memories, both bitter and sweet. How totally different were the living conditions of the shepherds I knew and the shepherds of the Scottish dales, and yet how identical they were in their love for the animals in their care. I would not have appreciated those books as much if I hadn't been sent to Changji, and so would not have had the pleasure of meeting with Nurseyt and his family.

I left them in late March to return to Urumqi and my husband left two months later. We did not have the chance to revisit there in the years that followed, but I have not, and never will, forget Nurseyt and family, not only because they were my first Kazakh friends. That experience endeared me to the Kazakh-speaking people among whom I lived for sixteen years later on. I hope that life has improved for this family of wonderful people, my unforgettable, first, but not last, Kazakh-speaking neighbors and friends.

It was now time that I went for a prenatal checkup in Urumqi. My husband was not allowed leave, and so I had to go alone by horse cart, driven by Ma Youfu, a Hui. (To me he was "Blessed art thou, Mr Ma" because in Chinese 'Blessed are the...' in Sermon on the Mount is 'you fu'.) "Blessed art thou, Mr Ma" was in his late forties, a very robust fellow. He had a short temper, and was known for his terseness. He remained single after his wife died at childbirth. He was very good with the horses, a diligent worker, but kept very much to himself so that he had few friends. No one ever found out where in Xinjiang he came from, because questions were always responded to by a grunt. We got along with him because we never asked him anything except for advice. I bumped my way to Urumqi with "Blessed art thou, Mr Ma" at the reins.

I went to look up Delia at the Medical College because she was head of the Obstetrics Department there. When she discovered that we had been sent to Changji, she advised me to stay in Urumqi until after the baby was born, which was to be around early June. She said that I would be needing a monthly checkup until then. I went back to my former dorm at the Mill, which, to my great surprise, was unoccupied, except for a new person, a Uygur girl by the name of Helman, from Toksun. The single girls with whom I had shared the dorm had all married during the time that we were in Ulanbo and Changji. I told my boss of the obstetrician's advice and he agreed that I could stay in my former dorm and not return to Changji.

My husband had bought a piglet early in the year and started to feed it in the hope that by the time I gave birth there would be some meat to eat. The piglet had just been weaned when he arrived. We treated it like we would a baby, and fed it soaked bread, chopped cabbage leaves and mashed potatoes. A hole was dug for it right outside our door and lined with hay taken from the stall where the horses were kept, and changed it every evening before the pig went to bed. The little thing thrived under my husband's meticulous care, and grew very attached to him. When it outgrew the hole we had dug for him, another one was dug further away nearer the stall, but it would insist on sleeping in its former hole which by now was only big enough to accommodate the front half of him. There was nothing we could do except to enlarge the hole if he insisted on not moving. We never gave it a name, but he was referred to as our "godson". By now, he was old enough to clean out his own sty. He did so by entering it head first and kicking out the dirty hay with his hind legs. We would throw away what he had kicked out, and he would go to the stall and make trips with a mouthful of dry hay each time to replace what he had cleaned out. Sometimes he would be over zealous and got so much hay that there would not be room left for him to even enter, not to say sleep, and he'd have to kick out the rest, and other times he would be so lazy that a few token bites of hay, hardly sufficient to cover the ground was good enough.

Before buying this piglet we first made sure that Nurseyt and the Hui workers in our courtyard would not be offended, since they were all Muslim. When my husband told them the purpose of buying the piglet and raising it, they were understanding and gave us their permission. A piglet, especially a male one, was cheap and therefore affordable. We wouldn't have bothered with it had our circumstances been better. But meat was very expensive and we were cash-strapped. We were still paying off my husband's debts, and figured they would be cleared in May if we were careful. The pig got to be so attached to my husband that he would follow him wherever he went. If my husband went anywhere on a bike and he couldn't keep up with the pace with his short little legs, he would squeal so hard, with his round belly pumping fiercely like a bellow that there was nothing to do but to slow down and wait for him.

Our first child, a boy, came a little after the dawn of May 27 after two difficult days. The Mill was being disbanded and most people had left and only one solitary male was left in my husband's former dorm, a Cantonese man, YK. He was a bachelor who had formerly worked for the import/export company and I think I could have married him because he liked me, and kept pestering me so for one of the two can-openers from WWII that I eventually had to give him one to stop him cornering me. My husband did not like him because of it. Being a college graduate, YK earned 88.20 yuan a month while my husband Gong got only 46.62 yuan, and I, 42.84.

The drawn out birth process was awful, but YK was there all the time. And I, bare from the waist down with only a towel over my belly, was in no position to care too much about it. When I felt the pains, I let him know. The mill was almost deserted and there was not a jeep, a truck, or any vehicle that could be used to take me to the Medical College Hospital which was at the other end of town. There was no way to get in touch with my husband because there were no telephones. It was very embarrassing indeed. YK went to get the midwife who served the factory staff and who lived behind the hill, and she directed him as to what to do, such as fetch water and boil it, make congee if he could find some rice, and so on. It gives me the creeps just thinking of it. I never saw him afterwards except for once twenty-one years later, in 1983, when I went to Zhongshan University. He was working at the Guangzhou Trade Fair building across from the Dong Fang Hotel as a representative of the Xinjiang Import/Export Company and he recognized me immediately. He was married by then and invited me to have dinner with him at his home.

As luck would have it, my husband had been sent to town to buy something for the farm, and he dropped by the mill to see how I was doing, only to find that he had become father of a baby boy the spitting image of himself, even down to the dark birthmark on the right side of his rib cage. He had to return to Changji to gather our meager belongings and come back to the Mill now that the baby was born. We named him named Jian, meaning healthy. My husband was also supposed to bring what "godson" was destined to become, but he returned the following day with our luggage, but *sans* pork. He just couldn't bring himself to slaughter the pig, so he had left quietly, very early in the morning before the pig had risen.

We were told to move in to an empty apartment on the other side of the hill, vacated by a family who had moved back to the Northeast when the Mill liquidated while we were away. The next day, a cadre from what had been the Personnel Department of the Mill came to tell me that I had been *jingjian*-ed (considered redundant, down-sized). I was not acquainted with that term, but was told that it meant I was temporarily laid off and that when the appropriate time came, I would have to go back to work. All I knew then was that some people had to be *jingjian*-ed when a company is down-sized or shut down for good, and others are assigned to work elsewhere. I was still in a state of euphoria at being a mother for the first time, and was delighted at hearing the news because it meant that I could now take care of my baby instead of having to leave him at the day-care center after my 56 days of maternity leave was over, as I had dreaded. I was so thankful that my prayers had been answered.

I had visited the day-care center once, and quite by accident, before I married. It was located in a quiet corner of the factory grounds, and run by some housewives headed by the wife of a workshop head. This couple's three year-old son was also in the same day-care center. One day, this boy managed to get one of the enamel potties (spittoon with a neck) on his head like a hat, and paraded around to scare the other kids when an *ahyee* or auntie, what the women who took care of the children were called, reprimanded him by hitting him on the head. What she had hit was the bottom of the potty and somehow it went down which meant that his head got into the neck of the potty, and stuck. All hell broke lose. First of all because his mother was the head of the day-care, and secondly, his father was a workshop head under whom that woman and other women's husbands worked. What's more, the child was crying and screaming himself hoarse because he could not get the potty off which came down past the bridge of his nose and thus obstructed his sight, but at the same time the other kids were all in stitches because he looked so ridiculous with an upside-down potty as hat. There was nothing to do but call for the boy's father, who eventually came with some workers with lubricant, scissors, and other tools. They could not get the potty off because the shape of that child's head was somewhat like the shape of a kidney. He screamed and kicked while his parents held onto him and a worker pulled in the opposite direction. The doctor came and advised them not to use brute force for fear of harming the child. He suggested that it was safest to put him under anesthesia and cut at the enamel potty. He was taken to a hospital in town and they managed to get the potty off his head somehow.

I had thought to myself then that if I had a baby and left him at such a day-care center, I would be worried to death. So being laid off, was to me then, a good tiding of great joy. I couldn't have asked for a better arrangement. I could now care for my baby until he was old enough to go to kindergarten, and then I could go back to work. What more could I ask for? How many working women then had the privilege to be full-time mothers? Almost none. Men looked for wives who brought along their own "meal tickets" as they did not earn enough to support them. I was elated. How was I to know then that being *"jing-jian'* literally meant being fired, and that I would be permanently out of work?!

After I knew that I was going to become a mother, I had written to Auntie Ellie about it, and she in turn informed mutual friends, mostly former Sunday School teachers. She began to send me one pound packages of sugar, cooking oil, dried noodles, lard, and condensed milk. The regulations during the three years of famine allowed us to receive unlimited food packages from Hong Kong, each package not exceeding the weight of 500 grams, and all we had to pay a 35 *fen* handling charge at Customs. Some of the food we received was saved for a rainy day while others were shared with friends. Auntie Ellie also sent used bed sheets for me to use for diapers and used clothing. They were of immense help. My mother sent me clothing that I had worn as a baby and all my four sisters and brothers had gone through, but were still in good enough condition.

The baby was healthy, but I had developed a symptom that took around a year to disappear. I couldn't laugh, cough, carry anything heavy, or hear running water without wanting to urinate, or actually urinating. Filling the thermos flask with boiling water from the kettle was one of the chores I avoided, among other things. There was something wrong with my bladder. But since I was now unemployed, medical care was not available unless we paid for half of it. After being fired, our already meager earnings were cut in half with an extra member in the family.

No explanation was ever offered as to why I was laid off. The half a dozen or more *mangliu* (aimless drifter) girls, most of them from Sichuan, were retained on the strength that they had married Party members who were cadres in the personnel department, the Youth League, and other offices of "importance", and were later assigned with their husbands to other companies, either in Urumqi or elsewhere in Xinjiang.

It is a fact I am a stiff-neck, and have never endeared myself to any of my superiors. And to make matters worse, I was married to someone with the same 'affliction.' Here, two minuses did not make one plus. My husband still had not received an assignment as to where he would be sent to work. We were told to wait. We did. In the meantime, my husband did what he could to find out why I had been fired. Could it be that we had displeased the man who ran the Personnel Department because I had not gotten a watch for him from Hong Kong? After this man had seen us carrying packages of food from the Post Office that Auntie E had sent, he asked me to have whoever it was to send a Swiss watch for him and that he would pay me for whatever it would cost. I told him that the person I knew was too poor to advance the sum needed for a watch, and left it at that. What would Auntie Ellie have thought? Here she was, sending me relief packages, and me, asking for an imported wristwatch for a man?!

Many of the cadres from the Mill had already been assigned to different places of work when it liquidated while we were at the farm and totally in the dark. We had to go to the Commercial Bureau under which the Mill had operated to inquire. The people there said that their job was to approve or not approve of whatever decisions had been made at the grassroots. But now the grass was uprooted, and where could we find each blade that had played a part in the decision-making? It was later that we were told that I was deemed to have "complicated overseas connections", and that "who knows what were in the overseas packages", and "what was written in the overseas correspondence", and a string of other guesses. There were too many "could be's" and "might have been's" and "what if's" circulating about me. So what was there for us to do? Where could we go to clarify matters? Any move on our part would merely give the impression that we had guilty consciences, so we just left matters as they were, innocently thinking that one day the truth would out and we would be cleared of whatever suspicion that existed about us. How extremely naive! That day never came.

Whatever that had happened three or four decades ago might as well have been ancient history. I have never seen the man or men who were responsible for me being made unemployed in 1962 even though I know that they are right here in Urumqi. I never looked them up, nor ran across them in town. I knew it would be futile to confront them because these are not people in power, and the reason they did what they did was because it was a part of their job. Although one of them, LES, a cadre in the Personnel Department who had been very stuck-up even though I never knew what he had to be stuck-up about except that he was a Party member, married a *mangliu* from Sichuan just when the factory was liquidating. Several other *mangliu* girls from Sichuan married at the same time so that they were transferred with their men to their new jobs as employees, while my name was struck off the payroll for good. Was it because my husband was not a

Party member? I, at least, had a file to show where I had come from, and where I had worked, while these *mangliu* had been all over the place, drifting from job to job with no records to show. At that time, those of us who had volunteered for work in Xinjiang looked down on the *mangliu* for various reasons. One was their kowtowing, accommodation to their superiors, and also their knack for trimming their sails to the wind. I suppose it is part of survival, and had we learned from them, perhaps we would have fared better. But human nature is hard to change, and in spite of it all, we were stiff necks, and we didn't want to have anything to do with the brown-nosers. To survive, I suppose one has to be a good sailor.

6

The Burqin Years (1962-1965)

THREE MONTHS AFTER our son's birth, my husband received news that he was being assigned to the Petroleum Station in Burqin. Where in the world was that?? I had never been further north than Urumqi, and neither had he. We had no map and there was no one around to ask for any information on the place where we were being assigned. GWB had had the guts to reject an assignment to Gulja when he first came, but now six years later, after the many political movements he had witnessed, he no longer had that same edge. Now he had more to consider because he was more mature, and married with a wife and child who depended on him for their livelihood.

He made the required arrangements of transferring our residential permits to where we were going, a place foreign to both of us. We had some forebodings, but there was nothing we could do about it except to go in the direction in which we were pointed. We feared it was a road of no return.

Unlike the young people of today, we were very docile, and never asked any questions, perhaps it was because we already knew what the answers would be. Both of us had an aversion to contact with 'superiors', or people who claim to be our superiors. Not being boot-lickers, our survival tactic was to steer clear of the "boss' but do our job well so that we would not incur his 'wrath'. Thus, whoever is boss is of little consequence to us, as most of them are about the same.

We were told that a two-and-a-half-ton Russian-made truck, a GAZ-51, had been assigned to take us to Burqin. So, on September 29, 1962, exactly six years to the day after we had left our hometown, Shanghai, as total strangers, we were leaving Urumqi for Burqin as a family.

The driver was a friendly man. The truck cabin was only big enough for two people, him, and another passenger. He regretfully announced to us that the seat next to him had been spoken for by a 'leading cadre'. That 'leading cadre' arrived after we had loaded our meager belongings onto the back of the truck, which consisted mostly of leftover coal and our bedding. The 'leading cadre', a northerner, standing by, seemed to be in a hurry to get going and prompted the driver to hit the road. We would have no choice but to sit in the open truck with no covering, not even a tarpaulin. The baby was just 100 days old, and it would take at least two and a half days to get to where we were going because that 'leading cadre' had some business to attend to on the way.

Even though we had already loaded our belongings onto the back of the truck, I refused to leave. I cried and complained to my husband in Shanghai dialect that 'that worthy-of-death man must be an animal with no heart, and that he must not have a wife, or if he did, she must be barren or else how would he have the heart to occupy the one and only seat in the driver's cabin and let a woman with in infant in her arms sit at the back of the truck under the blazing sun and strong wind on a nearly 1,000-kilometer-long trip.'

I asked my husband to unload our things because we weren't leaving. After a while, the 'leading cadre' reluctantly got out of the driver's cabin and offered his seat to me, with an awkward smile.

It turned out that this man's wife was a Shanghai girl who had come in to Xinjiang in 1954. He did not understand much Shanghai dialect, but I think he did understand some of the names I was calling him to my husband. He must have heard similar words from his wife. A few years later in Altai, he became my husband's boss for a short time. It's a small world. I have never spoken to him or his wife even though we lived in such a small town that there is no way to completely avoid contact. He later passed away, and she went to live in his hometown in Sha'anxi Province.

For the trip from Urumqi to Burqin, we had to travel north and northeast. First we had to pass the town of Changji. The Dianba Commune, where Nurseyt and his family were living. How I wished I could see them one last time!

After passing Changji, we arrived in Hutubi and then Manas. Further on was Shihezi where we stopped for a bite to eat. We were cheered by what we saw and what we heard there. Shihezi was much better laid out than Urumqi. The wide roads with tree-lined sidewalks were a feast to our eyes, and when we heard Shanghainese being spoken by people on the streets, we couldn't believe our ears! The many state farms there were mainly worked by demobilized members of the PLA and Shanghai youths, and even some reformed prostitutes from Shanghai and other cities, many of them were now married to former PLA men, most of whom were officers and some former KMT soldiers who had surrendered when Xinjiang was liberated. Shihezi was a brand new city established by the 7th Agricultural Division of the Xinjiang Production and Construction Corps, a semi-military organization. The food stands by the roadside and the restaurants sold Shanghai food. How we wished that Shihezi had been our destination instead of that unheard of place, Burqin!

After eating something, we were on the road again. We

pressed on to Shawan, and then to Kuitun where we spent the night in a small inn which was somewhat cleaner than the inns we had experienced in 1956. The ride from Kuitun to Karamai seemed to take forever. We went to Dushanzi, otherwise known as *maitaw* (oil mountain or oil hill) in Uygur, to the big oil refinery where that leading cadre had to attend to some business. Then we were on the road again for Karamai. After what seemed like an eternity, we came to a place called Qianshan Laoba (meaning the water-logged ground at the foot of the mountain). It was so unbearably hot that we had to stop and look for shade. There was none. The driver's cabin was like an oven, and the two men on top would have been scorched to death had the truck traveled at a slower speed. The ground temperature was at least somewhere near 45 degrees centigrade, if not higher. The paved roads were gummy and soft, and there wasn't a tree in sight. Had there been water we could have at least wet our towels and put them over our mouths to provide some relief. We just felt seared to our insides.

The driver stopped the truck and we got off to seek respite in the little shade the vehicle provided. We discovered that stopping or continue driving was a choice between frying on our bellies or on our backs, so we got in again and continued on our way. When we finally made it to Karamai, we were wilted. We had seen nothing on the road except derricks here and there, but we had seen more than a few mirages. They were almost identical – flowing rivers with tree-lined banks. They provided momentary elation and disappeared as soon as we approached them. Aside from that, it had been nothing but flat gobi all the way. We were still at least a day from our destination, and we steeled ourselves for the worst to come.

The next day, we left early in the morning. After we had driven for a stretch, a very different 'mirage' appeared in the distance. We felt as though we were entering Cambodia or Thailand because of the many delicately carved 'temples' of different colors that were getting clearer and clearer to our view instead of receding, like past 'mirages' had. What we were seeing is the phenomenon known as *yardang* landform, carved by wind erosion. The place was known as Ghost Town. I passed by it again in 1965, on a moonlit night. It made my flesh creep as the scene was eerie, with winds howling strangely, and not a single soul in sight of what seemed like a city of 'temples'.

We had to spend the night in Hoxtolgay because we were still almost 200 kilometers away from Burqin. The further we went, the more barren the landscape became, nothing except bare mountains without a single blade of grass in sight. As we were approaching Utubulak, the winds began to blow with great force. Because of the blazing heat, the two men sitting on top were in shirtsleeves, and were continuously assaulted by sand and gravel until we finally arrived in Burqin later on the third day. I stayed in this town until the spring of 1965 when I returned to Shanghai for medical care.

In Burqin, we were first given a room across from what would later on be the Party School. Our next door neighbors were Kazakh shepherds who were up in the mountain pastures most of the time, and across from us was a Uygur family with half a dozen children. When the wind was not blowing, I would stand outside sunning with the baby in my arms, and the lady from that family would be doing the same with her baby. We got to know each other, and I was very happy to discover that both she, Yitarhan, and her elderly husband, Semet, but always respectfully referred to as Semet-ahun, spoke perfect Chinese. They turned out to be natives of Hami. We became friends immediately. They invited me over to sit under the shade of their vine-covered patio, and walk around in their garden where different vegetables were grown, and huge, absolutely huge, bullet-shaped pumpkins were precariously hanging from their vines.

Semet-ahun had been a truck driver in his middle-age and had worked the roads between Hami and Mongolia. One time when he was away, his whole family was butchered by the bandits searching for hidden gold that they had assumed someone like him would have. Semet-ahun did not return from Mongolia until after 1949, and by then he was already in his fifties or sixties. He went to his hometown and found a young girl and started his present family.

The couple's eldest child was a son named Bator (meaning Hero, in Mongolian as well as in Uygur and Kazakh) who was about fourteen years old, then a daughter named Aysham, another son, Roze, a second daughter Zaynip, and then another son. The youngest then was Akmetjan, the baby in Yitarhan's arms. She had at least three more babies after him, one each year. Akmetjan was just a few days older than my son. One of the boy's ears discharged pus, and a piece of cloth was pinned to the shoulder of that side to catch the discharge and changed each day. The child was evidently suffering from the pain of his leaky ear because he was whiny. His head was permanently inclined toward the side of the bad ear. The local doctors didn't seem to provide any relief for his ailment. Next door to Semet-ahun's house lived a big Russian woman by the name of Maryam. But I never got to speak to her.

The courtyard where my husband had his office was locally known as the *ikinji skelat* in Kazakh, meaning No.2 Warehouse. Burqin is a very small town, located where the Burqin River converges with the Irtysh River, to empty into the Ob in Russia and eventually into the Arctic Ocean. In the rest of China, all rivers flow east, but in Xinjiang, where there are few rivers, this one flows west. *Ikinji skelat* was located by the Irtysh River, and in pre-Liberation days and days when Sino-Soviet relations were good, the town had thrived. In those days, each year after the Irtysh River thaws in late spring, Soviet boats would come to trade, unloading their wares, mostly petroleum and other things, in the warehouse in our courtyard. They then loaded supplies such as meat, grain, camel hair and other local products for their trip back.

Burqin is a county in the Altai Prefecture. Altai is rich in gold, precious stones, coal, mica, lumber, grain, water melon, potatoes, cabbage, sheep wool, camel hair, and many, many other things. All but one of the counties of Altai Prefecture shared a border with the Soviet Union - now Kazakhstan - and Mongolia. The natural resources of Altai were recognized by the Soviets very early on.

The *Ikinji Skelat* had a row of warehouses which other companies, such as the Foodstuff Company, the Textile Company, and the Hundred Commodities Company as well as the Cooperative stored their goods which were shipped from Urumqi to be dispatched to other counties and villages through the prefecture, so the *Ikinji Skelat* was like a transit center. In the winter and spring when roads were usually blocked by heavy snow, camels were used to carry supplies such as salt, tea, sugar, flour and other necessities to shepherds out in their winter pastures, usually in valleys deep inside the mountains, protected from the cold. The courtyard was a big one with warehouses lined up on one side where several trucks, or ten to twenty camels could be loaded or unloaded at the same time.

Burqin was known for its 'three mores'. It had more wind, more mosquitoes and more sand than anywhere else in the prefecture. The winds howled each and every day at fixed times, so sand dunes appeared after a windstorm was over, and people joked that even eggs had sand in them. As for the mosquitoes, they were bigger, fatter, and had longer stylets than any of their cousins, I think. Just prior to our arrival, the local flour mill had burned to the ground. After that, all the flour we had was sandy. The noodles and steamed or baked bread we made from wheat, bean, corn or sorghum flour could not be chewed, but had to be swallowed because they were so gritty.

A few days after our arrival, my husband was sent to Pingdingshan in Urumqi to participate in a three-month long course in metrology, which teaches the way of measuring the amount of oil in the big storage tanks of a petroleum station. The manager picked him because he seemed to be the only person in his department with the capacity to learn. With him gone, I was again on my own in this new environment, this time with a baby to care for. There was no central heating nor running water. The nearest well was in the courtyard of Gaochao (High Tide) Commune which was on the next street. So if I had to go and get water from the well, I had to leave the baby locked in the house as my next door Kazakh shepherd neighbors were with their flock in winter pasture (*kistaw*, in Kazakh). Since I could not carry anything heavy due to lack of bladder control leftover from childbirth, I had to double my trips and halved my loads to get enough water for our very basic needs. It was difficult. Since we did not live in the *Ikinji Skelat* courtyard like the other families of the Petroleum Station, I knew none of my husband's colleagues or their families. So I was alone all the time my husband was away.

One evening there was a knock at my window, and someone asked if GWB was at home. I said no, that he had gone to Urumqi and would not be back for a couple of months. The person then asked if I was his family member, and I said yes. He said that he had come to deliver my husband's pay. I was afraid to open the door and asked him to slip the money under it. I discovered that it was less than half of his usual pay. It turned out that what he had borrowed for the three months' food money while he was away, was being deducted from his monthly pay in one lump sum. The baby was growing, even though my diet was a poor one. I was later told that I should not have responded to the knock at the window, and that telling whoever it was outside the house that GWB was away, was the most stupid thing I could have done.

My friendship with Yitarhan and her family continued, and we would visit back and forth when the wind abated. It was good to have someone to talk to, especially someone from Hami. When we got to know each other better, she would send her daughter over with vegetables from their garden, and when it was time to harvest the pumpkins, Semet-ahun gave us a wheel-barrowful of them. Their gestures of kindness brought home the words of a hymn that I had so often sung in my mind. How I wish I could have been the one to help others, and not others, me.

Out in the highways and byways of life
Many are weary and sad
Carry the sunshine where darkness is rife
Making the sorrowing glad.

Give as 'twas given to you in your need
Love as the Master loved you
Be to the helpless a helper indeed
Unto your mission be true.

Make me a blessing, make me a blessing
Out of my life may Jesus shine
Make me a blessing O Savior I pray
Make me a blessing to someone today.

What vegetables Yitarhan and Semet-ahun gave us were deeply appreciated. But now, not only was I not a blessing to others, I was on the receiving end of blessings. Surely there was something I could do to help with household expenses.

Yitarhan taught me how to make 'sponge cake' using the big pumpkins they gave us. The flesh was one hand-span thick, the seeds, a delicacy, were saved for Chinese New Year. To make the cake, the pumpkin was cut, and the pulp, very little of it, was scraped clean, and pieces of pumpkin put in a pot to steam until it was thoroughly cooked. The skin, a mere layer of cellophane-like membrane, was peeled off and the pieces of pumpkin left to cool, then mashed. Flour is kneaded into it to the right consistency with a piece of left-over dough as a starter, and then it is covered and left to rise. After the dough has risen, a cast iron pan, if there is one, or a cookie tin, well-heated on a heap of dry cow chips, is greased by rubbing a piece of raw sheep fat along the sides and bottom, and the well-risen soft dough laced with baking soda water and thoroughly kneaded to counteract the sourness, was then put into the tin, covered, and buried in the heap of smoldering cowchips, to bake. The finished product is golden and tasted heavenly. I tried making it myself after I moved to *Ikinji Skelat*, and later to Altai, and shared them with a few Han neighbors, one of whom not only declined the offer, but sniggered that anything cooked with cow dung was bound to have a 'smell'. The stupid fool!

Yitarhan had no time to do any housework unless Akmetjan was asleep. To put him to sleep she first puts him in the *besuk*, a wooden cradle with a wooden rod above it that connects the two headboards. The board on which the baby lies has a big hole where his seat would be, and the mattress that is put on top of that board is also holed out. Under the hole was a drawer lined with either old ashes or just dry dirt or sand. Akmetjan, being a male child, had a wooden pipe, identical to a tobacco pipe but with a deeper bowl, put between his legs with his penis inserted into the bowl so his urine would drain through the stem into a container under the board. His bowel movements would fall into the drawer. His legs were securely tied together and a blanket wrapped around him and then tied just as an Indian squaw ties her papoose. The child is absolutely immovable in the *besuk*. He is nursed with his mother leaning toward him, and rocked to sleep afterwards.

The *besuk* is useful in that it can be easily carried. It is indispensable to the nomadic Kazakh shepherds. When a family with a baby moves from pasture to pasture, usually riding on horseback for hours, if not days, the *besuk* is carried by the mother on horseback by just putting it across the front of the saddle. Any amount of bumping does not harm the baby because he is securely tied – too securely, I think, because there is not even room for the baby to squirm. But generations of Kazakh were raised this way, and being tightly tied to a *besuk* as babies did not prevent them from growing up to be a very healthy and muscular people.

The *Ikinji Skelat* had two cows which were milked by an old Kazakh woman twice a day. The milk was sold to families in the courtyard. One day that woman came with someone who could speak Chinese and told the manager that she had to go to *Kaba*, or Habahe in Chinese, to take care of one of her daughter in-law who was about to have a baby and that she would not be coming to milk the cows the next morning. I had watched Nurseyt's wife milk in Changji, only I had been too clumsy with child to learn then. I told the manager that I would milk the cows the next morning. One was a Kazakh cow which was very benign and gave very thick milk, the other was what locals call a Russian cow whose hind legs had to be tied at the ankles before milking or she would attempt to stick a hoof into the bucket. This cow had originally belonged to a Russian woman, and after she sold it to the *Ikinji Skelat*, she was paid to come and milk it twice a day. Until she left, that cow had not been milked by another person, and that was why the Kazakh woman had to tie its hind legs to milk it because she was a stranger to the cow.

I got up early the next morning and donned my well-patched corduroy pants and a scarf covering most of my face to protect myself from the mosquitoes. The cows, like the people, were hungry. They would visit the outhouse in the courtyard to eat the human waste because there was more bran than flour in the so-called wheat flour that was part of every family's rationed diet. What the human system could not digest, the cows went after. That meant the cows stank and had to be washed before I could get near to milk them. After some struggling the two cows were milked, but not before letting their calves suck at them. They were then herded to a courtyard in the next street where all the family cows were gathered to be taken out by a *kuittuchi* (cowherd) to the pastures to forage for the day. A small amount was charged a month for the man's service. After that, I return to filter the milk to rid it of dirt and handed over the bucket to another person who was responsible for registering the weight of the milk before selling it. My reward for milking two cows twice daily, for clearing the barn of the night's waste, and covering the barn floor with dry earth, and giving hay to the two calves left there, merited me half a liter of fresh milk for each milking. It was sufficient for the baby, with enough left over to provide milk tea for both of us for breakfast. I was happy that I was earning a liter of milk a day.

I discovered that the mosquitoes of Burqin were so fierce that they could stab through several layers of cloth. My thick corduroy pants, with patched pockets and patches on top of the patched pockets, did not save me from being bitten. People went to the outhouse only went when absolutely necessary. Two hands just weren't enough to chase away the pestering mosquitoes that attacked with ferocity. Only one end could be protected. People often took fans along when they did their business, which were of little help. In the three years that followed, my husband suffered several attacks of malaria. The old-timers there seemed to have developed an immunity to the pests, but we were newcomers.

Famine was widespread throughout China at that time, and Burqin was no exception. However, we did have the Irtysh River at our doorstep. The *Ikinji skelat* and the local *poshta* (Post Office) pooled their resources and bought a boat and a 50-meter long net and a few strong men from both units would take the boat out to where the Burqin and Irtysh Rivers converged, a place called *Dulait*, to cast their net to fish. They would prepare everything the night before. The families made baked bread and some salted, pickled vegetables, for their men. Early the next morning they would leave Burqin and row their way to where they would fish. They would go to the furthest point and slowly cast their net along the way toward home. If they were lucky, and if the season was right, a day's catch would be around 150 kilograms of different varieties of fish. Carp was the most common. The catch was evenly divided between the co-owners of the boat and sold to their families at cost, just making sufficient money out of it to buy string to mend the net and pitch to paint the boat and other necessities. The men always brought along a big tin bucket to cook their first catch for lunch. Because there were rapids along the river, their families could not rest in peace until the boat returned safely.

On one trip they were gone much longer than expected and we all rushed to the waterfront with our babies, forgetting that the mosquitoes would devour us alive, to wait for our men. At long last they came into view, with one man looking more down-hearted than the next. They had returned empty-handed after a whole day's casting. The man who headed the team would not give up, and wanted to cast the net one more time just as they were about to dock. They cast their net, and guess what? A sturgeon was caught! The men were so elated that they forgot that they were being watched by a row of women on shore, took off their trousers, and jumped into the river to make sure that their 'trophy' did not escape. Everyone was overjoyed as the men came on shore, dripping wet, with their catch. (Some women must have wished that they had given their men cleaner underwear that morning!) How was one fish going to be enough for everyone? My husband was the designated cook. He made a big cauldron of fish soup and everyone had a taste of it.

Fish from the Irtysh River was the main source of protein for many families when we were there. Meat, with bones attached, was rationed at 1 kilogram per head, but fish was almost free so long as the company allowed the men to take out the boat to fish. We learned to make shredded fish with whatever fish that we could not finish, and it would last us until the following year. To make it, the fish is first scaled and clean, then steamed, boned, skinned, and dry-wokked over a slow flame until it turns light brown in color, resembling shredded tobacco. Flavoring in the form of table salt and some sugar is added. Since the fish itself is very fat, no cooking oil was needed. After it is done, it is spread out to cool and then packed into a jar or tin or any other kind of container. It takes a lot of fish to make just one kilogram of shredded fish. But a lot of fish was what most people had during the fishing season. There was no refrigeration in those days, and a way to use up what could not be immediately consumed had to be found.

Then when the fishing season waned with the weather turning

cold, the fish that caught were smaller and smaller. Salting fish and hanging them out to dry was not an option. Those who tried doing it soon learned a lesson the hard way. They discovered that the big, fat, green flies would swarm to the hanging fish and hollow it out in no time. We tried burning cow chip under the hanging fish to smoke out the flies, but discovered that the pests were immune to smoke.

In the winter when the river was frozen, holes were drilled in the ice and hook, line and sinker were lowered into them to catch whatever was available. In the summer, big fish were caught further out at a place called Dulait, and those who did not care what was caught as long as something was, could just sit by the river with a small stick and fish hook tied to the end of a nylon string that hung from it. If the day was good, a morning's work would yield half a tin bucket of tiny fish not longer than a few centimeters. These would be brought home, salted and spread out on the roof to dry. After a day or two they'd be crackling dry, and gathered into a bag and hung from a beam at the ceiling, to be eaten in winter when there was a fire in the room. The fish is toasted on top of the stove, the scales are pushed off from tail to head, by the thumbnail, and eaten with steamed bread as a 'dish'. Instead of the innards, there would just be a squirt of oil. Children and grownups would also eat them as snacks if there was enough.

There are many families in Burqin who were half-Russian. The head of the family, the father, were Chinese who had been mostly vendors or small merchants who had crossed the border to earn a modest living. They had married someone there, and later returned to settle on the Chinese side. Most of these families were big and their children were grown and working. Offspring of such families often intermarried because they had much in common.

One family with the surname of Liang had a couple of grown

sons who lived with their widowed Russian mother. The elder son, a truck-driver, was badly pock-marked and had an equally pock-marked wife who was also half-Russian. The younger son was single and in his late teens or early twenties. In 1962, many Russian, half-Russian and other local ethnic people wanted to leave for the other side of the border, whether legally or illegally. The more timid went through the formal channels to apply for legal departure, and had their residential permits revoked since they wouldn't be needing them anyway, which also meant that they would have no access to any ration coupons. In those days, everything from food to cloth for making clothes was rationed.

The old Mrs Liang, who spoke no Chinese, wanted her sons to leave with her, but the married one had second thoughts. Even though she had handed in hers and her younger son's residential permits, she did not want to leave without her elder son and his family, so now she and her younger son were stranded with no food rations. The young man went fishing everyday when the river was not frozen, which was only a few short months, to stock up enough fish and fish oil to last them until the next fishing season. They smoked and salted what fish they did not eat, and traded whatever they could for things they needed. One day, from the window of my room, I saw this young man passing by with a pole on his shoulder and a big, big fish dangling from the other end, the tail of which was dragging on the ground. The red fish from the Irtysh River was as big as a three or four-year old child.

Farmers in Burqin or nearby counties which had access to the river, would irrigate their fields and have fish swimming in the channels. The local non-vegetarian diet did not include fish. In the past, the local Kazakh viewed fish more as a fertilizer than a source of food.

There were other half-Russian families in other counties of

the Altai Prefecture, and a number of them later emigrated to Australia, with the help of the Christian Immigration Service in Hong Kong, headed by Pastor Stumpf, formerly of the Lutheran Church of Shanghai. That service was originally the International Refugees' Organization, or IRO, in Shanghai.

After Sino-Soviet relations soured, the last batch of imported petroleum came on a big barge after the river thawed in the early summer of 1963. Every able-bodied male in Burqin was mobilized to unload the barge so that it could depart in the shortest time possible. The Petroleum Station where my husband was working did not have enough people to do the job. The local government intervened and promised a reward everyone who pitched in to help – they could have their fill of steamed bread made of white flour, not bean flour, corn flour, or sorghum flour which had been the usual fare since the famine began some four years ago.

The Russians who manned the barge were not allowed ashore. What a change from the 'good old days' when relations were hunky-dory!! Didn't the town of Burqin grow because of the bilateral trade between the two countries? Later on, we heard that the trade then was one-sided – the ships left with more than they had come with. They came with petroleum and left with camel hair, sheep wool, mineral, mica, meat, flour and other things that Burqin did not lack. The people on the barge and their friends on shore were not allowed to communicate. The more discrete friends on shore stayed away from the barge for fear of incurring 'trouble' which they might have to account for later on.

The barge left in record time because all the men of Burqin helped in the unloading of the oil drums and the loading of ore from Koktogay, I guess materials that they needed to make atom bombs – uranium? The next day people were heard to say that the Soviets weren't that great after all. They had no 'white' bread to eat, and were all munching on 'black' bread and pickles. To many Chinese then, any grain that is 'white' is preferred to that which is not. The misconception that highly-refined grain is the most luxurious and therefore the most nutritious, and, least affordable, had been very common because they were only accessible to the moneyed people, the 'landed' and 'exploiting' class, and not the poor. Few then knew that whole grain is more nutritious.

At the end of each fall season, families would store up sufficient vegetables to last them until the following May. Potatoes, carrots and cabbage were the only kinds of 'fresh' vegetables available. By the end of summer, people would have salted as much as possible of other kinds of vegetables such as chives, cucumber, tomatoes and string beans. We were new to the area and had no idea how long the winter would last, or when it would begin, so we were unprepared for its early arrival.

Burqin was much colder than Urumqi. There was no central-heating and we did not have the proper shoes or adequate clothes to keep us warm. Each employee was given half a cubic meter of lumber to use as kindling and a sum of *dongtanfei* (winter coal money) enough for a ton of coal for fuel for the winter which was at least six months long. Fortunately, when we came in September, we had brought along what little leftover coal we had. We were told that the coal that gave the most heat and had the most complete combustion was from the mines at Hoxtolgay which was 176 kilometers away. With freight added, it was the most expensive variety of coal. The cheapest coal was from Jeminay, less than 100 kilometers away. We bought the least expensive kind and we had to be taught now to use it for it did not burn the usual way. First, the coal had to be mixed with water, but not before hammering the bigger pieces into smaller ones no bigger than half a walnut. Instead of being reduced to dust after being burned, like Hoxtolgay coal, Jeminay coal practically retains its former volume. The grate in the stove had to be changed to one with wider gaps. After the fire was kindled and few pieces of Hoxtolgay coal was added to lay the foundation, the wet Jeminay coal was added to fill the chamber of the stove, and an iron rod about two centimeters in diameter was used to poke nine or ten evenly spaced holes in the wet mass of coal so that the flame at the bottom would rise through them to the top. One drawback of using Jeminay coal was that too much steam was generated. The *huoqiang* (fire wall), which makes up a wall in the room to which the stove is attached, and serves as a built-in zigzagging flue before going out through the chimney on the roof, is usually made with sun-dried adobe. It cannot withstand all the moisture and would collapse with time. In later years, after some tragedies had occurred, kiln-baked bricks were used for the fire walls.

We noticed that many families had more than half a cubic meter of firewood stacked outside their door, and instead of buying coal for the winter, their winter coal money was used to buy winter clothing or whatever was needed. The next spring, my husband went each Sunday, his only day off, to gather firewood from the forest, sometimes making two trips. Whatever was brought home was chopped into pieces around 30 centimeters long and stacked up. We wanted sufficient firewood to last till spring so that the winter coal money could be used to buy cotton and cloth to make winter clothes for the baby and warm shoes and padded jackets for ourselves.

When time for giving us the winter coal money came, we discovered that ours had had deductions made to cover the rest of the debt that my husband had incurred from his three-month metrology course in Urumqi. We were left with what was only enough to pay for one sack of coal.

The daily subsidy for a business trip out of town was a paltry seven *fen* (cents), so that unless he fasted, there was no way that he would not overspend. When he left, he had brought along as much home-made bread and salted vegetables as he could, so all he needed was drinking water on the three days it would take for him to reach Urumqi. But what about the three-month stay to learn something that was totally 'Greek' to him? And what about the return trip? It is unbelievable how little, if any, sympathy those in charge had for their subordinates. Anyone who claims to be human would know that the paltry seven *fen* subsidy a day was far from sufficient to cover expenses. But that was the rule. Whoever had made that rule must not have ever been sent on a business trip.

I think the manager's wife was behind it all because she worked in the accounts department. Why couldn't she have deducted the debt by installment? We would not have run away as there was nowhere that we could run to, and even if we did run away, we would still be in China, and it would still be on our files how much we owed, to the cent. But, no, she had to deduct the debt in one lump sum. We had been eagerly looking forward to getting the winter coal money for a whole year, and my husband had gone on countless trips to the forest to gather firewood so that there'd be something with which to buy items we badly needed. I began to feel the intense pinch of not being employed.

The baby was still in diapers even though he was almost a year and a half old. I did not have him wear open crotch pants because it was so cold, and that meant the limited pieces of diapers, mainly made from old sheets and worn out clothing, had to be washed and dried in time so that they would not run out. With what limited fuel we had, there was no way to dry the diapers in time unless I turned a tin bucket upside down on the stove and covered it with the damp or wet diapers. This meant even less heat for the room. Since my husband's office was in the same courtyard and only a few steps away, and he was always working overtime in the evenings and late into the night, I would carry the baby and the wet diapers to the office to get ourselves warm and the diapers dry because the office was much, much hotter than necessary. After my husband finished his work, we would come home with diapers dried, and go to bed while we were still very warm from the hot fire in the office. There was at least a difference of 50 degrees Celsius between indoor and outdoor temperatures in Burqin during the winter, with outdoor temperatures around minus 30 degrees or lower, and the office room temperature at well over 20 degrees Celsius.

Christmas arrived. At this season, my nerves were at their most fragile state and my eyes seemed to have developed permanent leaks. The words of the well-sung carol kept resounding through my mind:

In the bleak mid-winter, frosty wind made moan
Earth stood hard as iron, water like the stone
Snow had fallen snow on snow, snow on snow
In the bleak mid-winter long, long ago.

Here, men's hearts were also like stone. I could not understand why our debt could not have been repaid by installment. My husband consoled me and said that there would be a way out. He did not want to give the accountant, the manager's wife, the pleasure of seeing us in misery because of what she had done. This woman had a chronic case of *schadenfreude*. Her husband, the manager, surnamed Hu, was the typical kind of official - 'a cigarette, a cup of tea, and a newspaper.' There was nothing concrete for him to do, so all he needed to do was to sit at his desk and smoke, sip his tea, read the newspapers and sign a piece of paper now and then. In those days, all state-owned companies or offices did not lack for such 'leading cadres'. Hu was an old, coughing, chain-smoker, and former PLA man. His asthmatic wife, a decade or two his junior, had been deserted by her first husband who had left for Taiwan from Hunan just before Liberation. She was from a landed family, but joined the PLA and came to Xinjiang, and was later assigned to marry an officer, many of whom were still single at that time.

Many young or even middle-age females (some of them were reformed prostitutes from cities) were recruited by the army for the purpose of providing wives for the older, single, army men in the Xinjiang Production and Construction Corp to make them stay in Xinjiang. This couple was later demobilized from the army and the man became a 'leading cadre'. They had a daughter and a son, and the latter was spoiled rotten. They lived in the same courtyard as everybody else in the company, but in a much bigger room, one door away from us, after we were moved to the company compound.

Manager Hu was not a bad person in that he recognized and appreciated how hard my husband was working to upgrade the company's operations. His wife was different. She wanted all subordinates to feel her weight through her husband, and many brown-nosers soon caught on. If her front door needed to be swept, all she had to do was stand outside the door with a broom in her hand and there would be at least one or two people going for that broom to do the sweeping. If she wanted some firewood chopped, all she did was to stand there with an ax in her hand, and someone would appear to do the chopping. It was disgusting, especially since those that catered to her the most were also the ones who liked her the least and spoke ill of her behind her back. For many, brown-nosing was a way of survival.

As someone said, some people lick the boots that kick them. In truth, most boot-lickers are people who want to eventually wear boots themselves.

In Chinese we have the saying, *feng bu da jian cao*, meaning the wind does not blow on a blade of lowly grass, the Chinese equivalent of "God tempers the wind to the shorn lamb'. In spite of the harsh winter and the lack of adequate fuel, the three of us passed the cold months in relative good health whereas both Hu and his wife suffered continuous colds. The old man was often seen bent double, coughing and coughing, a condition made worse by his chain-smoking, while his wife wheezed her way through the long winter with one attack of asthma after another.

Spring eventually arrived. We felt refreshed because we were now debt-free. The baby was thriving. The expiration date of cloth coupons from the previous year was March 31. We needed some cloth badly for a bed sheet because we had used up more than we had expected, for diapers. I had scorched some while drying them on the turned-over bucket. Each month, no matter how we scraped and scrimped, we were always around 5 yuan short till pay day.

The employees had a *huzhujijinhui*, the equivalent of a mutual-help fund, to which each employee put in 1 yuan each pay day and had the privilege to borrow a sum not exceeding 12 yuan within one month. At the end of each year, each would be given back the 12 yuan he had put in, and another round would begin. We had joined on our first pay day in Burqin, so we were eligible to borrow from it. We did not dare to borrow more than five yuan each month because debts accumulate and we knew only too well what it felt like to be burdened with one.

We needed to get five meters of cloth for a sheet which would cost another 5 yuan. I asked the accountant if I could borrow that sum from her since the coupons would expire the following day, and I could pay her back the next month, or I could do some knitting for her in return. She did not say no, but instead asked me to give her the cloth coupons since I had no money to use with them anyway, while she had the money, but not as many coupons as she would like.

I shouldn't have opened my mouth, and now I felt like a worm, but not so limp that I did not have the strength to tear up my coupons to her face. I did not know whether I felt more anger or pity for her. I don't know why I had such a knack for antagonizing those who were my husband's superiors. He, on the other hand, thought that what I had done was uncalled for. He thought that if she wanted the coupons, give them to her, she would not be the richer for it, and neither would we be the poorer because of it. Why make enemies unnecessarily? I guess we were just opposites, that is why we attracted.

When my husband returned from his three-month study it was January, just before Chinese New Year. The round trip to and from Urumqi was not by bus but by truck, with a piece of tarpaulin over it. It was now deep winter. Traveling on the same truck were people who had never been to Xinjiang before, and had no idea how cold it would be, judging by the way they were dressed. My husband had borrowed a *tohn*, which is a sheepskin coat with a big collar, from someone in Pingdingshan. It was long enough to cover him from head to toe. On the last day of the journey after the truck left Hoxtolgay, he went to sleep inside his coat because the journey had been very hard. He was awakened up by a fellow passenger, a woman, who was wailing her head off. She was a new passenger who had gotten on in Hoxtolgay, a woman from another province in China, carrying an infant inside her jacket, to keep it warm. The baby kept crying, and after she nursed him, he went to sleep. She must have been worried that the baby would suffocate inside her jacket, and kept uncovering his face to make sure that he was breathing. After a while she noticed that he was not. The extreme cold air must have entered its tender lungs and killed him. The truck stopped and shovel was taken from the driver's cabin, but the ground was rock solid that it was impossible to dig a hole to bury it. There was nothing to do except to mobilize all the passengers to gather gravel and rocks by the handful to heap around the dead baby and cover him up. The woman could not be consoled. Everyone pitched in to give her a little money to take her to her final destination. It seemed that she had been taken off an earlier truck because the driver warned her that the infant would not survive the trip, and that she should contact her husband to come for them with fur coats. Now she was afraid that her husband would not forgive her for insisting on making the journey. The poor woman!

My husband learned how to re-sole our own hand-made cloth shoes by slicing layers off discarded rubber tires from trucks and cutting them to the right size. I had never worn cloth shoes before I left Shanghai, but now circumstances were different and I had to learn to make them, uppers and soles. The first step in making cloth shoes is to cut square or rectangular pieces from less seamy pieces of material from worn-out clothing. Wet them in a thin starch and evenly paste them onto a board usually made of plywood, and make sure that the edges do not overlap, so that it's smooth. After the first layer is done, then the second layer is smoothed on in a similar way, but make sure that the edges of the second layer are not on the edges of the first layer, and then go on to the third or fourth layer. Then take it out to sun-dry. When it is dried thoroughly, peel it off, and you have a piece of leather-like cardboard which is then cut into the shapes of the shoes' soles. Then each is piped with a strip of bias cloth and stacked and glued. We bought the necessary tools which consisted of several thicker needles and an awl. The string used to stitch the layers of glued soles were hand-made by my husband by twisting eight strands of sewing thread together and waxing it by rubbing a candle on it back and forth. Then the twisted string threaded to two needles on its ends, and the awl is used to pierce the layers of the sole and one needle is inserted through it. Then a second hole is pierced and this time two needles cross over it, and so on. First the sole is stitched along the sides so that it will retain its shape. After that it is stitched widthwise from toe to heel until the entire sole is closely stitched, making it as hard as leather.

To make the uppers, first a layer of stronger cloth, preferably something new so that it will last longer, is pasted with starch on a board. That will serve as the lining of the uppers, then pieces of remnants will be pasted on, in the same way as they were pasted for the soles. The last layer would be the uppers, usually black denim or corduroy. Then when it is sun-dried, peel it off, cut the shape, add piping and attach to the soles. After the shoes are complete, rubber soles made from sliced, worn-out truck tires are attached to the bottoms to make the shoes last longer. Cloth-bottom shoes thus soled will last twice as long as ones which are not.

I learned from my Shantung neighbors how to make cloth shoes for the baby, and also to make padded jackets and pants for him. My sewing skills improved dramatically during my sixteen years in Altai. Necessity is indeed the mother of invention. We learned to do many things which we would not have learned had we remained in Shanghai. The Burqin days were to serve as our apprenticeship for much harder times that were in store for us in Altai. But we were young, and the baby was thriving, and except for the hardships, life went on. A silver lining could actually be found behind each cloud and there was little self-pity. I admonished myself with "Don't cry over spilled milk, it only makes it salty for the cat." I could see that the locals who had lived there for generations lived no better than we did, and did not complain, so who were we to be special?

I think survival would have been more difficult had it not been for Yitarhan and her husband Semet-ahun. I am grateful for their friendship and useful tips. Semet-ahun taught my husband how to find the buried bulb-like root of the wild red willow, which is a plant that looks like a cross between mesquite and tamarisk if living, but its root is buried deep in the sand, and is nearly fossilized because it's been in the ground for so long. The bulb-like root is about the size of a head of cabbage, and very light. It burns much, much better than coal. Semet-ahun would go on his donkey cart, equipped with water and bread, and a melon or two if the season was right, start out early in the morning for the desert. He would dig the loose sand with his *'juetou'*, an even-blade, narrow hoe-like tool on a long handle, and a day's work would yield him a cartful of bulbs. They served as fuel for both the outdoor *tonnir* (oven for baking *nan*) that is used in summer, and the indoor *dohofka* and *nan-mesh* (an oven, much like that which American Indians use) where huge loaves of bread were baked in winter. With the exception of meat, cooking oil and flour, Semet-ahun was almost self-sufficient in food for his big family. He grew his own vegetables, and was very generous in sharing them with us, especially his great, big, fat, bullet-shaped pumpkins (squash).

Yitarhan was a cheerful woman even though hers was not a life of comfort, not with the many children she had who were growing up. It wasn't uncommon to have a young one coming in just after the meal was over and the table cleared, and hear him calling out, *apahm, tamak,* meaning "Mother, I want food". He must not have been present when the family was eating. Semet-ahun was really more of a grandfather than a father to the children because of the age difference. His eldest son, Bator, told me that he has always known his father as an old man, when he heard his father tell me jokingly how handsome he had been in his young days. I can believe him by looking at his children.

When it came to making friends with non-Han people I always took the initiative. My husband was always in the background. He liked them, but not the way I did, because of the language barrier. Yitarhan and her family were our friends in Burqin during our stay there from September, 1962 to early 1965 when I visited Shanghai and my husband was transferred to Beitun. Yet when she saw my husband again in Altai in September, 1968, my husband did not recognize her. He was standing in line at the No.16 Hospital where I was having my second and last child, and Yitarhan was standing behind him, and she kept smiling at him which made him very uneasy. It wasn't until later that I ran into her and she told me about it. I did remember hearing my husband say that someone must have mistaken him for somebody she knew. To him, all ethnic people looked the same, as it were. Thank goodness Yitarhan knew us well enough to know that we were not the 'stuck up' kind or I am sure she would have been offended.

Semet-ahun has since passed away. Bator, the eldest son, worked in the local slaughterhouse, and died one winter from carbon monoxide poisoning, something that is not uncommon in cold places where the coal is the main source of fuel for heating. The daughter, Aysham, married her first cousin Teuyak, who was left a widower with several children after his wife, Tashburbe, formerly a nurse at the Altai Chipakhan died from heart disease. One of Yitarhan's sons, it was either Akmetjan, Roze, or Yimit, had trouble with the law and was sentenced. The last I heard, Yitarhan was still living in Burqin.

Maryam, the single, heftily-built Russian woman living door to Yitarhan made her living by white-washing houses and fences for local families. I was to discover that most Russian women were sought after to do janitorial work even outside of Urumqi. Most of these women were actually from Siberia who had married Chinese vendors or petty merchants and settled with their husbands this side of the border. There was one family in Burqin in the courtyard where I went to fetch water, with the family name of Liu. The mother was Russian and a chain-smoker. Her son and daughter were handsome and tall. The son married another half-Russian girl and their children were blue-eyed, platinum blonds. The children's aunt was selected to join the national basketball or volleyball team, did well, and later became a coach of that sport.

Not all Russian women who married Chinese learned the language of their spouses. Many remained monolingual, which, in retrospect, proved to be a bonus for their children who had to learn their mother's tongue, and that language skill later provided a livelihood. For the Russian wives who picked up Chinese, some became fluent in it, but their children could neither understand nor speak Russian, which was a minus. One obvious drawback of many children from such unions was their lack of education, as many of their parents were illiterate. There were some exceptions, of course. The offspring of many of these families emigrated to Australia.

I was still milking the two cows of *Ikinji Skelat* and they were doing fine except for the lumps along their spines. I was told that they were stings from a certain kind of insect and that these insects lay their eggs in the wound which grows in size when the egg develops into a worm that is as long as a silkworm, and twice as fat. One day after milking the cows, I steeled my nerves and got our awl and a bowl of table salt, and I dug those festering lumps from the cows' spines, one by one. Big, fat worms were actually extracted, and I added table salt to each gaping wound, to disinfect it. The cows were surprisingly still while all that was taking place. The wounds healed before long, but new lumps appeared after a few days. Whatever insect it was that had bitten them certainly must have been very strong to penetrate the thick hide of the cow.

Only one family on the entire compound had a radio. One day I asked if I could listen to it for a while. I started to fiddle with the knobs and accidentally got Radio Saigon. It was playing a Christmas carol. I turned it off and dashed out crying, leaving the family scratching their heads.

We had no money to subscribe to any newspapers or journals. The Renmin Ribao (People's Daily) from Beijing and the Xinjiang Ribao (Xinjiang Daily) from Urumqi were the only two newspapers the Petroleum Station subscribed to, the former was at least a week to ten days old upon arrival, and the latter not much 'younger'. We knew little of what was actually going on in the country, and next to nothing of what was going on in the world.

My initial interest in reading the 'old papers' resulted in a comment from one of my husband's colleagues which cut the endeavor short – "There's the State Council to take care of the domestic affairs, and the Ministry of Foreign Affairs to take care of diplomatic matters. The individual's duty is to be a law-abiding citizen. Any amount of newspaper reading will not bring employment." I sensed that there must have been something in my husband's files concerning my employment since I no longer had a file of my own once I was fired. We had left Urumqi with a letter asking the local authorities of Burqin to give me employment if the opportunity arrived, but that was as far as it went. For someone not to be illiterate and to be unemployed, especially someone from Shanghai, aroused many funny looks and much suspicion.

I can honestly say that most of the hostility that I had encountered up until then came not from non-Han groups or individuals but from people of my own kind. That I talked more to non-Han people than to those of my own kind accounted for some of that hostility. Many could not, and perhaps still cannot, understand why I was more attracted to these people than to my own kind. I think my early life had a lot to do with it. Life was complicated enough just trying to make ends meet instead of worrying about what others thought of my behavior. I had stuck out like a sore thumb since coming to Xinjiang and there was no reason why that should end since I was still there.

We had not seen a movie for ages, so when we heard that a documentary on what was called the First Asian Games that had been held in Indonesia was on in town, we felt that we shouldn't miss it (it was actually the third, after Games in India and the Philippines, held in a different era). We took turns. It was just not safe to take a young child to a public place with little ventilation. We hadn't had such an enjoyment in a long time and the documentary was so up-lifting. We hadn't realized how long and how deep we had been down in the dumps that even a documentary such as that could be so invigorating. Our eyes had needed a feast of colors because the surroundings had been so terribly bleak and drab. Our hearts had been so terribly heavy that just to hear the cheering of the crowds did wonders to our nearly frozen hearts and warmed them once again. I realized that too much had been taken for granted in the past. If I felt the way I did, what about those who had to spend their lives here generation after generation? It was hard to imagine. Perhaps 'ignorance is bliss' after all.

Chairman Liu Shaoqi and Foreign Minister Chen Yi with their respective wives' were shown in the documentary visiting Indonesia and meeting with the president of that country and his wife. Looking back, who would have thought that in just a few years, the Chairman himself would be persecuted to death, made to look worse than any criminal with a mug shot on a wanted list, and the other would also soon die, and their wives put through the mill. What was this country coming to?

There was a family in the compound with two boys, the younger of whom was my son's age. Both parents were working and naturally their life was much better than ours. One day, Xinmin, the younger boy, was munching on an apple and my son asked what it was. I told him it was an apple, and he said he wanted one, too. Well, I had to confess that I didn't have the money to get one for him. He had a great idea, "Why not buy the money first, and then use it to buy the apple?"

We were sad to learn of the death of that young boy's mother, ZZZ, the following year after we had been transferred to Beitun. The company had gone on its annual tree-planting spree in the spring, and she was assigned to boil drinking water for the group. She took a kettle to be filled at a nearby stream and never returned. Much time and money were spent to salvage her body, but it was never found. It seemed that she had stood on sandy ground, the underside of which had been washed away by water, and after the kettle was filled, adding to her weight, the sand collapsed and she was carried away in the undertow. The stream flowed westward, probably carrying her to the Soviet Union. That trauma affected her young son into his teens. Two and a half decades later when my daughter worked in the same office as he did, she found that he had no memory of his mother. He was now married with a family of his own.

A group of people from the China Petroleum Company in Urumqi came to inspect the Petroleum Station in Burqin. We discovered one of them, a Cantonese man my father's age, had been transferred from the China Petroleum Company in Shanghai, and had been my father's colleague! This man had been sent to Xinjiang after a certain political movement. He had a home-leave each year to visit his wife who did not come along because she was not in good health. They had no children. He had the good fortune of keeping his Shanghai residential permit so that he could return there after retirement. It turned out that he had only agreed to come to Xinjiang on condition that his residential permit in Shanghai – his *hukou* – remain intact, whereas when we came, we had to take ours along (our hukou was moved officially from Shanghai after we had a permanent address in Xinjiang). He was not a volunteer like we were, but someone sent from 'above'. For me to see him was almost like seeing my own father.

Burqin, like any other town elsewhere in the world, had its share of weirdoes. One morning, I noticed that the men on the compound were whispering in each others' ears, and the eyes of the one being whispered to kept widening and widening with each gasp of surprise and shake of the head. A little later, the women repeated the same routine, and instead of gasps of surprise, they screamed and covered their faces. I was itching to know what they were talking about, and when my husband returned for lunch at noon, I told him what I had witnessed in the courtyard and asked if he knew what it was all about.

It seemed that an old man had been found dead in his shack, with his private organ severed and minced to pulp, but all his belongings untouched, including the cash inside his pillow. It was rumored that two young boys were said to have been responsible for the crime. Word went around that the old codger had a habit of 'playing with boys', so I guess he must have been a pedophile. He had played toward his eventual fate.

Another old man, a weirdo of an altogether different sort, was a ragged, grime-covered, sullen guy who sat inside the lobby of the one and only local department store, selling odds and ends. The local people knew him and his story well. He was a native of Hubei Province but had been living in Burqin for many years. One day, many years ago, he had disappeared, leaving behind a wife and several children with no means of support whatsoever. The poor woman had a hard time raising them on her own. After the children were grown, they all went back to the parents' ancestral home, a town in Hubei Province. One day, some decades after his disappearance, this old man appeared on the doorstep of his old ancestral home, in rags and as dirty as can be, one hand holding a broken basket with a badly chipped rice bowl, and the other, a dirty, cloth-bound cane walking stick. No one recognized him. He was begging for food outside a house and when he couldn't be shooed away, a little food was given, grudgingly. But, still he wouldn't go away. Then, his wife recognized him. She let out a piercing scream and sat on the ground, pounding it with both fists, and weeping, howling, and yelling at him, all at the same time. She wanted to know why he wasn't dead yet, and wasn't leaving her and the children in a lurch bad enough, and now returning in his present beggarly state for them to support him? Fat dreams! She wanted to have nothing more to do with him and had already told her children that he was dead. That he had the nerve to look them up after so many years of desertion, and in this condition, showed that he was a good-for-nothing, and that her marriage to him was a sin, a punishment from heaven, but that she had atoned for it by raising the children who were now self-supporting. She took off a shoe and started beating him and pushing him away. She screamed for him to go elsewhere to beg, and if he ever dared show his face at her doorstep, she would see to it that she and her children maim him so he cannot return.

Any amount of begging and remorse on his part would not console her. The woman was beside herself, giving vent to anger accumulated over decades. There was nothing he could do but leave since he wasn't given a chance to even open his mouth. He spent the night at the train station, and returned to beg for forgiveness the following day, hoping that her anger had abated. He was wrong, and sure enough he got what he had been promised, the woman and her grown children pelted him with stones and chased him away. There was no way to prove that he was her husband and the father of her children. There were no marriage certificates those days. There was no alternative but to leave.

He returned to Burqin and spent the remaining years of his life there, living alone and selling odds and ends in the lobby of the department store. When he died, he was a charity case since there was no family member there to bury him. When his belongings were sorted, the little cash that he had from his vending was hardly enough to buy a humble coffin. The local government had to make up for what was lacking. All the junk that he had was dumped into the coffin with him when someone remarked that the dirty, cloth-bound walking cane seemed unusually heavy. It was examined, and the dirty cloth which was wound around it was unraveled, it was discovered that the cane was hollow, and one end had a cap on it. It opened to reveal irregular pieces of gold which looked as though they had been privately smelted. In his lifetime, no one had befriended him except a few other old men, and they had all passed away before him. He always smelled so bad that no one could stand to be near him for long, and yet when he was gone, he created a void in the lobby of the department store that was never filled. He had been there for so many years that he was like a permanent fixture of the store.

A new official was sent to Burqin who wanted to do something about the sand there. He mobilized the town people to weave *charbak* (fences) from fresh twigs and branches to keep the sand from piling up against the houses that faced the street. Everyone went to work. It was not unusual to get up in the morning and find ourselves unable to get out of the house because during the night the wind had piled the sand up so high that it had sealed our door. Our entrance was on the left, near the end of a cul-de-sac. Depending on the direction of the wind, either our door, or the door of our neighbors across from us, would be sealed with a sand dune. That meant either we had to dig them out, or they had to dig us out.

To my relief, Burqin had no *kara boran*. In the winter we did not even see snow on the ground because it was blown away before it could reach it. My husband, like the other office workers, had to take turns working at the *mai skelat* or filling station, which was at the old airport, a distance from where we lived. He would leave early in the morning and return after sunset. The walk there was usually against the strong wind so that by the time he reached his destination, what little nourishment his meager breakfast provided him was all consumed. With what he had learned at the metrology course, he had to climb up to measure and calculate how much oil was in the huge big tanks at the filling station. Lunch was taken along which consisted of a piece of dry bread, some salted vegetables and wind-dried fish to be toasted on the stove. After a day's work he would either be blown home or fought his way back against the wind, depending on the direction it was blowing.

One day, Manager Hu gave Yue Guyou, an armed watchman of the filling station where all the oil was stored in the huge tanks, a good talking-to and criticized him for his foul 'attitude'. According to regulations printed and posted, when vehicles came to have their tanks filled, no one is allowed in the vehicle except the driver, and he, too, must hand over his cigarette lighter or matches, to be returned when the vehicle is filled and leaves the gate. One day, a jeep drove in without even stopping at the gate. YGY ran up and stood in front of it, and shouted for the passenger in the back seat to get out. When he refused, YGY opened the door of the jeep and dragged the man out. That man, HYC, was the top man of the Altai Prefecture and Commander in Chief of the 10th Division of the Xinjiang Production and Construction Corps. He got out and immediately disarmed the watchman, YGY. The Chinese writer, Lu Xun once wrote something to the effect that there are 'people who use a tiger skin to protect themselves and scare others'. That was exactly what the driver of the jeep had done. What he hadn't realized was that not everybody in Altai would recognize HYC because such 'leading cadres' are sometimes remote from the people. HYC was in the wrong and he knew it, but, in the face of 'shrimps' this 'lobster' had to keep his 'dignity'. He called Manager Hu then and there, and advised him to better educate his subordinates, and left in a huff.

When we heard of the incident, we were so proud of YGY for doing his job. How was he to know who was in the backseat of that jeep? Shouldn't someone who was the 'head' of the Altai Prefecture have known better? Didn't everyone know the story of how Lenin was barred from the Kremlin by a guard because he had either forgotten his I.D. or had not produced it, and how that guard was complimented by Lenin for doing his job well? So what was wrong with YGY carrying out his duty? It is surprising how many cadres of that level have used Marx-Leninism and Mao Zedong Thought as batteries in flashlights, to shine them on others and not on themselves. The same is true of those who preach any of the different 'isms'. What they preach is a standard to judge others by and not a standard by which they themselves live. There are always Pharisees in different 'isms', and as for the different versions that had been preached to us, if only half had been practiced by the 'preachers', so much uncalled-for suffering would have been avoided, and we would have made much more progress so much faster as a country.

Because of that incident, we were all the more disappointed and thoroughly shocked when we heard that this same YGY was executed for murder several months later. It seemed that a Shanghai young man from somewhere further north passed through Burqin on his way home, and dropped in at our company to visit a friend, another Shanghai youth who was a colleague of my husband. Instead of looking for his friend in the office, he had gone directly to the filling station, thinking that that was the company. YGY, who was on duty, met him and told him that he would take him to his friend right after he was off duty, the filling station being quite a distance from the office, and this young man was a stranger in town, so he waited for YGY. On their way to the office, YGY found that this youth was going back to Shanghai to get married and that he had some money on him. YGY led him into a deserted house and murdered him by bashing his head from behind with a brick. YGY then took off his blood-splattered jacket and asked a woman to wash it for him, promising her ten times the normal price.

The body was discovered when someone went into the deserted house to relieve himself and found the corpse still warm, and reported it to the police. It seemed that 400 yuan had been taken from the dead man and hidden in a slot behind bricks in an unused fire wall. Clues led to him and his place was searched. He hadn't even had time to use one cent of that money. YGY was single, and perhaps had wanted to go back to his home in Anhui Province and get married, and didn't have the money for it.

That he was a murderer was a shock to one and all because he was not any different from any one of us. After the police took him away in handcuffs, he became a member of the chain gang from the local police station. From the window of our room, I could see the gang who clanged their way to and from their worksite across the wooden bridge, four times a day. By the time they had clanged their way through the sand to their worksite, it was time to clang back for lunch. It was difficult enough to walk on soft sand, not to say with ball and chain. They, like everyone else, had a siesta because the jail wardens had theirs. After the siesta, they would clang their way to the worksite again, do a little of what they were assigned to, and clanged back for the day. That daily 'ritual' was exercise for them, only serving to prolong the lives of the criminals and nothing else.

A family member came from Shanghai to identify and claim the murdered young man, and his body was buried locally. YGY pleaded guilty and was executed locally some months later.

The Altai Prefecture, to which the county of Burqin belonged, is known for its sheep. There were good pastures in Burqin and other nearby counties. For the slaughter season of 1963, Burqin was designated the task of selling tons of lamb to Beijing for the Muslim population there, and for use in Muslim and other restaurants. Muslim do not eat lamb, beef, chicken, or any meat which has not been bled, and no animal is slaughtered without a prayer from an ahun, mullah or imam. Pork is definitely taboo. To make sure that the meat was 'clean', even though all slaughtering in state-owned houses was done by local Muslim, Hui butchers were sent from Beijing and with them came a mullah, but tons and tons of lamb would involve several days' slaughtering and a whole lot more prayers. So I guess the mullah would just say a prayer for the first lamb to be slaughtered each day, and say "ditto, ditto" for every one that followed.

Political study in a work unit was a twice-weekly, if not a daily, ritual. But during the famine years, it was of secondary importance as all energy was centered on how to get more food. Individuals fished whenever there was a spare moment, and anything caught was appreciated. The watchmen were the ones who benefited most because they worked three shifts, and could spend the day fishing if they were on night duty, and sleep when they were supposed to be on duty at night. When word got around that they spent their on-duty time sleeping, the manager had the office workers go on duty at night to check on them.

Storage for petroleum had to be safe, especially because Burqin was a windy place. If a fire broke out in the storage tanks, it could wipe out the whole town. Xinjiang cities and towns had no fire hydrants. Unlike Shanghai where there were fire hydrants on every block and people from the fire station would come at fixed times to unscrew the top and let out rusty water on their inspection tours, to make sure that they were in working order. In Xinjiang, and especially Burqin, if a fire broke out, water was a problem. More often than not, fires were only extinguished when everything had burned out, even though Burqin was just by the Irtysh River. Its one and only flour mill had burned to the ground just before we arrived in September, 1962. Once a fire started, there was little to do but to wait for it to burn out.

The trouble with sending an office worker out at night was the threat of wolves. Plans were changed and office workers were sent out in pairs, each with a stick for self-defense. They were also warned that in case any one felt a tap on his shoulder, he should not turn around to look, but instead wield his stick and hit. It is said that the wolves were big and they usually attacked by putting a paw on the shoulder of the prey so that they can bite on the throat when he turned his head. Since anyone who was sent out the night before had to work the following day, some just made a show of going out and returned after a while. The manager's idea was almost like creating friction among the employees.

In mid-spring, the camel caravans came to our compound, the *Ikinji Skelat*, to be loaded with brick tea, sugar, salt, cloth and other commodities to take to the nearby villages. The housewives in the courtyard were busy tearing hair off the camels as they squatted down to rest for the night. A handful or even big patches of camel hair came off at a hard tug, and these women, with big aprons in front of them had their pick. I was new and did not join the crowd in stripping the camels. I didn't know if all that pulling and tugging hurt the camels, and I had no idea of how to clean the dirty hair, for it had a strong odor and was caked with the animals' urine and droppings. I remarked to Yitarhan what I had seen, and she put me wise.

Nearly every one of her children, she said, as well as most locals with children wore winter suits which were padded with camel hair instead of cotton. Camel hair did not harden or mat after washing whereas cotton or sheep wool, did. After washing and drying camel hair-padded clothes, all one needed to do was to lay them on a flat surface and beat them with a pliable twig or stick and they would fluff up again. The same cannot be done with cotton-padded or sheep wool-padded clothes.

She also told me that the Han Chinese women of *Ikinji Skelat*, being from elsewhere, really didn't know much about camel hair. She told me that the place to get the best hair is from the underbelly, even though that is the dirtiest part of the camel as they squat the whole night long in their own urine and dung and the hair on their underbellies is caked and matted. The finest and softest hair come from there, while the hair on the back and sides of the camels is rough and coarse.

When the camels came again in late spring, I again watched the women tear at them where the hair was the thickest. I got up early the next morning when the camels were ready to leave, and following Yitarhan's advice, tore at the underbellies of the camels, crouching from one to the next, making many trips, and I had a great harvest. The camels looked embarrassingly naked after we women were through with them. I stuffed what I had in a big burlap sack, to be used later.

Semet-ahun has a special place in his heart for camel hair for it had saved his life, so he told me. As a young man in Hami, he had been indentured to a local landlord and merchant as a payment for debts his parents owed the man. The landlord-merchant was in the camel hair business and he would send his men up to Barkol at the hair-shedding season to collect camel hair from the Kazakh shepherds for a very cheap price. It was brought down to Hami on camelback, and his servants fluffed it clean of all dirt and of all *kiltchik* – the coarse, stiff hair. Then they baled it to be shipped to other parts of China for use in the woolen textile industry. Semet's and other servants' job was to clean the camel hair during the day and take turns as watchmen during the night, to watch over the mounds and mounds of fluffed camel hair before it was baled, in case of fire, wind or rain.

One day, after a whole day's back-breaking work of cleaning camel hair, it was his turn to night-watch, which meant that he had to go up to the watch tower and walk back and forth keeping alert for accidents, usually fire. The piled-up mounds of cleaned, dried and fluffed camel hair were an 'eye-sore' for other competing merchants, and all precautions had to be taken in case of arson. After a hard day's work Semet was already dead on his feet, and yet he had to force himself to walk back and forth to keep watch over the camel hair below. Nights are very cool, if not actually cold, regardless of how hot the day had been. In the desert there is no moisture in the air to hold the heat, and the difference between daytime and nighttime temperature can be as much as 15 degrees Celsius, if not more.

Here he was, still patrolling in the cold of the night, with an empty stomach, an aching back, and eyes that simply refused to stay open. He must have fallen asleep walking and plunged headlong into the mounds of camel hair below. When morning came, there was no sign of Semet. His disappearance was reported to the landlord who came out and cursed and cussed till he saw something wriggling in a mound of camel hair. It was Semet, sitting there rubbing his eyes in the sun's glare. His master exploded, "I told you to watch over the hair, not in it!" Semet was in a daze. He could not remember how he had gotten into the hair. It took him a while to recall what had happened during the night.

From that day on, camel hair had a special place in Semet's heart. If it had not been for the camel hair, Semet would have had a bad concussion or been killed in his headlong fall. After he told me the story, I asked him if he had had some sweet dreams sleeping in that soft fluffy pile of camel hair. He said, "I must have, but I can't remember about what." There a faraway look in his eyes as he smoothed his white beard. He had fled to Mongolia after that incident several decades ago, and was now a pensioned truck driver with a very young family.

I brought my big burlap sack stuffed with camel hair with me to Altai when I moved there several years later, because by then the children were bigger and didn't need as much care as they did earlier, so I had more time on my hands. Cleaning the camel hair was a big and dirty task. The first thing that is needed is a big tarpaulin, the kind that is used to cover a truck. I had to borrow one and spread it out on a flat piece of ground. The dirty, urine-dung caked camel hair, not too much of it at one time, is put on the tarpaulin. Two very pliable, smooth and tapered branches, called *sabaw* in Kazakh, about 1.2 meters long which are especially used for fluffing either sheep wool or camel hair, and in this case, it always pays to borrow them from a Kazakh family who have used the branches so often for that same purpose so that they are nice and smooth. The longer the branches, the more unwieldy they are, but one advantage is that they keep the person further away from the pile of camel hair and the dust that would eventually fly from it. Before commencing the work, I made sure that I was well covered, especially my head, my nose and mouth. I usually wore a surgical mask with a doubled, sometimes tripled handkerchief inside it that has been dampened.

A little at a time, the caked pieces of camel hair is beaten by landing the branches on it horizontally, but pulling them away backwards so that no hair will fly up. In this way I would beat at the camel hair systematically until it was all fluffed up. Then the fluffed hair is removed onto a clean corner of the tarpaulin and the dust, sand, and dried dung is swept off. The process is repeated again and again until there is nothing left on the tarpaulin from the beating except the golden, fluffed camel hair resembling cotton sugar, but beige in color. A 40-square centimeter piece of dung-caked camel hair can be beaten and fluffed into a woolly ball the size of a child or bigger, depending on the quality of the hair.

Thanks to Yitarhan's advice, I got mine from the underbelly where there was nothing but downy, fine, soft hair. Because of the quality of the hair, it does not look like much when caked, but once beaten and fluffed clean, it contained more usable hair than what the other women got who had torn off patches of it from the sides of the camels. They had to throw away half the hair after it was beaten and fluffed because it contained a lot of coarse, hard hair, what is known as *kiltchik*. Whether the hair was eventually spun into yarn for knitting or just used as wadding for winter clothes or quilts, *kiltchik* has to be discarded because it is much too stiff. The lesson I learned from this was, when in Xinjiang, do as the natives do, and learn from them. That was one thing not many people with a language barrier did, and they were the worse for it.

It took almost an entire day to rid a burlap sack of camel hair of all its dirt. Each batch had to be beaten four or five, sometimes six times. Then it was removed to a clean place. The tarpaulin was swept, and the process repeated until there was no more dirt left on the tarpaulin. Then the light and fluffy hair is stuffed again into the burlap sack to be taken to the river to be washed. It is a very arduous task, and usually done when the weather is hot so that it will dry in a day or two.

So one hot day in summer, the sack of fluffed camel hair, a big tub, a bag of laundry detergent and a basket was taken to the river on a shoulder pole. More than just a couple of hours were spent at the job as the hair had to be divided into several batches to be washed. First, the tub is filled with water, then detergent is added and dissolved, then some hair is soaked in it for a while and stamped on with bare feet. The water and detergent have to be changed three times because the first wash results in black, muddy water. The second wash is the color of third-brew coffee, and it is not until the third or fourth wash that the water is clear. Then the hair is put into the basket in the water, wedged in by rocks so that water flows through it to make it thoroughly clean, but not wash the entire basket away. Then little by little it is wrung dry and brought home.

The now-cleaned camel hair is pulled apart and hung on the clothesline to dry. In the drying process, the bunches of hair are pulled apart, a little at a time so that they will dry quicker. When it is thoroughly dried, it is placed on a bed sheet on a tarpaulin and beaten and fluffed all over again. The camel hair this time is several shades lighter than when it was first given the same treatment. Because the hair has now shed all its dirt, it is much lighter and I need not keep myself covered because there is no dust in it anymore. The cleaned hair can be hand spun into yarn for knitting or it can be used as wadding for clothes or comforters.

Fluffing camel hair the Kazakh way has many advantages to it. The main one being the preservation of the length of the fibers. After all, it's the individual fibers that contribute toward the fluff. Camel hair that is machine-fluffed and later used for wadding for clothes or covers, soon balls because the fibers are cut short by the iron spikes of the machine that forcefully tear at the bunched-up and matted hair. Unlike cotton or sheep wool, camel hair has a much longer 'life' if hand-fluffed.

Forty years later, we were still using the comforters padded with that camel hair which I had hand-fluffed myself! The difference between fluffed camel hair taken from the sides and the underbelly is almost like the difference between plain wool and cashmere. One is coarse, the other is silky. I think I got the latter because it had been taken from the underside. It was very time-consuming to clean all that camel hair, but when one has more time than money, sometimes that time means more than money. Camel hair, a much more expensive commodity than cotton, was not utilized as it should have been those days. Now, it is mostly for export. Camel hair lasts and lasts if it taken care of properly.

It was now early 1965. A man by the name of Jiao and his family of a wife and several children were to be transferred from Urumqi to take over my husband's job. A clear demotion for him. My husband was to be assigned to Beitun and plans were underway to set up a similar station in Beitun where the headquarters of the 10th Agricultural Division of the Xinjiang Production and Construction Corps was located. My husband was asked to draw up the blueprints and plans for the building project, and to be on site for its construction until completion. By this time, my health was giving me trouble again, and so with some money that former Sunday School teachers and friends had sent me, via Auntie Ellie, I returned to Shanghai for medical care, with my son, Jian, who was now almost three years old. My husband had to go to the head office in Urumqi for the final approval of the blueprints, and he went with us to Urumqi and put us on the Shanghai-bound train. By that time, the railroad tracks had been laid to Urumqi.

7

A SHORT VISIT HOME (1965)

THE TRAIN RIDE home took nearly four days, a total of eighty-eight hours. We could not afford a hard sleeper, which meant that we had to sit all the way. The child did not need a ticket, but he did need to lie down, so that meant next to no place for me to sit. It was murder to sit and stand that many hours, and so on the last day of the trip I had no choice but to stretch myself out under the seat on an old newspaper because my back was giving way. When I finally got to the entrance of the building of my parents' place, my mother was on her way out, and she passed me by and did not even recognize me. I must have looked like a ghost.

My stay in Shanghai lasted several months. Neighbors were surprised that I could be given such a long "leave", until I told them that I had been unemployed since the child was born. They could not believe it since there were people from Xinjiang still recruiting Shanghai people to go there to work, and that youths were going there by the trainloads, and how come someone like me who volunteered in 1956 to work in Xinjiang could be unemployed. There were funny looks, as though I had committed some crime and was fired as a punishment. There was no way to explain what had actually happened. How could I make anyone understand something when even I could not understand it myself?

After seeking some medical care I was physically better, and I decided to leave. After all, it was December of 1965 and what turned out to be prelude to the Cultural Revolution was already in the brewing. What was more, since I had no permanent residential permit to stay in Shanghai, the policeman would come and ask when I would leave. That never failed to make me feel like an outcast even though I was born and bred in Shanghai, the only place in China I call home because my parents and brothers and sisters were there.

I did sense much disillusionment from people who had returned from the U.S. at the end of 1956. Although they were "untouched" by the anti-rightist movement according to a directive from Premier Zhou Enlai, they were not blind to what they had seen happen to their closest colleagues, friends and family members. They came to realize that had they not had the "advantage" of being so-called "returned overseas Chinese" they would have been in their colleagues' shoes and become targets of the movement just the same. Most of them agreed totally with their "rightist" colleagues' point of view, and what they had said, so in theory, they were also "rightists" except for that protective layer. It was true in 1956 that the government had promised that if things in China were not as they expected after their return, they were free to go back to wherever they had come from. That is easier said than done. Would the U.S. open itself once more to these people who had left through the backdoor? Many had not left the normal way, but went via Canada, supposedly on a trip, then took a boat to Italy, and another boat to Hong Kong before coming into the mainland. Others supposedly left for Taiwan, but changed course mid-way, leaving behind most of their belongings. All for what? All out of love for their own country, all wanting to contribute their bit toward the new system which they believed was better than the old one, and many had skills that were badly needed by the country.

In the years that followed, these folks became very cautious, always on edge, it seems. Many had returned at the prompting of their parents who truly believed that this generation of highly educated people could put their talents to use in New China. They were Chinese, and should naturally think of their own country first and that the U.S. did not lack the skills and talent that these folks had. As the political climate worsened, I wonder how many of them secretly blamed their parents for giving them a "wrong" picture? As time passed, I am sure many of them came to realize that their well-meaning parents could not have predicted the way circumstances had developed. If these "returnees" were left unscathed during the anti-rightist movement, their "protective layer" wore off with time, and the Cultural Revolution made up to them in double-dose what they had 'missed' in the previous movement. By then they had more understanding for their parents, many of whom also became targets. That the system antagonized those it needed most, was, and still is, beyond comprehension. In later years, some people thought that the Cultural Revolution just happened when it did, on a certain day of a certain month, in 1966. But I think it was the culmination of all the political movements since 1949, especially the Anti-Right Movement which was directed against the intellectuals. "Preludes" were orchestrated, and since it was already sixteen years after Liberation and many political movements hence, people were more or less conditioned to going through the rituals.

My being at home for the several months did not go by unnoticed by the lane committee, and the family was constantly being asked when I was leaving. I was told that trainloads of youths were leaving Shanghai for Xinjiang, and other faraway places, and not all of the departures were voluntary, either. The trains, instead of departing from the North Station, as was the rule, were changed to another station because the crying on the platform of those leaving and of family members seeing them off, was so loud that it was having a "bad influence" on the neighborhood. Untold suffering was involved in the departure of these youths, and those sufferings remained to haunt them and their children decades later. A few years after the Cultural Revolution officially ended, the surviving persecuted were rehabilitated so that their children who had been sent to faraway places could return to be with them, but some of them were kept from coming back because they had married in the meantime. Whoever made the rule that anyone who was married was not allowed to return must have been a sadist. The policy resulted in some of the young people deserting their spouses and children for a chance to return to Shanghai or other cities from which they had come. Others hid the fact that they had married, and committed bigamy, only to have their spouse and children come to the city to look them up years later. A TV series was later broadcast which reflected exactly that problem. Its theme song with the words to the effect that "Beautiful Xishuangbana (it could be Xinjiang, Inner Mongolia, or any other remote place in China), could not hold onto my father (or mother), Shanghai is big, but it does not have a home for me. Daddy now has a home, and Mommy also has a family, they gave birth to me, but where do I fit in now? Daddy, Mommy, tell me why this is so?"

Unlike most of the other Shanghai youths, my husband and I came to Xinjiang voluntarily and ten years earlier, so our fate was better than theirs, to a certain degree.

I left Shanghai around Christmas 1965, from North Station. The trip by train back was not pleasant in that I could not afford a hard sleeper, which meant I had to sit all the way again, but the child could sleep stretched out on the seat on most nights. I was very depressed when I was in Shanghai because the pinch of poverty was keener now that there was a child to care for. I have always thought that people had no right to have children when they cannot afford to offer them a decent living – I knew first-hand what it was to grow up in poverty. But here I was making the same mistake that older generations had made, and I felt very guilty and hated myself for it.

In those days, traveling by train had no limits for carry-ons. Unless what one had was so big and clumsy that it could not be put on the luggage rack, one carried it on. Since most people traveling on that train had Urumqi, or other far off places as their destination, they naturally had a lot to take back with them. At that time, anyone who bought a platform ticket (月台票) could get near the train, and so those with a lot, and I mean a lot, of carry-ons had their friends bring them and occupied most of the length of the luggage rack over head. They would use a rope to link each piece of carry-on so that should the train stop at a station and they were asleep, no one can take away (steal) a piece of their luggage.

I did not have much except thick clothes to put on as we progressed westward. I did have a square biscuit tin full of soy beans, green beans, and red beans. There was no room for it as the luggage rack was already fully occupied, and leaving it beneath my seat was no a choice as I could not see it, and leaving it under the seat of the person I was facing was not possible because he already had occupied it with his own things. I had no choice but clamp onto it with my feet as I sat there with my child in my arms.

To describe the toilets in detail would be nauseating, and so would the description of the washbasin. Imagine not being able to wash for such a length of time. As for the various stops along the way, if I had an agreeable person sitting across, I could actually get off the train with the child to get a breath of fresh air. My one drawback was that I don't like talking to strangers, so it makes me kind of look snooty, but I am not the snooty kind, and have no right to be. My constant crying must have left the impression that I was someone who had a baby out of wedlock since I had no man by my side, and very little spending money.

The fact that I felt like an outcast and unwelcomed in Shanghai was that I was unemployed whereas Xinjiang was still recruiting people from Shanghai, and how can I, someone who had volunteered in 1956, be unemployed? It must be that I had committed some 'crime' or was expelled for some reason. Well, they were not too far from wrong, and I don't blame them for it. Too bothersome to explain, and what's more, I couldn't, not understanding it for myself.

On looking back, I am surprised that I did not go bonkers, but all that pent-up frustration resulted in the frequent mid-night weepings because my 'cup overflowed', and good thing it did or I really would have landed in the loony bin, as several times I knew I was heading in that direction.

My son was brought up to use the potty, and so on our trip to Shanghai, I had brought along a biggish enamel bowl for him to use, and that meant on the return trip it had to be carried with me. Train toilets were a hole over which you squatted, but how could a child squat over it? It would be too scary. For myself, I would limit my food and drink since whatever food was available was often undownable, and I did not have much money since I had to go back to Beitun where my husband had been transferred while we were in Shanghai, and I had no idea where it was.

The entire trip (Shanghai to Urumqi) took about 84 hours, I think. As for conditions on the train, well, it was dire. For me, it involved lots of tears and self-pity, and with a child to care for, it was really quite heart-rending, but fortunately my son was too young to know of the deprivations. He could sleep and have regular hours for his 'meals'. At that time, train tickets were sold without regard to the number of seats available, which meant that lots of people who got on half-way would have to stand to their destination if they could not find a place to squat. Some occupied the toilets, much to the dismay of other passengers who might have wanted to use them. In such cases, the conductor used his key to open the toilet, and chased the people out. I witnessed people getting on in Henan province and standing or squatting all the way to Xinjiang, days away.

You may wonder why I chose to return at such a time. Well, the truth is that I felt I was an outcast in Shanghai and not welcome. I had that same feeling in 1959, and this time, with a child, it was double-dosed. I went solely because I needed decent medical care because the drawn out childbirth, with only the help of an unqualified midwife, left me with problems.

Almost immediately after I had left for Shanghai, my husband was transferred to Beitun to set up the Petroleum Station there, and his Burqin job was taken over by ZBJ who was demoted from Urumqi. This meant that I had to go to Beitun instead of Burqin. I had no idea where Beitun was. After arriving in Urumqi I went to Wangjiagou, the Petroleum Station from which Burqin gets its part of its oil supply. There would be oil tankers from Burqin and I could ask my way to Beitun. Winter was cold and we were clumsily clad and the child being only three-and-a-half years old, could not walk fast or long, so he had to be carried most of the way. We had a friend at Wangjiagou who helped me find a Burqin driver. He turned out to be that nice friendly man who had taken us to Burqin in September of 1962. He said his destination was Burqin, not Beitun, but he could give us a ride all the way to Dushanzi and then find a Beitun truck to take me to my final destination. We made our way to Dushanzi, and after entrusting us to the truck dispatcher, he left for Burqin.

I had trouble finding a driver willing to take us as they all claimed that we were not wearing sufficient clothing for the cold. I told him that we had spent three years in Burqin and were very hardy people who were used to the cold, but still, no one would take us. By then I had run out of what little money I had because staying at night in the hostel costs, and instead of just staying for one night, it just dragged on. I had to go to the dispatcher's office every day to try my luck. Finally he sent a message via a driver, to my husband in Beitun and told him to send out two sheepskin coats with the next truck that was coming out so that we could leave. This man had just gotten tired of my going to his office and crying there every day.

We finally got on the road, not on a truck to which my husband had entrusted the sheepskin coats, which would not arrive until a few days later, but on another passenger truck. A young PLA soldier had an extra coat that he could let us use on the way. So we bumped for two whole days and finally reached Beitun in the middle of the night. But where was this Beitun Petroleum Station? The truck terminal was outside of the town where all the passengers were to get off to go their separate ways. There was no way that I could find my way in the middle of the night on New Year's Eve, to where my home now was, not in the wee hours of a cold winter night. If there had been a place or a person, someone I could leave the child with, I would have gone out to look for the Petroleum Station. But I was already penniless and staying the night at the inn was unthinkable especially since I was already at the doorstep of home. I was more than frustrated, and sat down to cry once more. The PLA man who had lent us his sheepskin coat was staying the night at the inn because he still had a stretch to travel, and he, bless him, volunteered to go out and look for me. Someone pointed to a brightly-lit hilltop some distance away, and said that that was the new Petroleum Station. I gave him my husband's name and he left. It seemed like an entire day had passed when he finally returned with my husband and a worker with a pushcart. We thanked the PLA man, and stumbled our way home in the dark.

Beitun was much like Burqin only it had a little less of the "three mores" the latter was known for. But the wind, the sand and the mosquitoes were still there. It was a desolate town, very poor and further from the Irtysh River than Burqin was. The only industry seemed to be a woolen textile mill which had been moved, lock, stock and barrel from Tianjin. Almost one hundred percent of the population there were Han. There were state farms nearby which were worked by farmers from the 10th Agricultural Division of the Xinjiang Production and Construction Corps. The only blessing of that place was that the Irtysh was there where people could still go and fish to supplement their poor diet. Otherwise Beitun was even bleaker than Burqin.

Early the next morning everyone came to have a look at "Lao Gong's Shanghai wife", expecting to see some pretty young thing, but what they saw was a prematurely old woman with sunken cheeks and panda eyes. Our new home was a unit in a row of two-room, one-story brick houses. I was surprised to find that there was not one single non-Han ethnic family on the compound except someone from an unheard-of Tujia group. The woman was at most in her early thirties, very pretty and demure. Her husband was one of the watchmen, a man named Qi, and they had a year-old baby girl who was the sweetest little thing. I almost fell over dead to discover that this pretty young woman had bound feet which were later unbound! It was pathetic to see the poor thing mince her way around the gravel courtyard.

When I got to know her better, I asked her why she allowed her feet to be bound, she just smiled and lowered her eyes. Actually they were no longer bound now, but since they had been when she was a child, she found it difficult to walk or balance herself if she did not have on tight shoes. Later on, her husband said that he had called for her to be with him to have the baby fearing that if it were a girl, his parents would also bind her feet. This couple was from some unheard of nook in Qinghai Province.

Among my new neighbors were three young Sichuan couples, and each of the men were veterans. All were newly-married and expecting their first babies. The man in charge of the Petroleum Station was an old veteran named Ma, from Shantung Province, someone my husband knew from the Motorsala and Dongfeng Steel Mill days. Temperamentally, Ma was amiable, benign and candid. But where knowledge and work was concerned, he left much to be desired, and he knew it. He did not have "airs" like most "leading cadres" did. The word "bureaucracy" in Chinese is made up of "guan" and "liao" meaning bureaucrat, or official, and the suffix is "ism". So we usually criticize a "leading cadre" for putting on "airs" by saying that his officialdom may not be big, but his bureaucracy is certainly not small. (guan bu da, liao bu xiao). Ma was just like one of us. This "normality" was seen as an abnormality by the compound's radical, a watchman, a native of Shantung by the name of Li.

This Li (HL) had a big family. A mother in-law, wife, and six children. They were as dirty as can be and lice-ridden, and no one went near them. The wife worked as a farmhand on one of the nearby state farms belonging to the 10th Agricultural Division of the Xinjiang Production and Construction Corps. Their youngest child was still nursing, and when it cried, the grandmother, always in a padded black jacket buttoned on the right, would unbutton her jacket and have the baby suck on her dry breasts. She was grime-covered but the part near the nipples where the baby sucked, was of natural color. Every evening there would be a sort of gathering at our place where Ma and others came to listen to the news. I had brought back from Shanghai a clumsy old transistor radio which belonged to my parents after they bought a smaller one. Ours was the only radio in the whole compound and we usually listened for the news. After that they would stay behind for a fun game of poker (*zheng shang you*) with my husband, or they would chat late into the night. All this was noticed by Li, and pretty soon he and his wife spent most of their free time squatting under our window and eavesdropping. We were totally unaware of it all until one day we heard a loud slurping outside the window, and found this husband and wife team, each with a big bowl of soup noodles in their hands, having their meal. I am sure they did not hear a word because of their noisy eating habits. Little did I know that this Li would make a mountain out of a molehill for us later on.

As usual, political study was part of every employee's life. A ritual to be gone over at least once week, and practically once a day if a political movement was taking place. Housewives were spared. Since the Beitun Petrol Station was newly established, everything was done to set it on the right track. The housewives contributed in taking care of the women's side of the public outhouse. We competed with the men to keep it as clean as possible. We did not have much trouble since the men outnumbered us. When my turn came to clean the outhouse, the other women bet that I would go in wearing a mask and that I would just swish-swish and call the job done. After all, Shanghai people were known for their disdain of dirty work. They were wrong. My job was inspected and found acceptable, and therefore it made me acceptable to them, and I found that by sweeping and cleaning the outhouse I also had swept away the barrier that had separated me from them.

I got along better with one of them, Chen, than with the others. (She has since died of cancer of the liver). One day, the wife of Li Mingzhu (he committed suicide ten years later), who was my height which is five feet nothing, had her first baby and we visited her several days after the birth. She was sitting up in bed, but I noticed that the teats of her swollen breasts touched down to her thighs! My eyes popped. After all, this was her very first child. I could not resist remarking to Chen about it. She said that many Sichuan women had what were called 'sandbag breasts'. First of all, no one knew what a bra was, or had the luxury of one, and secondly, most women did heavy farm work in the fields in their puberty, mostly in a bending position, and later on when they became mothers, they would still do the farm work carrying their babies on their backs, and if the baby was hungry, they would either let the baby suck from under their armpits, or over their shoulders, like their mothers did, their grandmothers did, and their great-grandmothers did, all the way back. (I guess the laws of evolution caught on and extended the milk bar which made it easier for Sichuan farm babies to survive on the backs of their mothers.) Chen told me all that as matter of factly while I was doubled up in stitches and almost rolling on the floor just picturing how some Sichuan babies nursed. She couldn't understand why all that seemed so hilarious to me. Couldn't I see how difficult life was for women to work the fields and be nursing mothers at the same time? Didn't I know that the farming season waits for no one and that the livelihood of everyone depended on how well the rice grew? She realized that this Shanghai person, me, was more stupid that she had thought. I understood her point, but what I saw just tickled a funny bone.

Another new employee, Gao, someone we were acquainted with in Burqin, a much older Sichuan veteran, joined the Station, and came with his family. One day he went fishing and caught a big, big sturgeon. It's called "*Qinghuang yu*" by the local Chinese. It looks like a shark, with the mouth in the neck, and has a brownish skin with no scales but a layer of slime where the scales should be. It has no regular bones but semi-transparent soft, plastic-like bones which are edible. The meat of the sturgeon is white, very smooth, tender and tasty. Gao attracted a crowd on his way home, carrying it dangling on a pole on his shoulders. Just as he was preparing his fish, someone came and offered to buy it from him for a good price, to use in a banquet that evening. HYC, the No.1 of Altai Prefecture and Commander-in-chief of the 10th Division of the Xinjiang Production and Construction Corps was in town on an inspection tour, and the local leaders wanted to fête him with this rare fish, the sturgeon. Gao refused to part with his trophy saying that he did not need the money. The man tried to intimidate him, asking if he knew who HYC was, and Gao said he didn't and couldn't care less. Actually, there was no one in Altai who did not know who HYC was. But Gao said that whoever he was, if he liked sturgeon so much, why didn't he go and catch one himself, or better still, why didn't this boot-licker catch one for him and get a promotion at the same time. Talk as he did, the man could not get Gao to part with his fish, not even for a high price, and the man left empty-handed. I could just picture his "promotion" going down the drain. There are no lack of brown-nosers wherever one goes, it seems.

"*Shacong*, a kind of wild green onion, sprouted around the foot of the two huge oil tanks on top of the hill. Since that was a forbidden area for anyone except workers on the site, my husband would come back with some of it at noon and that would be our source of green vegetables for the day. On the whole, life in Beitun was easier on my husband in that he did not have to be blown on his way to and from work since where we lived was only a short distance away from both the office and the oil tanks. As for me, I missed my Uygur neighbors Yitarhan, Semet-ahun, and their family. Ma, as a leader, was certainly a lot better than the Burqin one, Hu, in that Ma did not have his wife and children with him. They were all in Urumqi. It's amazing the difference a "good" and "bad" wife of a superior makes, especially in China, as our history has attested to.

Now that the Burqin and Beitun Petrol Stations were on the right track, my husband received orders again, to be transferred to Altai this time and JZB, several years my husband's senior who had replaced my husband in Burqin, was once again designated as the man to replace him in Beitun. We left after he arrived with his big family. Our stay in Beitun lasted only six months for me, but several months longer for my husband. The China Xinjiang Petroleum Company Urumqi Head Office decided that instead of having only Petrol Stations, Altai, the prefectural seat of Altai Prefecture, should have a Petroleum Company as a branch of the Xinjiang Petroleum Company, in addition to its petrol stations. My husband was transferred there to work in the business office as he had in both Burqin and Beitun. As I said, we went where we were told to go, no questions asked. But I could not help wondering where we would be sent after Altai. Was there still another place that was even further north than Altai? If there were, it could only be the Soviet Union. Going there would be "involuntary" exile. The time then was June, 1966, the beginning of the abominable Cultural Revolution.

8

THE ALTAI YEARS (1966-1978)

THE MOVE FROM Beitun to Altai took about three hours of bone-rattling on a truck on the unpaved highway. (It has now been cut to a little over an hour since the roads have been paved) It was our shortest move yet. I was very happy to find Altai different from either Burqin or Beitun. It was a town surrounded by mountains and there was no sand, no wind and no mosquitoes even though there was also a river.

We were taken to a hilltop where there were two rows of houses built with sun-dried bricks, and we were told we had been assigned to the room on the left inside the first entrance of the row on the right. The entrance was in the middle which opened up to a room which was supposed to be the kitchen in summer, shared by two families living on either side of it. Cooking was done in the room in winter because there was a fire wall, (*huoqiang*) inside. Our room was small, only big enough for two single beds put side by side, and our one and only piece of big furniture, a cupboard made from an old crate that had held bicycle parts, and a tiny table and three low stools. So that room was our bedroom, living room, kitchen, and all. The ceiling was news-papered, like most adobe houses are.

The making of a newspapered ceiling is now a lost art except in some rural areas where people still live in one-story houses built with sun-dried or kiln-baked bricks. To make the newspapered ceiling, a hanging "frame" of tied up bunches of dried reed for scaffolding had to be made to hang from the rafters. Each square was the size of a spread-out sheet of newspaper. The newspaper is brushed with starch made from flour, stuck onto the frames until the entire ceiling is covered, then another sheet of newspaper, again fully brushed with starch, is stuck on to cover the first layer of newspaper entirely, one layer lengthwise, the other layer widthwise. It looks like an easy job, but not everyone can do it just right. The newspapers cannot be too tightly stretched or they will tear apart when the starch is dried.

Newspapered ceilings have their advantages and disadvantages. In the winter, it keeps the room warmer because less heat escapes, and it also keeps it cleaner because no dry hay or loose particles of mud will drop from the underside of the mud roofing. But the disadvantages far outweigh the advantages, because the ceiling is a breeding ground for mice. Throughout the day, I could hear mice scurrying back and forth, as they had through passage in that row of houses, and they enjoy nibbling at the newspapers because of the starch. Sometimes if too many congregated in one spot, they would drop through. Another thing is that when it begins to thaw in the spring and the roof, which is slapped-on mud mixed with chopped up hay, is dripping wet and leaking, slowly soaking the newspapered ceiling until it is too heavy for the reed frame, then the entire 'ceiling' falls down.

The courtyard in which the two rows of adobe houses stood was actually a slope on the side of a hill. Unlike our row, the opposite row of houses had an entrance for each family each with two rooms. From left to right, they were occupied by a Kazakh-speaking Hui-Kazakh family of Hassan, the *shopir* (Hasan, the truck driver. The word *shopir* comes from the French '*chauffeur*'), which consisted of a widowed Kazakh mother who had married a Hui, her son, Hassan, and his Hui-Kazakh wife, Kalile, who was childless and adopted a niece and nephew, children of her younger sister. The family next to them was "Pockmarked" Zhang and his family of a wife and two sons and two daughters, the latter two were in Sichuan. Then came another Zhang, who was a watchmen, and his wife and two sons, and the family next to them was yet another Zhang, and the last family were the old Meng couple, Grandma Meng and Grandpa Meng, both in their late fifties if not older, and both equally queer, but in different ways, especially the grandma.

After we had settled down and begun to be acquainted with the neighbors, we were told that Grandma Meng had been a very comely girl in her youth. She was the only child of a rich merchant in Qitay (Gucheng), and many local young men had sought her hand. But her father was reluctant to give her to any local eligible young men because he had thought that they were really after his money. One day, a raggedy man from Shanxi Province came begging at their door. The rich merchant gave him a job as a watchman in their courtyard for three meals a day and place in the hay loft to sleep at night.

This man proved to be not only diligent but also very honest and after a year or two, became the accountant for his master. He was most useful in going after debts owed to his master, and with time, became his employer's right-hand man. The rich merchant decided to marry his daughter to him so that he could carry on the work. This marriage was not what the daughter had wanted, but she had to go through with it. They eventually had four children, a daughter and three sons. After the youngest was born, the woman wanted to marry someone she had fallen in love with for a long time, and who would have married her had he not been under his parents' pressure to marry someone else whom he did not love. Now, he was divorced and if she also divorced, they could marry.

Her husband, Grandpa Meng, refused to divorce her on the grounds that the children needed a mother. He would only agree to a divorce after the youngest son was grown. By that time, Grandma Meng's intended had already remarried. She then began to take to drink and kept to herself. She developed into an alcoholic and a very mentally disturbed one of the pacifist kind. Grandpa Meng went queer as well. Grandpa Meng had not spoken to her since the day she asked for a divorce.

I saw Grandma Meng again in 1994 when I revisited Altai. She was now all shriveled up and gray in complexion, with skin the color and texture of elephant hide. She no longer drank, but she wandered around and was known as the local "traffic stopper" because she liked to stand in the middle of an intersection, and all drivers would slow down and skirt her. She was known to have caused more than a few local traffic jams. Grandpa Meng was still around. Their youngest son and his wife took care of these two old people.

During the second half of the sixties when we were still living in the same courtyard, Grandma Meng would often provide the neighborhood with "entertainment" whenever she was drunk. One day, in the deep of winter, and probably on Grandpa Meng's payday, she came home with bottles of liquor under both arms and in her hands, she stood outside her own doorstep like the Colossus of Rhodes, opened the bottle caps with her teeth and downed one bottle after another, standing on the ice-covered ground, at the same time cutting through the ice with a steamy, yellow stream flowing from under her. After all the bottles were emptied, she went into her room and picked up bowls and plates and began smashing every single window pane in their two rooms. Then she went down the hill and came back laden with discarded card-board boxes from the courtyard of the local Commercial Bureau which was also the backdoor of the department store. She then borrowed nails and hammer from a neighbor, and began to seal the window frames with the folded cardboard boxes.

This woman withstood the cold better than anybody else in the neighborhood, and was never once bedridden. She wore a single padded Chinese jacket that was opened on the side, the buttons of which she had ripped off, and a straw rope was used to tie the jacket at the waist. She wore the same pair of padded pants most of the winter and they were permanently frozen from the crotch down, a pair of padded shoes which were in fact worn as clogs because she had never bothered to pull them up, and she never wore socks. She shuffled down the hill and up in them the year round. With the exception of her eldest daughter who had eloped with her teacher, the other three children were away in the countryside for re-education. The eldest son was a very active element during the Cultural Revolution, and most of us would freeze at the sight of him whenever he came to visit his parents. He was always armed with grenades hanging from his waist, and swaggering and brandishing a gun that he would pretend to aim at someone.

The housing units on our side were all occupied by Han families, all of them belonging to the different companies under the Commercial Bureau of Altai. There was electricity most of the time even though the voltage was not normal. If we used a 220-volt bulb we would only get an orangey glow, if we changed the bulb to the 110-volt kind we would get reasonable light, but the bulb would burn out once the voltage fluctuated. There was no running water. What water we used had to be carried from the river on a shoulder-pole with a bucket on each end. A one-way trip was thirty minutes' walk downhill unloaded. The return trip with two big buckets of water would take longer, with frequent stops on the way. Sometimes, water would come from upstream of the river to the ditch which snaked halfway up the surrounding hills in late spring, summer and early fall. That water was mostly used for irrigation for the nearby fields of the local communes, and used by residents who lived nearby. The one and only out-house was down the hill, the men and women sections were separated by a wall of old flattened cardboard boxes precariously stapled together, with wooden planks across a one-man deep ditch for people to squat on. The ditch was slanted to make entrance easy for nearby farmers who came to collect the human waste every now and then.

My husband's work place was down the hill in the courtyard of the Commercial Bureau which faced the main street of the town, and it was half-way between home and the river where we got our water. It was the same place where nearly all the heads of households in the neighborhood worked because they belonged to the different companies that were under the administration of that bureau.

Just a few days after we settled down, a big family moved into the room across from us. This family consisted of a short, little elderly lady who was very fair in complexion, and whom everyone called *Ahnee*, meaning mother. A middle-age couple, Ashat and his wife, Sonya, and their four daughters, Gulchat, Demonar, Aliybe, and Adiybe and the youngest, a son, Elyar. They were a Kazakh-speaking Tartar family. At first, I did not know who they were but did notice that there was a lot of whispering going on among some of the Han neighbors and the Hui-Kazakh family across. I was glad that I had Kazakh-speaking neighbor again as I missed Nurseyt and his family and wanted very much to learn the language. I think this new family sensed the hostility around them and perhaps thought that I was one of the crowd instead of just a newcomer to the courtyard like themselves. Their youngest child, the son, was just two weeks younger than mine and once the two children got to playing together, the chemistry was there and we clicked. The friendship between us developed during the following years we stayed in Altai, and through the years after we moved to Urumqi.

It wasn't until much later that we were told that this family was twice related to the one-time governor of Xinjiang, Burhan Shahidi. Burhan's eldest son by his first wife married *Ahnee's* first child and eldest daughter, Mariam, sister of Ashat, and Sonya, wife of her son, Ashat, is the youngest sister of Burhan's wife, Rashide. *Ahnee* and her late husband, someone by the name of Hussein, had been rich Tartars from Zayzan across the border. They had escaped to China, to settle in Kaba (Habahe), Xinjiang, just before or right after the October Revolution when Tartars were persecuted in Russia. The couple had two sons and seven daughters, the youngest daughter was born several months after her husband, Hussein, died. The eldest daughter, Mariam, was married to Nusrat, the eldest son of Burhan Shahidi, the second child was Labiybe, a daughter, married to a rich Kazakh herd owner, and when he died, she married his younger brother, and she had a son from each of them. Both her sons, Kurash and Riis, were over six feet tall of the Clint Eastwood type. After Labiybe came the elder son, Mithat, and then Ashat, the younger son, then five more daughters, Powsiya, Periyde, Adiyle, Hatiya, and the posthumous child, Ediye.

Ahnee's name was Paerzinae, but no one ever called her that because there was no one around older than her in years. She must have been in her late sixties or older when we first met her. She was meticulously clean and tidy in dress. Physically, she looked as though she were somewhat dehydrated. Her skin was like *crepe de chine*. She lived with her fourth child, the younger son, Ashat. The elder son was in Burqin with his family where he worked in the bank. I had noticed him in Burqin, a tall blond man, and had thought that he was a Russian. With the exception of a daughter across the border in Kazakhstan with her family and the eldest daughter in Urumqi, the rest of the children were all in the different counties of the Altai Prefecture, and the three youngest daughters, all married, were in the same town of Altai, in nearby neighborhoods.

It was in the 1920s or even earlier when Burhan was banished to Kaba, for political reasons, with his parents, wife and children, that was when he first made the acquaintance of *Ahnee* and her husband Hussein. Burhan and clan were destitute, and *Ahnee* and her husband then were living in a big courtyard of their own, and seeing that Burhan was also Tartar, or at least part Tartar, and he seemed to be a refined person, this couple offered them rooms on one side of the courtyard where they settled down. It was here that Burhan's eldest son, Nusrat, started a school with *Ahnee's* eldest daughter as teacher, and many of the earliest local Kaba intellectuals received their initial education in that school. Nusrat spent his life working in education, retired as president of the Xinjiang Normal University.

Sonya, wife of Ashat, the younger son of *Ahnee*, was originally from Semey which is also across the border, but she later moved to Gulja where her sister Rashide was an educator before her marriage to the former governor. Her other sister stayed across the border. Ashat was a jack-of-all-trades in the local Hardware Company in Altai. From this family it was evident to me that the Chinese saying of "if one person in the family gets converted, even the household chickens and pet dogs ascend to heaven" did not apply, since this family did not benefit from Burhan's position. The Shahidis were transferred to Beijing in 1955, and Burhan was a vice-chairman of the People's Political Consultative Committee (PPCC), under Premier Zhou Enlai. One would have thought that anyone in such a position could do much to relieve his relatives' poverty. It was true that the Shahidis did make an attempt to adopt their youngest daughter, Adiybe, and that she had stayed in Beijing for a while and even went up to Tiananmen to stand beside the dignitaries on a national holiday, but as the 'clouds' began to gather in the early to mid-sixties, the Shahidis felt that their own fate was unknown, and so they sent the little girl back to her parents in Altai. That was in late '65 or early '66. The stay in Beijing accounted for her speaking Chinese with a Beijing accent which at first had puzzled us. Adiybe grew up to be bilingual as she attended Chinese school as her younger brother did. The other three children attended Kazakh school. Both their parents could speak little Chinese.

Further up the hill lived several other families among whom was an old Uygur couple, and an old Kazakh couple, including a crippled wife and their adopted daughter, Nurisa. A few Chinese "mangliu" (aimless drifter) families who made bricks for a living, both adobe and kiln-baked; and another Kazakh family, whose wife, Zahiman, was bed-ridden with TB of the lungs. She was of a Kazakh family from Urumqi who had fallen in love with Kabedan, a former cadre, who, because of one reason or another, was made a farmer and commune member in one of the earlier political movements. They had three children, two sons and a daughter. Her father in-law had a woman who tended to all his needs and who also took care of the family, which was poor. Kabedan was an alcoholic and the children were more or less left on their own. When Zahiman was dying, her mother came from Urumqi to take her back and she never returned.

Members of this family met tragic ends after Zahiman died. The old father in-law died of old age, and the woman who had taken care of him, returned to her own children. She had actually been the one that held the family together all along because Zahiman had been too sick. This woman often went to Sonya or to Halile's mother in-law to ask for tea to brew for the family. After she left, the job fell to Gulsade, the only other female of the house, to take care of the family. Her father remarried not long after Zahiman's death, but this new wife died at childbirth. Kabedan died from drink not long after that. Kalmen, Gulsada's elder brother, was later assigned to work in an office of a local commune and he met with some financial trouble and committed suicide. Her younger brother was later executed for a crime. Gulsade grew up and married, but being a poor commune member, she had to work extra hard to make ends meet, and one day she just laid down and died. Actually she had been complaining of abdominal pains for quite a while, but circumstances did not allow her the luxury of prompt medical care. So that was the end of that family.

Down the slope was a courtyard which belonged to the Kazakh family headed by the old man, Testembek. He had several sons, one of whom was mentally disturbed in a nice sort of way, as a result of several days' high fever which must have short-circuited his nerves. He was almost always pleasant and smiling, and quite clear at times. He would go around asking people for the meaning of certain words. One day he came and asked if I knew what the word *kwanish* meant, and I shook my head. He then went into details and gave example after example which meant nothing to me because I knew little Kazakh then. He was married and had several children. He wandered all over town, but could always find his way home. One day he wandered into the courtyard where the local tannery was, probably looking for a drink of water, and accidentally scooped up what he thought was water from an open barrel in the courtyard which contained liquid sulfuric acid instead, and he died. His wife, who was a commune member and the only breadwinner in his family, was left with the children. When I revisited Altai in July, 1994, I inquired about her and was told that this spunky woman never remarried. She worked as a local tinsmith, and saw her children through school. She is now mistress of the courtyard after the death of her old father in-law.

Altai had several mentally disturbed people whom everyone knew and whom no one bothered or teased, as is so often the case in small towns. One of them was a middle-age woman from the No. 3 Ore Bureau who was an alcoholic. When there was no alcohol available in the shops, she would go from family to family asking for a drink. One day, people saw her at the local department store buying bottles of *eau de cologne*. These came in green glass bottles with long skinny necks. With her purchase, she went out and breaking the bottles by smashing their necks against the corner of the wall, downed all the contents and happily went off home.

Another mentally disturbed person was a very unkempt man called Adehai. He was in the prime of life, and always walked around holding a small hand mirror in front of him and looking into it. It was said that when he went away for his college education, his girlfriend, who had promised to wait for him to return, got married to another man instead, and that drove him crazy. His own family turned him out after that, and he became homeless, doing odd jobs for families which needed someone to do their heavy work, such as carrying water from the river, chopping firewood, or shoveling snow in the winter. Adehai was not violent, on the contrary he was always in a good mood, and always smiling. He was not so mentally disturbed that he could not talk coherently. During the Cultural Revolution people heard him in hot debates over what was "right" and what was "wrong". He was even temporarily detained when he was suspected of being a "spy", sending out "signals" with the mirror in his hand, with the help of the glare from the sun. I think the person who suspected him must have been more mentally disturbed than he was. It was said that the reason he always walked looking into his hand mirror was that his girlfriend had married someone handsomer than he was, and he just couldn't take it. He was probably asking the mirror if he wasn't as handsome as the man who finally got his girl. An Altai version of "Mirror, mirror, on the wall, who is the fairest of them all?" His was perhaps, "Mirror, mirror, in my hand, who is the handsomest of Altai men?"

Yet another mentally disturbed person was a young Uyghur girl by the name of Hernisa. She was very tall and slim, and was betrothed to a local young man from the same ethnic group, and everything was set for the wedding after the parents from both families had completed all the formalities. Then just a day before it was to take place, the man called off the whole thing with no explanation offered. The shock of it all caused poor Hernisa to take to her bed, and when she finally recovered, she would walk the streets of the town, scouring them for her beloved, and she behaved much like Ophelia did. It was sad to see her pine and slowly waste away, and she eventually died from a cold which had been too much for her in her weakened state.

Old Man Yao, head of the Altai Petroleum Station had just died from cancer of the liver leaving behind an idiot wife and four idiot children, the two older ones already in their thirties. The eldest was called "Liujin", meaning six *jin*, (a '*jin*' equals half a kilogram) probably it was his weight at birth. Yao had worked for the Sino-Soviet Mining Company in the early fifties. In those years, the Soviets took exploitative mining measures to get the precious stones that they wanted by dynamiting, and workers were paid by the day, and according to the weight of the ore that they could turn in. Yao's two idiot sons, who were little more than animals, not knowing the danger of falling rocks, were always the first to grab whatever they could, and in doing so, earned a lot of money for their father. So Yao was known for being a rich man, but few envied his riches because he was burdened with a family of idiots.

His wife was a simpleton with a permanent grin. The front of her jacket was covered with Mao badges the size of saucers which always drew a lot of attention from people, and no doubt wore out a few jackets because of the sheer weight of the "medals". His eldest son Liujin, even though an idiot, was the most likable member of the family. He was a sorrowful sight because he was always dirty and always in rags. Like his brother, his face resembled a tightly stretched skin on a drum with randomly poked little holes where eyes, nose, and mouth should be, and his teeth were uneven, few and far between. He was quite clear at times and whenever he was free he would wander around the town, and would sometimes come and visit. Whenever he came, we would offer him whatever little food we had in the house, and he would enjoy himself. Workers who hated his father would befriend him and teach him all sorts of dirty words to say to his father, and Liujin would go home and do exactly as taught, and run away when he saw a beating was coming his way.

His brother, the one around his own age, was an even more sorrowful sight because he looked much worse than Liujin, and was not one bit likable because he was very mean and cunning even though he was an idiot. Whenever he was sent out by his parents to gather firewood, he would steal from neighborhood stacks of firewood instead of actually going up into the hills to gather it for himself, and so the neighbors just detested him, but there was nothing that they could do because he was very good at retaliating. Their sister, a homely girl, was at most half the age of her two elder brothers, and she was also wacky, and grew worse with age.

The youngest was another boy who also deteriorated in mentality as he grew so that he dropped out of school before completing his elementary education. Because he was the youngest and the most pampered member of the family, the father gave him whatever he asked for, and he usually asked for money to give to people whom he hardly knew because they had taught him what to ask from his father. Just before Yao died, he sent for a nephew from his hometown in Gansu, and married his daughter to him so that at least there would be one sane person in the family to take care of it. We guessed that his own children were the result of inbreeding, and shuddered to think what the result would be of his own daughter's marriage to her first cousin. On the solemn occasion of her father's funeral, all those present had to keep themselves from smiling, if not actually laughing out loud, at what she had to say of the deceased. The mercy of it all was that she thought herself no different from any other person.

There were several people in Altai that really stood out, in a nice sort of way. Among them was a couple, the wife was a middle-age lady who worked in the local Xinhua Bookstore. Her name was Ezart, and she was a Kirghiz, her husband was Commander Aysan of the PLA, who was a Kazakh. They made a very handsome couple. Ezart was tasteful in dress, wore gold-rimmed glasses, had long, thick braids which reached below her waist, and was multi-lingual in that she spoke perfect Chinese besides her own native Kirgiz, plus Uygur and that of her husband's, Kazakh. Commander Aysan was handsome, tall and straight, and had the imposing air of an army officer, which he was and a high-ranking one at that. The couple had several children. I met him and his son, Talhat, many years later at the local airport. His son was taking him to Beijing to have a health check-up. I greeted them, and I was a little surprised to find that Commander Aysan looked and sounded rather down-hearted. I had thought military people were made of sterner stuff. He has since passed away here in Urumqi, and the funeral was not well attended. Had he died in Altai, the whole town, and representatives from the seven different counties and the other northern Xinjiang prefectures would send representatives to pay their last respects to this man. He had been one of the highest ranking army officers in northern Xinjiang. One of the reasons the old people, especially those with certain positions, are reluctant to retire outside their 'powerbase' is that they fear "once the man leaves, the tea gets cold". When they are in office, they merit certain "considerations", those "considerations" are no longer available once they retire to a place where they had never held office. Many just become ordinary citizens who carry no weight, and that kind of "weight loss" is hard to adjust to after being used to "gravity" all their working lives.

Old Testembek was the first environmentalist of Altai that I was aware of. Nearby there were several families of "mangliu" from Jiangsu Province who made their living by making adobe and kiln-baked bricks. The nearby grounds were carved up and the ground cover of green vegetation was destroyed. Old Testembek would stand up on the rock in his courtyard and bellow and holler at these people who were carving up the ground. When we first moved to Altai, we could see stretches of green from the hilltop near Abdulreyim-aka's, but before long they disappeared and instead, big crater-like holes appeared here and there where the earth had been carved out to make bricks which were in demand in the building industry. Neither the "manglius" nor anybody else paid any attention to Testembek's 'voice in the wilderness,' but during the ensuing years nature took its revenge.

Several of the "mangliu" families lived in the two renovated abandoned kilns across from our window. The men worked in the day time for the local construction company while their jobless wives made adobe bricks to earn extra money. The men would relieve their wives after they got home from work while the women went home to cook the meals. Many had small children whom they left in their rooms while they were out making the bricks. One family had a young child of a little over a year old who was left sleeping on a bed made up with a few wooden planks supported by bricks on either end, while the mother was out making bricks. The father, a construction worker, worked during the day, and as usual, when the baby girl is asleep she is usually put on the bed and the mother goes off to her brick-making, and when her elder brother comes back from school, he would go home, and if his baby sister happens to be sleeping, or awake, he would carry her to the mother to be nursed. One day after he returned from school he claimed that he could not find his baby-sister. The mother thought that perhaps some neighbors next door must have heard her cry when she woke up, and had taken her to their room, and she left it at that. When the husband returned from work, he relieved her and she went home to cook, and when she went to the neighbors to get her baby, they said they had heard no crying, and that the baby was not with them. She went home and searched high and low, and finally, she looked under the bed, and saw the baby dangling between the planks of the bed and the wall. The child must have woke up and discovered that there was no one in the room, and had attempted to get off the bed, but got off on the wrong side, her legs got down, but her head was too big to go through the gap which lay between the planks and the curved wall of the kiln, and in her struggle, she had pulled the covers on the bed over her own head and suffocated. I don't think she even had a chance to cry out, being only less than eighteen months old. The mother cried her heart out, but most women on our side of the neighborhood blamed her for killing her own baby.

If the "manglius" are to be blamed for having carved up the ground to make bricks that were used to build all the houses that now dotted the hillsides of Altai, then the entire population of Altai, regardless of ethnicity, are to be blamed for denuding the mountainside of what is locally known as "*torbil*" in Kazakh, or "*tu er tiao*" in local Chinese, a shrub resembling mesquite or tamarisk, for firewood. The "*torbil*" branches are covered with a dark maroon/brownish skin which contains oil so it emits sparks when burned. It was ideal for kindling because just a few twigs would do the job. When we first arrived in Altai, every Sunday we would see people passing by our hillside going to the mountains with a hoe and ropes. A roundtrip would take half a day. As the population grew, the nearby mountains were denuded, and people had to go further away for *torbil*, which meant that a round trip would take the entire day.

My husband joined the *torbil* gathering people and made his trips with them. We had to buy the necessary tools such as hoe, ropes, and other things. One trip would net about 70 to 80 kilograms of *torbil* bundled tightly and carried on the back with two worn-out soles of foam-rubber slippers to ease the cut of the ropes on the shoulders. The men returned in pairs because resting on the way required assistance. First, sitting down was a problem because of the weight and the length of the burden, and getting up after resting was another problem. They had to help each other down and up. With the heavy load, their trip uphill or downhill was equally difficult. But still, when the weather allowed, a trip a week was a must except for those who could afford to buy firewood. Coal was expensive and so the men who did not have extra money to spare all went for *torbil* on their one and only day off on Sunday.

As time went on, they had to go further and further away for *torbil* which meant that they had to leave on Saturday right after work with a pushcart, ropes, hoe, a kettle for boiling drinking water, bread and some salted vegetables, and a sheepskin coat for the night, and be on their way because by now the *torbil* was much further away than when we had first arrived. The trip with the pushcart was even more tiring. It had to be unloaded before climbing each hill because even two able-bodied men were not strong enough to push a cartful of *torbil* uphill, nor to control it going downhill. Each trip took so much out of the men that they needed an entire week to 'recuperate' and then it was time for yet another trip. The last few trips that they took were with the help of donkey carts borrowed from friends because they had to go even further away and there was no way that they could make the trip on foot with push carts. Even with a donkey cart, when going uphill half the burden had to be unloaded to reach the top, in other words, the work was doubled. The cart had to be unloaded and reloaded after climbing each hill, and there were many hills they had to climb on their round trip. Such trips were made as long as the weather permitted, which was from mid-to late May through to late September as frost-free days in Altai were limited.

When the nearby hillsides and even hillsides a day's distance away were stripped naked of their *torbil*, Nature took revenge. After we moved to Urumqi at the end of 1978, flash floods each summer would devastate the town and would always claim several lives. A big flash flood occurred in 1992 on a public holiday, the Muslim Korban Bairam. On that day, the non-Muslim people get one day off and the Muslims get three days, which means the whole town was on holiday that day. The flash flood came from the hills and carried with it all the loose dirt it had collected on its way, and when it reached town, it was a wall of over three meters high of thick, "chocolaty" ooze. It pushed through all the doors and windows of the local nursery on its way to the river across from it. If that day had not been a holiday, few children would have survived the disaster, and it would have been a day of great mourning as many of them were from one-child families.

After a flash flood had passed through, the streets would be caked with mud several inches thick, and the whole town would be mobilized to clean up the aftermath. It has been several years now since local environmental protection laws prohibited the chopping of *torbil* because it is now a protected species, but much of it had been literally uprooted and there is no way that the hillsides would be able to regain their former lushness within a decade or two, even if humans lend a hand. We were among the people who had aggravated that problem unknowingly. In retrospect, we feel very guilty.

With what *torbil* that was accumulated before winter arrived, there was enough kindling so that the half cubic meter of lumber that each family got the first couple of winters could be saved. My husband spent his spare time in the winter months, when the days are short and the nights are long, making furniture from the logs. Sawing them into boards, drying them and drawing out the 'blueprints' for the next piece. The wood was locally known as "red pine" or "hybrid pine", and another kind was white pine. Red pine was very heavy and had a coarse grain while the hybrid variety was lighter but in short supply. My husband saved the best to make a pair of skis for our boy who wanted to learn how to ski like the other boys in the neighborhood. With what little firewood we saved, my husband also made a wardrobe, a cupboard, a table for our meals, and several small stools. Unfortunately, the wooden planks were not professionally dried like planks in a sawmill were, and the furniture we made soon began to warp, and later on, to crack with a loud noise when the bone glue used to attach the boards could no longer withstand the shrinkage and warping of the wood. It was not unusual to hear a noise like a firecracker going off in the middle of the night from our furniture.

Even before the *torbil* was gone, I had started to gather dry cow chips to subsidize fuel. With two rusty, leaking buckets and a shoulder-pole, I left my son to play with Elyar in Sonya's care, and her daughters and I would go on our gathering trips. There was one place I went for chips that the girls or other Kazakhs wouldn't go, that was the Chinese cemetery which was on a flat piece of high ground to the east on which the sun shone almost the whole day. The local cows would go there to enjoy the sun and chew their cud every day all winter long through to the spring. It had a lot of chips, but most of them were only shells as the dung beetles had done away with all the insides.

Chip gathering got to be an obsession with me because it was the only way I could contribute toward fuel. At first I was finicky, and would only pick the dry, whole ones because they stacked up nicely outside our door, and I just loved to see the pile grow higher and higher by the day. Then we discovered that the Petroleum Company and other companies sold coal dust (the coal residue in the coal shed after the big pieces of coal had been used for heating the offices) for one yuan a burlap sack. First, I would use a sieve to sift the whole sack of coal dust to separate the marble-size pieces of coal to put aside, then the finer coal would be hand-kneaded into the buckets of fresh cow chips brought in each day to make cakes and slapped on the walls or on the roof of our adobe house to dry, and peeled off after they did and stacked up for use in winter. To make stacking easier, I later used a metal ring-like mold for my "cakes". It was a daily ritual to make them, and there was a quiet competition between the girls and I. Fuel was so precious that anything that could burn was picked up wherever we went, whenever. It was like a natural reflex to bend down and pick up the smallest wood chip or cow chip to take it home.

One day, we saw a neighbor using a bellows, a wind box where one pulls a handle to make the fire burn better. My husband found the necessary boards and started to make one himself. It really did work, after some renovation of the stove. As time wore on, the 'wind-box' was replaced by a hand-operated air blaster with a four-blade propeller, also hand-made. How proud I was that my husband was such a handyman around the house, little knowing that more surprises were in store for me.

One drawback of the hand-operated wind-box or air-blaster was that it needed two people to do the cooking. When the wind-box was first installed the neighborhood kids fought to operate it to the point where they had to stand in line to wait their turn. Then they all got over it and when I needed someone to operate it while I cooked, no one would be found. The same thing happened with the hand-operated air-blaster.

I was very happy that at last I found friends in Sonya and her family. Their four daughters were well-behaved girls, each with a personality of her own. Gulchat, the eldest, was a model student, always prim and proper, very much the pillar of the family. Demonar was pretty and sweet-tempered, the softy of them all. Aliybe was the most outspoken member of the family, and very clever with her hands whether at doing fine work such as knitting, crocheting, cross-stitching, embroidering, or *reshelia* making, or at coarse work such as cleaning *bas serak* (the head, hooves and insides of a sheep or cow), cow-dung cake-making with coal dust, or any other work. She was not afraid of anyone and would have her say regardless of the consequences. She often vocally expressed to relatives what her parents only dared to think, and more often than not, left her parents in very awkward positions with their different kin. She has since died of cancer, leaving behind a husband and two children.

With three very different elder sisters as examples, the youngest, Adiybe, managed to develop into an independent young lady embracing all the better qualities of her sisters in addition to developing her own personality. Her having had a Chinese education made her unique, and a very close relationship developed between her and my family which lasted until she got married. Elyar was too young to show any personality of his own, but I did notice that even as the only son, he had not been pampered and grew up to be a very nice young man. He later married the maternal granddaughter of his father's eldest sister and had two daughters. His wife, Glara, died of leukemia several years ago and three years or so following that he, himself, died of carbon monoxide poisoning when he was sleeping in his office one night.

Ahnee, the paternal grandmother of the Ashat's children, could speak no Chinese at all. She was toothless and was like a child in that she had to be taken care of by her daughter in-law as one. She was quite removed from what was happening around her and no one took it upon himself to enlighten her. I supposed everyone believed that "ignorance" of what was happening to her sons, daughters, and sons in-law at that time would be "bliss" for her.

Not long after they moved next door to us in the summer of 1966, Ashat was branded a member of the Black Gang – *Hei Bang* – together with a group of other people. While they were not physically in chains, they were almost treated as though they were. They were assigned the most menial labor and had to engage in 'political study' half the day. Sometimes Ashat would be cleaning the gutters alongside the road while his mother, blind in one eye and very little vision in the other, walked by without seeing him, clad in her well-pressed dress and leather boots polished like mirrors, on her way to visit her youngest daughter a short distance away. Ashat's daughters went to school every day, passing by their father in the Black Gang working by the roadside, cleaning the sewer or doing other such labor, and their young hearts bled, not knowing why their father, of all people, had been singled out for that kind of treatment. They had not benefited from having a relative like Burhan Shahidi when he was in power, so why should they now suffer because of association to him? Burhan, though transferred to Beijing in 1955, became one of the primary targets in Xinjiang during the Cultural Revolution. In that day and age, very few knew why they had to suffer.

Sonya was always busy. She suffered from high blood pressure and now and then she would be unable to get up from bed, and lay there retching the whole day. Whenever she took to her bed, the girls would be in a frenzy as their elderly grandmother also had to be taken care of, and their father, after a hard day's work expected his tea and meal upon coming home, and they themselves had to go to school since being children of a Black Gang member they had to be careful never to be late or in any way cause criticism at school. The girls were also called upon to help the different aunts do their cleaning up, laundry and other odd jobs on Sundays, their one and only day off from school.

Going to the different aunts to help out was something that they had took for granted that they should do until much, much later in life. As an observer, I felt indignant for the girls that they should be treated as washing machines or household maids by their relatives. But Sonya's reaction was different. She said that hard work never killed anybody, and that the girls would eventually benefit from it. Sonya did nearly everything herself at home and spared the girls because they had their homework to do. Friction between sisters in-law is common in all households, regardless of ethnicity and Sonya was an exception. She turned the other cheek too often, for the sake of peace.

Altai was a small town with one main street that stretched from *Lagir* on one side of the river to *Chirimtahl*, meaning mica, at the other end after crossing the bridge under which the river flowed. Streets on the *Chirimtahl* side of the bridge were perpendicular to the flow of the river, and they were named in numbers, beginning from first to tenth, such as *Birinji Kurshur* (1st Street), and so on. After that were the outskirts. The *beyis*, as the landlords, or rich men were called, all had their homes beyond *Besinji Kurshur* all the way to *Ooninji Kurshur* (10th Street), whereas the salary-earning people and therefore poorer people, all lived on this side of *Besinji Kurshur*. Altai had two hospitals, the Prefectural one known as *Aymak Doktorhan* was across the bridge in the beginning of *Lagir*, next door to where the former Soviet Consulate had been, whereas the county hospital, known as *Chipakhan* was on *Besinji Kurshur*. The other hospital was an Army Hospital known as the No.16 Hospital which was further down in *Lagir*.

For the Han population, pork was seen once a year at Spring Festival and it was rationed, so coupons were needed. Ordinarily, lamb was the only meat. As time wore on, our systems were no longer adjusted to pork. Each Spring Festival when the Han families were given a ration of pork we would all get bad tummies, and by the time we had adjusted to it, the pork would be finished.

Ashat being the only breadwinner of his big family and ours with a very modest income, we saw a little meat only once a week. When the annual slaughter season came around in winter, we would go to the slaughter house in Lagir to buy *bas serak*. *Bas* means head, and *Serak* is hooves in Kazakh, and it can be either sheep or cow. It is the name of a set which includes head, hooves and all the innards except for the lungs in a cow which are fed to the hawks or discarded, and the kidneys of lamb which are sold as meat separately. The price of a set of cow bas serak then was 7 yuan while the sheep's was 1 yuan. We only bought them when it was slaughtering season when they were plentiful and the weather was below freezing so that they wouldn't spoil. The water to clean them had to be carried (with shoulder pole and a bucket on each end) from the river. The price for one set of *bas serak* was equivalent to one kilo of lamb with bones, and it yielded much, much more meat and cooking fat than one kilo of lamb did. But *bas serak* entailed much, much work, too.

Cleaning a set of *bas serak* is very time-consuming, but since there is natural refrigeration in winter, what cleaning cannot be completed in one day can be left to the next. To clean the sheep's head, first the wool is cut off and put aside and accumulated to make *keygiz* which is rough felt use as mattress or covering for yurts, or to knead into mud when making the 'mouth' of a *nan*-baking oven or *tonir* to keep it from cracking, and then a wooden stick is stuck into the severed esophagus of the sheep's head to hold it over a fire to burn off the remaining wool and a knife is used to scrape off the burnt wool until only the skin remains. The four legs are first un-hoofed and a stick is inserted into each to hold it over a fire and burn in the same manner as the head. Then these are put in a big tub of water laced with baking soda to be scraped clean. The head is opened up by slicing both sides of the jaw as there is much cud in the gums and under the tongue and everything has to be cleaned out and scraped clean of slimy saliva.

The spleen, the heart, and the liver are easier to clean in

comparison to the lungs, stomach and intestines. To clean the lungs, water is poured in through the esophagus and slowly patted to inflate both lungs to their fullest and then keep on pouring in the water to wash the pink lungs until they are white. Then a thin, spiced batter of flour is poured into the lungs to fill them, and then the tube is tied with a string and the lungs are cooked in a big pot together with the head and legs. After it is done, the lungs are cut into slices and fried.

Washing of the stomach is the hardest job. First it is turned inside out to empty it of the cud, then rinsed clean. Then it is dipped in a cauldron of very hot, but not boiling, water to harden the dark gray fuzz inside of the stomach so as to make it easy to scrape clean. The whole stomach is scraped until it is spotlessly white. The big intestine is usually wrapped in fat which is stripped and put aside, and later mixed with vegetable oil to use as cooking fat, as without vegetable oil it would harden too quickly once it cools off. To wash the intestines, a kettle filled with water is poured through one end of the intestine to clean it out, and then the outside is cleaned before turning the intestine inside out, with the help of a chopstick, and rough, crystal salt is added. The intestine is to squeezed and kneaded it over and over again to rid it of the slime until it literally 'squeaks' to make sure that it is thoroughly cleaned. The narrower section is braided and tied to put into the cauldron to be boiled with the rest of the *bas serak*, and the wider section is cut off and tied at one end, and with chopped up spleen, and sometimes liver, a little rice, chopped onion, with a little salt for flavoring is stuffed into the intestine tied up to be boiled in that same cauldron. After a few hours, chopped raw onions, fresh cilantro or coriander, or dried, powdered, celery leaves, salt and pepper are put into each bowl before soup is ladled on it and the rest of the *bas serak* is taken out and placed in a big tray and the head of the household - in

Sonya's family's case, it was Ashat - would cut up and divide the ingredients among the family. The ears from the sheep head is usually cut and given to the youngest member of the family. The sheep's heart can be used to stir-fry with vegetables which will be good for another meal. The cost, labor aside, for one set of *bas serak* was equivalent to one kilogram of lamb with bones, but provided much more nutrition for that family of eight people.

For us, a family of only three, a set of sheep *bas serak* would last us for a week with some meat every day. We usually prepared our sheep *bas serak* a little differently from Sonya because there were fewer of us and we didn't have such a big cauldron to hold the entire set of *bas serak*. We usually boiled the head and legs, and after they were all done, the meat from the head would be stripped and cut up to make a dish with or without vegetables. The skull was then cracked open with a hammer, and the blob of brain, containing high protein, went to our son. As for the four legs, after the skin, tendon, and meat was eaten clean, the bone was cracked open and the marrow extracted – marrow is a wonderful source of lubricant for the wheels of horse carts, ox carts or other carts because it doesn't harden in cold weather, and it can be saved in a bottle as a source of cooking oil. The bones from the head and legs are saved to be boiled once more to extract any fat that might still be gotten, and then they were taken to the place which bought bones to make fertilizer. The scooped-up layer of fat from the water in which the bones had been boiled would be used to make soap.

During the slaughtering season in the winter, sheep *bas serak* is usually bought by the dozen or more sets, so that meant we had to deal with them in an "assembly line" manner. A whole day would be devoted to the cleaning of one thing, such as the head, the legs, the stomach, the intestines, or the lungs. We borrowed blow torches from friendly truck drivers to do the head and legs which saved much firewood and time. The cleaned, halved heads and legs were carefully lined up and put into cardboard boxes between thick layers of snow. The boxes would be left outside buried deep in snow with firewood and cow chips stacked on top and around them to prevent stray dogs or wolves from getting at them at night. If we were nearing the season when the ground began to thaw, then the cleaned *bas serak*, if any were left by then, would be put into a big sack of crystal salt to seal in the moisture and give an extra flavor to what was stored.

Altai is not far from Burultokay which has a salt lake from which we got all our salt for salting vegetables at the end of each fall. Salt was one yuan a bag, regardless of its size. One truck driver, a prankster, sewed together an old tarpaulin as a 'bag,' and got a huge bag of salt for the same price, which he divided among all the families in the courtyard, providing enough salt to last for several seasons of pickling.

Because the winter was long and the varieties of vegetables limited to only cabbage, potatoes and carrots, people just pickled and dried whatever vegetables could be had. Each family had at least one baked-clay container big enough to hold an adult, in which to pickle their veggies. Tomatoes were bought when they were most plentiful and at their cheapest, washed clean and salted in another big container. One layer of tomatoes, sprinkled with one layer of salt, and then another layer of tomatoes and salt, until the container was filled to the brim and covered with a wooden cover held down with a piece of rock on top. After all the salt had melted and the tomatoes, many crushed by the weight, were floating in the salty water, other vegetables such as chives, string beans, cucumber, carrots, celery and cabbage were added. Families traded their salted vegetables and it always seemed that a neighbor's tasted better than one's own.

Heads of garlic would be pickled separately in a glass bottle or a much smaller container, in vinegar and sugar or honey, or if either was too expensive, then with a little saccharin. Vegetables such as eggplant and a zucchini-like squash which could not be pickled, were sliced and hung up to air-dry. Also coriander (cilantro). Ripe tomatoes were sometimes cut into thin slices and placed on a board to be dried for use in winter. After they dried, they were put in a muslin bag and hung up where there was a draught to make sure they didn't get moldy. They were precious in winter, especially for soup noodles. They were soaked and softened in hot water and then chopped up to provide color and flavor to dishes. Pickled vegetables such as tomatoes, carrots, cucumber, cabbage, celery and string beans sometimes served as snacks for children because they were not very salty, and the children in our courtyard could not afford any other snacks. So they munched on salted vegetables, of which cabbage and tomatoes were the favorites.

Each family would also dig a *bahz* (cellar), which was a vertical shaft into the ground with tunnels dug out in all four directions. Our *bahz* was in the middle room which was used as a kitchen for the families on either side. *Bahz* were necessary for storing fresh vegetables, usually unsaltable vegetables such as potatoes, and sometimes cabbage and carrots. Potatoes would grow white sprouts on them after the winter was over, and then we would have to snip off the sprouts and move them from one hole to the next. Our *bahz* was easy to dig because it was all sand underneath. The sand was moist and very cold, and was ideal for storing our vegetables or even for home-made beer, *kvas*, in summer. The hill on which we lived, and the surrounding hills were actually piled-up boulders and sand.

The local *kuush-hahn*, or slaughterhouse, was in Lagir, by the river. It had one faithful "employee" whose name was not on the payroll – that of a big billygoat with a shiny coat of black. His job was to bring a flock of sheep from the corral in the yard into the slaughterhouse where they would be slaughtered. The flock of sheep would follow his lead into the slaughterhouse, and once they were in, the outer gate would close, and he, the billy goat, would leave through a hatch that was the same color as the wall, leaving behind the flock. And once they are all slaughtered, bled and skinned, he led in another flock, and so on until the day's slaughtering was done. He was well-fed and his job was a cushy one. But not all goats, whether they be nanny goats or billy goats had such an easy life. Because goats are known for their hardiness, they are not as well cared-for by their masters as sheep are. But, unlike ewes after they lambed, nanny goats provide enough milk for their masters after they had kidded, and the quality of their milk is much superior to that of cow's milk, though it cannot be compared in quantity.

One nanny goat which had recently kidded belonged to a family way up the hill at *Chirimtahl*, was left to roam the neighborhood during the day. She would dig with her front hooves at the wheat sprouts from the roofs of nearby adobe houses which had been slapped on with wet mud mixed with dry straw the fall before, for added insulation against the cold. Now that spring was here, some of the straw had sprouted, and this hungry nanny goat dug with her front hooves at the sprouts, making holes on the roofs which caused leaks in rainy weather or when the snow melted, and she would not only eat whatever vegetables that were growing in the patches of nearby families, but would also mess them up in the process. No one in the neighborhood knew exactly to whom that goat belonged, but everyone was sick and tired of the destruction she was causing. One day, the man in one of the families that had suffered from her antics decided to put an end it. He caught the nanny goat and extracted two of its front teeth with pliers, and then set her free.

Sure enough, she was never seen again in the neighborhood.

Each winter, most families would buy a set of cow *bas serak* either from the local slaughterhouse or from the nearby county of Kaba. The price was equivalent to 6 or 7 yuan, or what it would cost to buy six or seven sets of sheep *bas serak*. Cleaning a set of cow *bas serak* entailed much more work than one dozen set of sheep *bas serak*. First of all, the horns had to be sawn off. Then the head would be torched of all the hair. People who thought that was too much trouble just skinned it, and if skinned the right way, as done by the Kazakh shepherd, the hide would make wonderful rope by cutting it in such a way as to make one continuous strip. If the hide is boiled long enough, it was also chewy and edible. The cow head is first sawed and halved like a sheep's head, then quartered, to make it smaller and easier to cook. The meat from one cow head was at least five kilograms, not including the tongue. Again, a lot of work is involved to clean the inside of the mouth. The legs from the knee down, had to be unhooved first, and then torched to rid them of hair and scraped clean like one would sheep legs. Then they were cut at the joint (ankle) so it would fit into the pot. The eyes and the brains were also eaten, but the tongue was special. I would take it out and thoroughly wash it, then bury it in salt till the next spring when the weather turned warm. I then took it out to be dried with smoking cow chips and sent it home to my mother in Shanghai. She said it tasted exactly the same as the smoked tongue which had once been sold in Cosmopolitan, a delicatessen near Central Arcade on Nanking Road.

The cow stomach is huge, and so is its heart and liver. Unlike the sheep *bas serak*, the cow's come with the kidneys but not the lungs, which are usually thrown away beforehand, to feed the hawks. The fat on the intestines alone when melted is a whole bucketful which served to supplement the year's cooking oil. It took just about a whole day to clean out the stomach because of its sheer size. After it was emptied and rinsed clean, it was cut into pieces to make further washing and scraping easier. Because we live up a hill which was quite a distance to the river, it meant many trips were necessary to bring back enough water for all the cleaning that had to be done. Sometimes it would take days to clean just one set of cow *bas serak*, and the work was back-breaking. And yet because we had more time than money, we had to get the most out of it. Labor power was what we had, and it was free. Meat from the head would be ground to make hamburgers or filling for dumplings, or simply stewed with potatoes and carrots. We enjoyed the sinew (tendon) of the legs best. My husband boiled them in a pot with soy sauce, sugar, and spices which included cinnamon, star aniseed, and other herbs and spices tied up in a muslin bag.

Lamb was always priced by the kilogram regardless of the cut. So for the same price per kilogram, some got a lot of meat from it while others got a lot of bones. It depended on how one's relationship with the butcher was, and also on if one belonged to the same faction or held the same viewpoints as their butcher, since this was during the Cultural Revolution. The two local butchers were Mametjan and Idayet. Mametjan became Hajj Mametjan because he had made a trip or two to Mecca.

For as long as Ashat could remember, he never got a better cut of lamb from the butcher than the neck. He saved all the neck bones and strung them out like a big necklace-like wreathe that he said he would present to the butcher after his fate turned and he would "deserve" some cut better than just the neck. Most preferred customers got the hind leg with all the fat attached. When anyone complained that he also wanted a hind leg, the butcher would bellow that Allah only gave each sheep two hind legs. When anyone asked him to please give a cut with less bone and therefore more meat, he would holler that bones are places on which meat is grown, that without bones there would be no meat. In a word, the disfavored customer is always in the wrong.

Altai sheep are known for their "bustle" of solid fat. In the 1960s, and 1970s, sheep fat was rationed. After that, when times were better and people became more health-conscious, and vegetable oil was more available, people started to disdain sheep fat, and the butchers had to sell it by adding 100 or 200 grams of sheep fat to make up a kilogram of meat because the weight of the sheep included its bustle. In the early 1990s, when Sonya's family as well as other Altai families had relatives visiting from Uzbekistan or Kazakhstan, they would slaughter at least one fatted calf or sheep to treat their relatives, and naturally they did away with the "bustle" of fat, thinking that their kin from the other side of the border must be much more health-conscious than they were. So how surprised they were to discover that their relatives viewed the sheep "bustle" (fat) as a delicacy! They said that the sheep fat boiled in salt water, cooled, and sliced was ideal for sandwiches for either breakfast or lunch. No wonder many of the ladies were so generously endowed.

Only old cows or male calves are slaughtered for beef. A few steps from where we lived was the *kirmahn*, a level piece of ground for sunning wheat, and later used as a playground for children and for people learning how to ride the bicycle. That was the only piece of flat ground near us. To tenderize the beef of an old cow or ox before being slaughtered, it is force-fed with cheap alcohol and then led on to the *kirmahn* by a rope tied to its nose ring, with one person whipping it from behind, and another tugging it by the rope in front and running around and around on the *kirmahn* until the exhausted animal is puffing like a steam engine and foaming at the mouth, and then the man leading it wrestles it to the ground with one tug and plunges in a knife to finish it off. Meat from this old cow is supposed to be tenderized by the alcohol and by all that running around with its heart pumping fiercely and all the blood vessels dilated. That is what all privately-owned old cows or oxen had to go through before being slaughtered in order for their masters to get less tough meat.

Now and then, a family's milk cow would suffer from intestinal colic (spasm) or the animal had *ishek tuenipkalde*, meaning its intestines had knotted, and the animal would lie down in a death-like trance with its eyes wide open. The one remedy for such an ailment, if diagnosed correctly, was to scorch the area with a red hot branding-iron, with several men holding down the animal. That usually worked. As soon as the "knot" was "untied", the animal got up on its feet and went around as though nothing had happened.

Most privately-owned milk cows were taken to a cowherd after the morning's milking, to be taken out to pasture, for a few yuan a month. To save money, a few families just let their cows wander around the town during the day, picking up what they could on the streets. Discarded cardboard boxes in the Commercial Bureau courtyard and the backdoor of the department store, the hardware store, and other stores were a source of food for these wandering cows because the cardboard was made from pulped hay and pasted together with gruel. But devouring discarded packaging proved to be suicidal for the animals because they also swallowed the staples that held the boxes together. These animals eventually died a lingering death from starvation. After their stomachs were cleaned out, fistful of staples were found in them. However, if discovered earlier, a probe with a piece of magnet on the end would be inserted into the cow's stomach through the mouth, and usually whatever staples or small pieces of wire that were in the stomach could be extracted.

The Petroleum Station had some surplus oil drums to sell to their employees for next-to-nothing, and we bought two and opened them and smeared the inside with hot pitch, after we had cleaned them out and burned what residue oil there was inside. We used these oil drums as containers for water. Sometimes when the water appeared in the winding ditches on the nearby hillside, we would fill each pot and pan we had because it beat going all the way to the river. Sometimes the water would run all day and the hillside would be dotted with women from the neighborhood doing their laundry there. Coming from Shanghai, I did not know how to carry things on a shoulder pole like all of my neighbors could. We had two buckets and I would carry one with each hand. It wasn't until after my second child was born in September 1968 that I learned to use a shoulder pole and became quite good at it. At first I could not balance and walked from side to side, following the weight instead of controlling it. There were many painful lessons of walking on icy ground with a bucketful of water on either end of a shoulder pole, and whoops, slipping and landing on my seat, upsetting the two buckets of water, making the ground all the more slippery, and having to make the trip to the river once again. I think the tread on the bottom of my shoes were too worn out and made it that much harder to walk on slippery ground, especially uphill with a load. It took some practice to keep the water from spilling from the buckets as I walked. I would leave the river with two full buckets, and by the time I got home, at least one-fourth would be spilled. In the winter, the river was frozen and holes were made here and there for people to get water. It was especially slippery near the holes and being inexperienced, I never went to the river alone but always with one of Sonya's girls.

Abdulreyim-aka, who lived up the hill a little further from us, was the water man who drove an ox cart with two big oil drums lying side by side, each with a square opening on top and a short stretch of bicycle inner tube attached to where the cap should have been. He went to the river every day to cart water and to supply the families in the courtyard of the company he worked for, the Foodstuff Company. Sometimes he would make an extra trip to the river after he had completed his daily round and would come back with enough water for himself and some to spare for Sonya's family and I. Abdulreyim-aka was in his eighties and still in reasonably good health when I visited him July, 1994 in Altai. Amina-atcha, his wife, had died a few years prior to that. He told me that most friends his age and younger have already passed away and that his having engaged in physical labor all his life accounted for his durability. He was living with his adopted daughter, Rahiman, and her family. I went to Altai again in 2005, and wanted to visit him but his neighbors told me he had passed away.

Like Burqin and Beitun, Altai was very cold and the winters were also very long. But unlike either of those places, each flake of snow that fell stayed on the ground because there was no wind to blow it away. Altai was surrounded by hills and had little wind. Here, all Christmases were white. We needed wooden shovels for snow which could be more than a foot deep. The early snow had to be cleared from our roof otherwise it would leak. But as the temperature dropped, the snow was left on it for insulation. By spring, the snow on the roof would be compacted into ice crystals, and it served as a source of water for washing and cleaning. We needed to clear a path to walk on, especially a path to the outhouse down the hill. My husband picked up some discarded iron rods from the company's garage and soldered it to make a *chana* (sled) with a few pieces of board on top. The girls with their brother and I with my son, would take our *chanas* and walk up sideways to the top of the hill near Abdulreyim-aka's place and then slide all the way downhill, and repeat the trip over and over again until we were tired. That was our recreation. On a fine day after a snowfall, Altai, was absolutely beautiful with clear blue skies and crisp air.

Even though all non-Han families used rugs either for hanging on the walls, or laid on top of their *sak*, a wooden platform, usually half the size of the room, there was no need for a vacuum cleaner for the rugs. Instead of being beaten to rid them of dust and dirt in the other seasons, in the winter they needed only to be taken out by four people each holding onto one of the four corners, or by more people holding along the edges, depending on the size of the rugs, and beaten on the snow, one-two-three bam in unison, and changing round until the rug was spotlessly clean and with its design left on the snow where the rug had hit. Altai had no dry cleaners either, people snow-cleaned their winter clothes as they did their rugs. But there was no pollution except for the smoke coming from chimneys of homes. The sky was a beautiful blue, reminding me of the Irving Berlin song "Blue Skies."

Blue skies, smiling at me, nothing but blue skies do I see.
Blue birds, singing a song, nothing but blue birds all day long.

At night, the sky was even more beautiful. It was like a canopy made of dark blue velvet with huge, big, sparkling diamonds pinned on it. And they seemed to be within reach. The night air was cold and crisp, and breathing deeply would actually hurt because the air was so icy cold.

The skies were blue, but politically speaking, in the late 1960s, storm clouds were gathering. Letters from home were getting fewer and their contents were vaguer, and eventually the few that came said nothing at all. Pamphlets of every kind were being passed around, some in secret, others openly. They told of so-and-so, usually a high-ranking government official, being a what-and-what in no uncertain terms, and yet if the information in these pamphlets were true, why did the news not appear in the newspapers or on the air waves? All we could get on the radio were the eight modern Peking operas, otherwise known as *yangbanxi*, supposedly put up by Jiang Qing, wife of Chairman Mao.

Sometime after that, we also read pamphlets sent to me from my brother which provided some negative news of this woman. Something clicked inside my head. I remember not long after Liberation in 1949, a new girl had entered our class at school. She was cross-eyed and spoke no Cantonese, but she was especially eager to be friends with the rest of the class, most of whom were Cantonese-speaking. She told us that she had been in the movies. We didn't believe her. Then she said it was a bit part in the Chinese film *San Mao*, as one of the beggars who pushed a pedicab up Sichuan Road Bridge, and that her face had been smeared with soot. She told us that she had a secret she wanted to share with us. Her aunt, a pretty movie star named Shangguan Yunzhu, knew Chairman Mao's wife as the "Rotten Apple". (SY committed suicide during the Cultural Revolution). Now and then, a letter from home would hint at someone being "taken in" in a round-about way. Letters were brief, but I think more could be gotten from them between the lines than the actual written words. I think white terror was reigning all over China at that time. I was equally cautious in my occasional short letters home.

Being a *semiya haten*, literally a "housewife" I was not obliged to attend any political study sessions, but I noticed that my husband's political study sessions were lasting longer and longer. But whenever I asked him what was being studied, he would just answer vaguely and seemed unwilling to talk. I did not press. My husband's boss was a sourpuss even though his name was "Always Happy." He was bespectacled with beer-bottle-bottom lenses. Before long, a clear demarcation appeared between the people, they were divided into what amounted to the "loyalists" and the "rebels". People who held opposite views did not hide the fact. There also appeared a third group which straddled the wall; they were not well thought-of. After some observation, we developed our own opinions concerning the three groups and discovered that the people that we had gotten along with were nearly one and all members of the second group, the 'rebels'. Our sympathies sided with them because they were definitely the weaker group. The stronger group wanted to keep the status quo and had the means to do it. It seemed to be the trend then to "belong" to one of the groups or one would be considered "worthy of suspicion". We identified ourselves with the second group but discovered that we were not "good enough" to be accepted as its members, which later proved to be a plus for us when it turned out that all the groups diverged from their original principles and took to arms.

Not being "good enough" literally meant that we were under suspicion. Why, we were not sure. By this time there were posters appearing all over the streets, some with mug shots of former top government officials who were beaten black and blue and made to look worse than anyone on a "Wanted" list. We did not know what to believe because Beijing was so far away. There was a yawning gap between what we saw around us and what we heard over the radio. Later on, that difference was switched - what we saw on TV and what we heard around us. "Sourpuss" was a zealous loyalist as was nearly everyone else in my husband's office except for a few "oddballs". My husband, not being a member of any faction, worked all the more diligently, as those belonging to the factions were busy 'making revolution' during office hours and nearly all the work was left to him, as the company still had to function, if only minimally. The slogan then was "stop production to engage in revolution" but not being a member of any one group, there was no "revolution" for him to engage in, and "production" had to go on.

In the winter of 1966, employees from the different companies of Altai were "selected" to participate in the "Socialist Education Movement". My husband was dispatched to a remote commune in *Kaba* (Habahe) in the winter. The first leg of the journey was by truck, and the second leg was by horse-drawn *chana* (sleigh). I still can't quite understand what that movement was about and who benefited from it. To those who were sent, it was a sign that something was "wrong" with them. The authorities of the places to which they were being sent got the signal. But, thank goodness, the time that he was sent was "right", as in the countryside, even the remotest countryside, the local authorities were paralyzed due to the upheaval that was spreading through the country. Having these people on their hands was a burden as food and housing had to be found for them, and the local authorities, who were not functioning in their former capacities, wanted as little responsibility on their hands as possible. So after a couple of months, my husband and those like him were "returned" to Altai.

The first leg of the return journey back was by *chana*, made in 35-degree-below-zero (Celsius) weather, so that to keep from freezing even with his long sheepskin *tohn* on, he had to get off and walk beside the *chana* until he was too tired and get on again for a short ride, and then get off to walk again just to keep his blood circulating and to keep awake. His luggage (bedding) was on the *chana* so it had to take him to the place where he could catch a truck to ride back to Altai. He came back to say that Kaba was a much poorer and colder place than Altai, and that we should be grateful that we had not been sent there. By this time, we had begun to compare ourselves to people less "lucky" than we were, as a source of comfort.

While my husband was away in Kaba, a Cantonese woman with whom I had gotten acquainted, and who worked in the local department store behind the counter where knitting yarn was sold, asked me one day if I could knit, seeing that I was from Shanghai, and as it was known that many Shanghai women were good knitters. I told her that I could. She remarked that the local Geology Division had a lot of field workers who come to buy yarn and requested that she find someone to knit sweaters, vests, and pants for them. I told her that I would be glad to take on whatever knitting there was. Well, such a thing could not be done just like that, it had to go through the "housewives organization". If they approved of my doing it, I could, and they would deduct what amounted to 15% of the income for their permission. It turned out that there were also other women who wanted to earn some money, but since we were paid by the piece, it was fine with me. I only had myself and my boy to take care of, I would make one big pot of gruel and heat it up for every meal until it was finished and then make another pot. All the rest of my time was spent in knitting as much as I could, as fast as I could. I sat up night after night doing my knitting and devised my own patterns for vests. After the first batch was finished, more requests came in. I was actually earning money, however modest the sum was. Hurray for me!

Early in 1968, I discovered that I was pregnant the second time. I had been in bad health since the birth of our boy in 1962, and did not conceive even though no precautions were taken, since none was available. I had taken it for granted that that was it, I was unable to have children anymore. I was relieved by this fact because we were very poor, and especially since having grown up in a poor family myself, I knew what deprivations would be in store if I had more children. So when I found I was pregnant, I wanted to have an abortion because I knew there was no way we could afford another child. Having come from a poor family of five children, I am convinced that it is humane that parents should not have more children than they can support.

There was no family planning in 1968 as there is now. Any couple with only one child who wanted an abortion needed to have written permission from the boss before the hospitals were willing to perform the operation. That meant we had to have permission from Sourpuss. I was indignant and refused to bend that low to ask for his permission even though the person who would apply for that permission would be my husband. Still, I was the one concerned, and why should he have a say over me. He was not my boss, and he clearly looked down on me, like most of the people in the office did. My husband left the final decision up to me. He said he could see no harm in having another child, especially if it were a girl. He was convinced that since our needs were very modest, we could afford it. Altai was a healthy place even though our circumstances were still relatively harsh. I racked my brains to come to a decision because the political climate was so unstable then and what if my husband was to go through what my father had gone through and was still going through? What if something happened to him? What was I to do with no job and two small children to support?? Even though my reasoning told me that it was best not to have another child, I just could not submit my husband to the indignity of asking Sourpuss for the written permission for an abortion. I decided to go through with the pregnancy and then have a sterilization right after birth. I stuck to that decision, and have never regretted it. I did not think I could survive another birth, and what was most important was that I felt it inhumane to have more children than we can afford. On September 10, 1968, the day that the Xinjiang Revolutionary Committee was established, my daughter was born at the No.16 Army Hospital in Altai (my son had been born on May 27, 1962, the 13th anniversary of the Liberation of Shanghai). I remember the "loyalists" had mobilized the herdsmen into town, and the surrounding hillsides were dotted with men on horseback, for what, I didn't know. As we were not members of any faction, we were left very much on our own, and we were careful not to ask questions.

I had an operation the following day.

When my daughter grew up, she became my best friend and confidante, and I could talk to her in a way I could not talk to my son, or even to my husband.

My daughter was born with two teeth right in the middle of her lower gum. Probably as a result of my having drunk too much *irkit* (buttermilk) during my pregnancy, when other food could not be downed. Her teeth raised a stir in the hospital as the doctors claimed that they had never heard of, nor seen, a child being born with teeth, two fully grown ones at that. A Han neighbor, an old lady, advised us that it was an ominous sign. If born with one tooth, one parent would die, and two meant both would. I was in no way superstitious, but was scared by what she said since the Cultural Revolution was going on and I could see, and heard of, a lot of lawlessness in Altai. It would not surprise me if one of us, or both of us, would end up in the soup before long. I was advised to extract the two teeth, but just couldn't bring myself to do it.

After my daughter's birth, I had double vision for a while. If I used both eyes I would see double, or overlapping pictures, but if I used only one eye, everything else was fine. It was very uncomfortable to have to go around with one eye closed to keep from stumbling. A month after the baby's birth, I took her back to the No.16 Hospital for the doctors to check on her to see if there was anything abnormal about her, and also to see what was wrong with my vision. Nothing radically wrong was discovered in either of us although I was told to closely monitor the child's growth, and compare her with babies her own age to see if she was bigger, taller, or slower in reflexes. As for my own malady, they said that some nerve must have been damaged, and that if no other symptoms developed, the double vision would go away in time. It did, after some months. And my baby daughter was normal, except for the two full-grown, lower teeth.

We lived on the hilltop and seldom ventured into the streets below. Our grain and cooking oil rations, and tea for the month was bought right after pay day. Those were the most important items of expense. Our diet was very Kazakh, and has remained so even to this very day. For breakfast we have milk tea and bread. Instead of baking bread in a "*tonnir*" like the Kazakh and Uygur did, we either steamed or baked bread in a flat cast iron pan, or in an old cookie tin buried in the hot ashes of burning chips. Sonya's girls fought to baby-sit my daughter, which was fine with me as that gave me time to either pick my chips or do my knitting. With an extra child, I could feel the pinch of poverty much more keenly than I did with only one child. But physical deprivation was easy to bear since I had grown up in anything but luxury. It was emotional deprivation that was hard to tolerate.

We were in a daze at what surrounded us. So much was

happening, so many people were put through "struggle sessions", paraded on the streets. Some were maimed or killed, or committed suicide out of fear over the uncertainty of where it would all lead to, when it would end, or whether we would one day be the targets of persecution ourselves. Hostility among neighbors was surfacing. Except for the relationship between us and Sonya's family, there was no one we could trust. Most of our neighbors were very zealous 'loyalists', and the one or two who were 'rebels' were under control and going through a hard time. Since we belonged to neither faction and were, more or less, on the same footing as Ashat, a member of the Black Gang, our two families were in the same boat.

Since coming to Altai in June, 1966, almost ten years to the day after we had left Shanghai as volunteers, my husband had worked in the Business Department of the Petroleum Company and was about the only person who did not "stop production to engage in revolution" when it was fashionable to do so. For a time, he ran the company almost single-handedly, looking after the office, the petrol station, and the coal business which had come under the management of the petroleum company. He knew the whole petroleum supply system of the Altai Prefecture, the capacity of the petroleum stations in each of the seven counties of Altai: Burqin, Beitun, Burultokay, Kaba, Jimenay, and Chingil inside out as he had visited each one and, being in the Business Department of the company, had all the necessary figures.

Sourpuss and his gang of lackeys - one of whom had a name containing a word with the same sound as "sugar" but actually he was cyanide - decided that my husband knew too much. Li (HL), the radical watchman from Beitun, had made a special trip to Altai to "denounce" us to the authorities, claiming that he and his wife heard us listening to "enemy radio" and that I "wore a pair of headphones even during the day". (I did wear a blue plastic band on my head to keep my hair in place). My husband had all the figures he needed to "tell the enemy" the exact location and content volume of each oil storage tank in the Prefecture and he had a radio and an operator (me) to transmit the messages.

That was exactly what Sourpuss and his gang needed to relieve my husband of his work. His one-man job was divided among eight people (!!), and I don't think those who got the jobs were happy about it. The work was light enough, but still they had to work whereas prior to that all they needed to do was report to the office on time, and loll around the rest of the day, often times wandering here and there to enjoy a "struggle session" that was going on somewhere, having a go at the victim or victims with the clubs they had fixed to their belts, or huddle in one of the sessions to devise ways and means of torturing their next victim, or compiling a list of future victims.

The Army Propaganda Team was stationed in the Commercial Bureau under which the Petroleum Company and other companies operated and the loyalists were that much more active as a result. Outrageous and obscene tales floated around town about MLS, the local Army Head, so many in fact that I decided those in the opposition were responsible for most of the rumors and the tales lost much of their credibility. Then again, the saying of "no waves without a wind" left some of the doubt. The fact that the head of the Army Propaganda Team often had his meals with a single lady who someone nicknamed "crooked neck" because of her physical deformity, supported the rumors to a certain extent. In Chinese we have the saying that "if the upper beam is not straight, then the lower beam will be crooked" which literally means that if a superior is not as exemplary as he should be, than subordinates follow suit because the superior had set the precedent.

The following years showed that anyone who abused the power that came with his position usually had a "backstage boss" who, perhaps unknowingly, empowered his subordinate to walk in his footsteps. To do bad things one needed "backing" or "capital" and the best capital to have during the Cultural Revolution was the possession of the "three steel plates" - membership in the Communist Party, service in the armed forces, and being of poor, lower-middle peasant origin.

Sourpuss's chief lackey, Cyanide, had the needed steel plates, and he, in turn, hand-picked his own lackeys. The most evil one was SKM, a workman at the petrol station, who spent his days wandering about town looking for "struggle sessions" where he could lash out with his club at the victims, mostly people he did not know. SKM was a *mangliu* (drifter) from somewhere in Shandong Province. Another lackey was CL, also a mangliu, but from Henan Province. Before my husband was relieved of his duties, these two men worked at loading and unloading oil drums at the petrol station and my husband, even though he was supposed to be an office clerk (cadre), joined them in their work whenever he was up there, and they had gotten along.

By this time, it was clear that Burhan Shahidi was one of the chief targets of attack of the Cultural Revolution in Xinjiang although he and his family had been living in Beijing since 1955. That he was accused of having pro-Soviet sentiments, among other things, was unbelievable. It had been him, and no one else, who had prevented Ashat and family, and countless other families, from leaving for the Soviet Union in 1962 when so many families in the Altai, Gulja, and Tarbagatay Prefectures crossed over, legally or illegally. As for his being accused of having "Splittist sentiments", that was yet another laughable falsehood. Wasn't he one of the key figures who had engineered the peaceful liberation of Xinjiang? The accusations against him held no water, but then, nothing in the Cultural Revolution was waterproof. All those related to him were in for a bad time. That the Beijing authorities allowed the old man, who was then in his late sixties or early seventies, to be dragged back to Xinjiang and jailed, clearly proved that either they were in cahoots with the Xinjiang "baddies" or else there was no authority existing in Beijing at that time. The fact that he was jailed about as many years pre-Liberation during the rule of Shen Shicai as post-Liberation under Communist rule during the Cultural Revolution may be a mere coincidence, but it is ironic nonetheless.

Life for Ashat and family, and all those who were related to BS one way or another, was anything but easy. Poor Ashat was accused and questioned, and accused and questioned over and over again, beaten and tortured, but he could supply no information. Here was someone who was hardly educated and had never had a better job than a gofer even though he could claim to be twice related to Burhan.

Not long after Burhan was taken from Beijing to Xinjiang and jailed, his wife, Rashide, was also taken back from Beijing and jailed. His children, three daughters and a son, were all in different parts of China for "re-education" being children of such big targets. Even youths with good family backgrounds had to go through "re-education" away from their hometown.

BS was not released until the late '70s. His wife suffered a very serious nervous breakdown and was for a time considered mentally disturbed. Somehow, news of her aimlessly roaming the streets of Urumqi, scavenging, and in doubtful health reached Beijing and it is said it was Premier Zhou Enlai who sent someone to get her back to Beijing for medical care. After BS was released, he stayed in his Urumqi home for a short time to recuperate before returning to his family in Beijing. By then he was already in his late seventies.

There were different tales circulating about his imprisonment in Urumqi. After he was released, many old people who had known him all along beat a path to his house to see him. He lived more than a dozen years after his release from jail and died in the summer of 1989. The name BS was only known to the young people of that time as a Cultural Revolution target. It was said that one jail warden delighted in making life miserable for the old man and would then go home and boast to his father of what he had done to that "bad old guy'. One day, his father asked him who the "bad old guy" was, and the son said it was one of the people in the slogan that everyone had been shouting since the Cultural Revolution, "Down with WLZBY". The bad old guy was "B" in the slogan. His father jumped to his feet, took his son by the scruff of his neck and threatened to deal with him personally if he dared to touch the old man again. In those days, many young people were involved in torturing the old cadres who were imprisoned, and many of them moved on to positions in different levels of leadership. I hope they will do all they can to prevent another Cultural Revolution from taking place as I am sure that if it does, they would be the victims next time around.

Ashat's two eldest daughters also had to leave their parents for "re-education" in a very remote commune in Burqin. Some of those with them were also offspring of other Black Gang members. Fortunately, the two sisters were allocated to the same production team at the same commune so they could help protect each other. Other classmates and friends of theirs were not so lucky. Sometimes a girl was dispatched to an unheard of production team out in the middle of nowhere, and her fate was sealed.

One girl, I saw as the local "Audrey Hepburn" because she was a doe-eyed beauty with black hair and fair skin. She was a tall girl of over 1.7 meters, and carried herself well. She had a certain elegance about her that made her stand out from the rest of the girls in the town. Her parents had crossed the border in 1962 along with so many other families, but her grandmother, who must have been a beauty in her own right in her youth, kept her behind. This girl, K, was very spoiled by her grandmother, but she was also sent to a very remote village and soon we heard that she was pregnant and married into a local shepherd family. She took to drinking and smoking and aged before her time. Later whenever I had the chance, I asked people from Altai for news of her, they all told me that I would not recognize her now even if I met her face to face. She had turned into a typical old woman smoking hand-rolled cigarettes the size of cigars, and could drink any man under the table. She had several sons, one of whom was studying in a college in Urumqi. Pictures of him reveal strong traces of his mother's youth-time beauty which made him all the more handsome. I was also told that his mother was especially strict with him, which partially accounted for his diligence at study. I think K wanted to relive her lost youth through her son who looked so much like her.

Just how many Ks lost their youth in the Cultural Revolution is anybody's guess. Many city girls married local peasants as a source of protection from sexual harassment, or worse still, because of it. When the Cultural Revolution finally ended and their parents rehabilitated, many were allowed to go back to where they had come from, but not if they had married and had children. They had little in common with the husband and had married often unwillingly because of sexual harassment, or to seek protection. Or else the family of the husband did not allow the girl to return to the city. Some families persuaded their daughters to divorce their husbands, and other families bought off the peasant family by offering a handsome sum with the back-pay they had received for their years in jail, but more often than not, the couples stayed together, if awkwardly.

The same happened to male offspring of the Cultural Revolution victims. The young men married village girls who were often illiterate or under-educated and had children. There was much cleaning up to do after that, and who knows how many such families were broken up after the holocaust was over? The lucky ones were those people who held out, stayed single and remained uncommitted. The tragedy these people went through was actually a repetition of what had taken place after the Anti-Rightist Movement in the 1950s when intellectuals, single university students or teachers of the sciences and liberal arts were exiled to the remote countryside as punishment for their outspokenness during that political movement. These people, mostly men, were in the prime of their life, and some married local peasant girls from families who were kind to them, thinking that they would be condemned to live in the countryside for the rest of their lives. Less than twenty years later, when the Cultural Revolution was over, these men, by now in their forties and fifties, were recruited from the remote places to return to their former schools or were assigned to schools elsewhere which were in dire need of teachers. They found that they were useful once more, but their spouses felt very out-of-place in the new environment.

There were also some couples who "divorced" for the sake of their child or children's future when one spouse, usually the male, was labeled a rightist in that anti-rightist movement of the late 1950s. Not all such divorces were real ones, some were just on paper with the mutual understanding that each would remain single until the times changed, and that the move was necessary only for the sake of the children who would otherwise suffer needlessly, deprived of a chance of a better, or higher education. Such couples, if they lived to see the day of rehabilitation, were united once again, in their fifties. It just absolutely cannot be that the highest authorities were not aware of such tragedies taking place all over the country, especially among the intellectuals, and yet little was done to alleviate all that uncalled-for suffering. Physical pain is so much easier to endure and recover from than that which is inflicted on the heart, which can sometimes be fatal, What is lost can never to be recovered and the victim is left permanently scarred.

Very early in 1970 when the Cultural Revolution was going on full-steam, a so-called "Yida Sanfan" (one hit, three against) movement began. My husband's political study sessions were getting to be more frequent and lasted much longer, often into the night, and with it he became more silent than ever before. I could sense something was wrong, but didn't know what, since he would not talk. I was scared because someone we knew, ZZQ, had gone home and hanged himself after a political study session in which he witnessed how Ashat was beaten up. He left behind a wife, a son who was a classmate of my son's, and a daughter. ZZQ had been forced to witness how Ashat had been strung up with his arms behind his back and beaten, and he was scared that he would have to go through the same thing himself, as clearly he was one of the candidates in line. After he died, he was dragged out to the slaughterhouse for pigs near our hill, and buried there.

When the "mangliu" adobe brick-makers heard about the nearby burial, they raised a rumpus saying the ghost of anyone that died from suicide will haunt the surrounding neighborhood, and insisted that the body be dug up and taken to the Chinese cemetery. "Manglius", ordinarily looked down upon by people who were not "manglius", were socially elevated when they sided with the "loyalists", and so Ashat and other Black Gang members were ordered to dig up the body and put it on a plank.

Four people carried it to the Chinese cemetery, doused it with gasoline and burnt it, with the widow and two children watching. No one was ever held responsible for this death because it was a suicide. As for what led to it, no inquiries were ever made even after the Cultural Revolution was over.

One evening when my husband's arrival home was several hours overdue and I was getting very nervous when CL came in and said that he needed my husband's bedding as he had to be detained to "clarify some matters". That was another way of saying that my husband was being prevented from coming home. He was being detained and confined in his office. I asked CL what would be done about his three meals a day, and he said that he would eat at the company dining-hall and that I needn't worry about it. I had been dreading all along that one day he would be taken, and now that dread became reality. Didn't my own father go through the same thing in the 1950s, and going through it again? It was like a coming-of-age ritual for some men.

I was to learn later that my father was again taken during the Cultural Revolution even though he was forcefully retired just prior to it. One day he had gone to work as usual, and in less than an hour, he was back, with a big red paper flower pinned to his chest, and a group of people banging on drums and cymbals and blowing horns had sent him back with a banner which said "Honorably Retired". He was too dazed to react, and accepted his unexpected retirement unquestioningly as he had accepted so many other indignities in the past. That he would be dragged back to be confined in his office after being 'honorably retired' was a total shock to him and to the family. His being in isolation affected us in that it meant I was from a suspicious background, otherwise why would my father be confined? Another ground for suspicion was that both Dr Tu and Chum were also in isolation. Correspondence with her and with Auntie Ellie stopped as soon as I sensed the political climate was worsening. I had no news from home or anyone, and no news was good news, or so I had thought. Happy thinking!

I was now also required to participate in political study sessions each afternoon, in a group with other housewives, 95% of whom were illiterate, or semi-literate. The group was headed by a short, wrinkled old man, an old "mangliu" from Shandong Province who had two sons, both truck drivers and both very zealous "loyalists". This Old Man Geng, someone I had never laid eyes on before, was very "progressive" and took it upon himself to "expose" me to the rest of the group. His accusations amounted to the charge that I was a spy. I did not know whether to cry out in indignation at what he accused me of or to laugh at the absurdity of what he had to say. I was now clearly a target among the housewives, and there was no sense in "troubling" any neighbor to care for my children in the afternoons when I had to attend these sessions. My son was left together with Sonya's son at home, and I carried my daughter on my back with a home-made Cantonese "*Meh-dai*" (baby-carrying belt) to attend the daily afternoon struggle sessions. It was late winter and early spring and the ground thawed at noon but froze again when the sun did not shine on it, and it was very slippery to walk down or back up the hill to where we lived.

Not having my husband at home was bad enough. But now I also had to go to the river for water at least once a day, do the cooking, care for the children, worry about my husband, and now these sessions to attend and my "material" to write every day, and not knowing if I would return in one piece after the sessions. It was nothing uncommon to have people go into these so-called political study sessions "vertical" and leave "horizontal." It was very hard on the nerves because they were being so badly strained. I had a feeling that I was soon going to snap. The afternoon "struggle session" was just the time for the baby's nap, and she usually slept right through them. One housewife barked that I had taken the child along for protection because with her on my back I would think that they would not dare to hit me. I was told to put her down, and I did. I let her lie on a wooden plank on the cement ground in one corner of the room while the session was in progress and she always slept through them. She was about eighteen months old then. After each session, I was told to write down my history, so that meant working late into the night after the children were asleep.

Whether what I wrote was ever thoroughly read, I cannot tell. But judging by the fact that they kept asking the same questions over and over again when the answers were already clearly written down, told me that nobody seriously read what I had written. I guess that if there had been copy machines then, and if I could have afforded it, I could have made a stack of copies of what I had written and handed one in each day instead of going through to the trouble of writing it all out every single day.

A typical afternoon session was always pre-orchestrated, just as the sessions of the anti-rightist movement in 1959 had been. The only difference was that the people then had not been so physical. As one Cantonese saying has it, "Gentlemen move their mouths, and not hands, but when thugs move their hands, they become fists." Well, it was now the 1970s, and "gentlemen" or "gentlewomen" were extinct. Those who remained, the ones who were lucky enough not to be targets in political movements, became bystanders or thugs. And if they were the latter, they would lash out at those whom they knew nothing about except what they had been told by official sources.

A typical 'struggle session' would have me in the middle of a room, surrounded by women, many of whom were former neighbors or nodding acquaintances, and I would be told to kneel down and confess my "crimes" in front of a poster of Chairman Mao. The women would all begin to move behind me before they got physical so I would not see exactly who were the ones that hit me. But they themselves knew who did and who did not. One day during a session, the Petroleum Company thug, a lackey of Cyanide I will call SKM, grabbed me by my neck and a piece of the cloth jacket that I wore came off in his hands, which no doubt surprised him, and that kept him from getting any rougher with me. My seamy old jacket saved me from what would have been a bad roughing-up.

Once, during a session, I had remarked that beating up a person did not solve problems, I said that I would never do that, and that even if Chiang Kai-Shek were standing in front of me, I would not move a finger against him, because hitting him would not change him. To save my hide, I could admit to everything I was accused of, but how could I prove to them that I was actually what they accused me of being, and would they believe me if I admitted to everything they said I was? Did they really think I was really that "clever", even though I had secretly wished that I were? A CIA spy because of some letters sent and received from overseas? A potential member of the East Turkestan Clique just because I could speak some Uyghur and Kazakh, and got on better with my non-Han neighbors than those of my own kind? That started another round of name-calling and finger-pointing, in addition to my having said that I "would not move a finger against Chiang Kai-Shek"! It really was a case of damned if you do, and damned if you don't. Sometimes I had difficulty in deciding whether the people struggling me were pitiful or just plain laughable.

Several days passed and still my husband did not return. Instead, his colleagues came and poked under our bed, looking for what, I did not know and they did not say. My clumsy transistor radio was taken apart by someone who later became my husband's boss. Nothing unusual was found and they put it back together again. Then two Shanghai female colleagues of my husband came. Nearly every single Shanghai girl who had come to Altai in 1954 later married northerners years older than themselves who had been previously married to wives in the countryside, instead of marrying fellow Shanghai males around their own age. I guess people around their own age earned too little, like my husband. These Shanghai women had always looked down on me because I was unemployed, and because I spent all my spare time picking cow chips, carrying water, doing knitting for next to nothing, and mixing with members of the Black Gang. They came to ask me to confess and write down what was wrong so that my husband could return home earlier. I was at a loss. What was there to confess to, what was there to write? They said that there was nothing wrong with him, and that he was detained simply because of my problems. But what problems were they??

Another day passed and a soldier came with CL to tell me that from now on I should take my husband three meals a day because he 'refused' to go to the dining-hall for his meals, whereas the truth was that he was not allowed to. They said that I should also take the children along when I took him the first meal because he missed them very much and wanted to see them.

I did as instructed. I made a bowl of soup noodles in an enamel pot with a handle, and with my daughter on my back I set off, one hand holding the pot containing the hot noodles wrapped in a baby's blanket to keep it from getting cold plus a piece of bread and a pair of chopsticks, and the other hand holding onto my son. We made our way down the slippery hill to the courtyard of the Commercial Bureau where my husband was confined. A PLA soldier at the gate refused to let us in, instead he took the pot of noodles and stirred it thoroughly with the chopsticks, and broke the piece of bread to see if there was anything inside it, and told us to go back and that he would give my husband the food, which by then was cold. I was under so much pressure that I was tempted to lash out at the soldier right there and then, but I controlled myself just in time. After all, I think he was just acting according to orders from his officer.

I was called to attend an outdoor meeting in which many people, especially one by the name of ZFL, were being denounced. I went with my daughter on my back and sat several rows behind where my husband was sitting. I let her down and pointed her father out to her and asked her to walk to him. She was about eighteen months old and could toddle along. She recognized him and went to him. He looked at her for a while and told her to go back without turning around to see where I was sitting. It was very painful, perhaps more for him than for me. I still cry when I think about it.

ZFL, one of the targets to be denounced, was taken by his armpits and dragged onto the stage. He had been beaten black and blue, and was being accused of "playing the dead dog" by refusing to walk on stage. It was later revealed that his kneecaps had been smashed by his torturers so that it was impossible for him to stand up. The people standing nearer by the platform could see that he had left behind a trail of blood where he was being dragged and that his legs from the knees down were twisted in an unnatural way. I can't remember what he had been accused of, and only knew him as someone who had worked for the Foodstuff Company. His crime was that he had been an active member of the rebel faction. A day or two later, word got out that he had committed suicide by hammering a rusty nail into his own head'. Just how many people believed that crap, I will never know. He was wrapped up in old cardboard boxes and dragged out and buried. As far as I know, no one was ever punished for torturing him to death because it was a 'collective effort'. He left behind a wife and several children.

Following that, another person from the Prefectural Construction Company, a man known as 'Big Neck' Sun as he had a very prominent goiter, hanged himself in an empty room in a warehouse a few dozen yards from where we lived that was used to store matches. He was accidentally discovered by someone who crept into the warehouse hoping to steal some rafters. There was news of yet another person who worked in a lumberyard who committed suicide by cutting himself in half by putting his head against an electrically operated saw. One horror tale after another had me imagining the worst that could happen to my husband and I. To be killed was one thing, to be maimed for life was quite another. My husband was our family's only breadwinner and if something happened to him, my children and I would be left high and dry. On the other hand, if something happened to me and not my husband, the children would still have a livelihood. I had to do something about that quickly, before it was too late.

I decided that I would go to the Army Propaganda Team leader himself and have it out. I was desperate. I went that very afternoon and plunked myself down in front of a man known as Soong Duizhang (Team-leader Soong), and had my say regardless of whatever consequences it would bring. I just could not contain myself any longer because of all the emotional pressure that I had been bearing up until that moment.

I ranted and I raved that my husband did not understand English and that he could not have known what I had written in my 'overseas correspondence' and could not offer an explanation on my behalf. Detaining him any longer would not help, I said, and I should be the one to be detained. And I am willing to be detained, I said, provided that he find a family or a place that would take my two children, because it would then not be possible for me to care for them, take food to my husband, write my history over and over again, attend 'struggle sessions', carry water from the river, gather cow chips, and cook. Provide evidence, I shouted, for all they were accusing my husband of knowing about me. If I deserved a jail sentence, I was there for them. But detaining only my husband meant that they were afraid of me, otherwise why didn't they come straight for me instead? Wasn't I the one that was causing all the "trouble"? Here I am, I screamed, lock me up!

I guess I must have been beside myself as I cried and shouted at the same time. I called him a coward and shamed him for being in that uniform because all he and his men did was to smear the image of the PLA. I told him that I had met better PLAs, and in my limited lifetime, had not even seen a KMT (Nationalist) soldier worse than him. I was beside myself, and could not stop ranting. I wanted to goad him into jailing me so that I could have a fair hearing. Or so I had thought.

After I eventually cooled down, I was ready for the worst consequences of my outburst. But nothing happened. I was told to go home and think things over, write an apology for my behavior, and wait. I did think things over but wrote no apology, and waited. Nothing happened.

The next morning, my husband came home carrying his roll of bedding. He came in and sat down glumly. I asked him how he had been treated, and at first he kept silent, then after a while said it had been okay. From that day on, both of us had to attend afternoon meetings and neither of us could go anywhere without permission from one of the people from the "loyalist" faction, except for him going to work and both of us attending those meetings. One day, my baby daughter was running a fever, and I had to take her to the *Chipakhan* county hospital on *Besinji Kurshur*, but I had to first ask permission from people in my husband's office. I went there but could not find anyone who could give me the needed permission as they were all involved in "stop production to engage in revolution" activities elsewhere in town. I was frantic. Without thinking twice, I went directly to the hospital and had the child seen to and then returned home. The pressure I was under and the fear was huge, but no one questioned me about not asking for the needed permission to take the child to the doctors, and I did not make up for it afterwards.

Before the PLA Propaganda Team had arrived, the fighting had been between the two factions, loyalists and rebels. The loyalist faction was much the stronger of the two, they were more numerous and had more weapons, and we knew where they got them from. The rebels was more or less in hiding, or on the run. The few that staked it out tried making their own Molotov cocktails and hand grenades, and several people were either killed or permanently maimed in this endeavor. But after the PLA came, the demarcation that had existed between the two factions was blurred. The cards had been reshuffled, as it were, but the animosity between the factions was still there.

The Cultural Revolution not only involved the Han people, but the other ethnic groups as well. There was talk about an East Turkestan Clique and many people from the ethnic groups were arrested. Ashat was questioned on his relationship with us as it was open secret that our two families got along well. By then, I could freely converse in Kazakh, and I had even started to teach myself to read Kazakh because the script, instead of being in the former Arabic, was now in a modernized Latin-based script. I opened my Chinese language and English versions of *Selections of Chairman Mao's Works*, and then the new Kazakh script version and figured out for myself what word was which. With some help from Gulchat, the eldest of Sonya's children, I could recite many sections in Kazakh. The adoption of the new Latin script made the older generation of Kazakhs illiterate overnight, but provided a shortcut for me to learn to read. Kazakh has since reverted to its old Arabic script and I have become illiterate.

Years later, a Kazakh friend told that my ability in learning to speak Kazakh and my interest in the written language had raised many an eyebrow and thus provided new grounds for suspicion that I was indeed a CIA spy. I had no idea what "CIA" was. I had known about the FBI from the many detective stories I had read as a young girl, but having been in Xinjiang since 1956, I knew nothing of the existence of the CIA.

It was also suspected, my Kazakh friend said, that perhaps I was connected to this East Turkestan Clique, or maybe that I had been earmarked to become one of its future officials since I was trilingual. And so on and so forth. In short, I had been completely overestimated by these dumb clucks, and I felt really flattered to have been thought of as someone that important, even though I didn't know anything about that Clique, if there was one. It turned out that many who had been accused of being clique members and jailed were eventually rehabilitated and reinstated in their former jobs.

A lot of rumors were floating around town, and for people like us who had little access to what was really going on, we were always in a state of 'wait and see' as to which rumor would eventually prove to be true.

One rumor persisted which eventually did prove true. One day, an afternoon struggle session turned into a political study session, which was contrary to the normal run of things. It was usually a political session that turned into a struggle session and not the other way around. We were told about the Lin Biao incident. Actually we had heard rumors about it earlier, and because it was so unbelievable, we kept mum about it. News of this nature was usually relayed top-down, one tier at a time, reaching the grassroots when everyone who should know already knew. First, top-down means it was the governmental leadership tier, then the provincial leadership tier, then the prefectural leadership tier, county leadership tier, and the village leadership tier, when finally everyone who was in a leadership capacity knew, then the general public was the last to be informed. But, as is always the case, walls have ears, and when it came time for the masses to know, they already did. Hearing it officially just confirmed that what we had thought were rumors, were not, after all.

Thanks to the Lin Biao Incident, our struggle sessions were terminated. We still had to attend political studies but we were no longer the target of group hatred. To be relieved of the worry of whether one of us would return maimed after a meeting in the afternoon just lifted the dead weight off our hearts, and I found that I could once again breathe normally. Now the big bad egg was not one of our neighbors but Lin Biao, and he was the target of people's verbal wrath. To me that was like directing the anger at the person who had hand-picked him to be successor. We knew nothing more, and believed nothing less than what we were told at meetings. We asked no questions, and attended these meetings as necessary rituals. I was especially careful in my occasional letters home to my parents or my brother, and never dared to mention anything that was remotely connected to the existing political climate as I did not want anyone to answer for anything that I had said. Letters received from home were equally vague. I think we had all learned to read between the lines very well during those years.

Not long after the Lin Biao incident was announced and the

general public was informed of it (when they already knew), and much steam had gone out of the ongoing movement, three movies were shown for the State-owned enterprise employees (the SOEs being the sole employers) of cadre or office worker level. Not the workers. They were shown all three at one sitting, meaning that the viewers took a *mantou* or two along with them, and temporary toilets were set up behind the movie house. The movies shown were "Tora! Tora! Tora!", "Yamamoto" (the Japanese Admiral of the Grand Fleet)", and "The Battle of Midway Island" (Charlton Heston), which was later also shown publicly.

In those days, all movies shown usually were either Chinese or East European or even Soviet ones, and, of course, North Korean.

The Petroleum Company was moving out of the courtyard of the Commercial Bureau to a courtyard in *Chirimtahl* on the slope the opposite end of *Lagir*. We were also moved to that same courtyard to live. In other words, we were moved from one hilltop to another, and *Chirimtahl* was even further away from the river and up a steeper hill. This time we were given an extra room, a big, old coal shed which had been partitioned into living quarters for three families, each with two rooms and a small warehouse right next door to our two rooms where all the spare parts for the company's trucks and Isuzu oil tankers were kept which were in the care of my husband. He was reinstated to his job, although not in his former capacity, but he was equally busy in that he had to look after the oil transporting done by the seven-ton Isuzu tankers and other Jiefang tankers that handled all the oil transporting from Karamai, Dushanzi, and Wangjiagou to Altai.

Leaving my old neighborhood of the past six years or so was not a happy event for me even though we were only moving three small hills away. It was especially hard for my daughter who was then around three years old. Frequent visits back and forth to see our old neighbors were just not the same as being next door to each other.

One day, a girl from our old neighborhood, Lanfen, came to visit, and my daughter hung on to her and refused to let her go. After a lot of promises that she would return to visit us the next day, my daughter finally agreed to loosen her hold on the young lady. A few minutes later when supper was ready, we called for my daughter, but she could not be found. We were frantic. We went into all our neighbors' homes to look for her, but she wasn't there. We went to the outhouse, thinking that she might have gone there with the older girls in the courtyard, but she wasn't there either. We enlisted the help of several neighbors and colleagues to the search for her. There were several abandoned kilns not too far from us, and we were afraid she had dropped into one of them and no one would hear her cry for help. We searched and searched, and asked everyone who passed by if they had seen our girl. No one had.

I then went to Sonya's in our old neighborhood to enlist her girls in the search, and lo and behold, there was my daughter playing in their courtyard! She had stealthily followed Lanfen all the way to our old neighborhood without being discovered. When Sonya had seen her and asked her where her mother was, my daughter told her I was on my way. To her, our old neighborhood with Sonya and family right next to us, was home and very familiar, and now our new surroundings were not as friendly since we were not well-acquainted with our new neighbors. For several months after our move, each time an old neighbor came to visit, saying goodbye for her was like bidding farewell to someone never to be seen again. It was also tearful for the visitor to encounter her sad goodbyes. However, with time, she got over it.

Lin Biao was dead, as he deserved to be. So were several other top people in the Central Government, but rather from persecution. Friction between the different factions had not lessened with the arrival of the PLA. On the contrary, it had gotten worse. But not long after the Lin Biao Incident, the PLA upped and left. The officers of the team were not exemplary in their behavior, and the few soldiers who had shown sympathy to those who were detained in their offices, like my husband, and to those who were the targets for persecution, were soon assigned elsewhere. Without even a send-off, the PLA team quietly departed. It was very unusual. When they had arrived, people were organized and sent out to welcome them with great fanfare, beating of drums and clanging of cymbals, and welcome speeches from each company under the Commercial Bureau being read out. One would have thought that a send-off would be similar. If we had been more informed of the political struggle going on in the government and in the military then, we would have been less surprised at the low-profile departure of the PLA team.

The people who died during the Cultural Revolution whether from torture or suicide, were dead and gone. Of those who survived, some were reinstated in their former jobs and others were transferred to other companies, all within the confines of that one town. For those who were sentenced to serve time in prison, it took longer for them to be cleared. But the sudden dying-down of the Cultural Revolution was good news for the persecuted because it meant the end of isolated detention, and better still, the end of being beaten. For the persecutors, it was altogether another thing. Here they were with their prey trapped, and suddenly they had to let them go.

I think that for some of them there was an ulterior motive in all their persecution, which was power, whatever that stands for. Take Cyanide for an example. Even though he had hardly any education, he did have all the then-required ingredients for becoming a "leading cadre" — poor peasant origin, army veteran, and Party member. These were the three steel plates, considered the "musts" in a desirable male suitor by parents who had daughters of marriageable age. Anyone with those qualifications would be free from persecution. But Cyanide was only semi-literate, having had next to no schooling, so he had been unfit for any work except that of a watchman in the oil storage area of the gas station of the Petroleum Company. Through his active participation in the Cultural Revolution, however, he could be promoted several rungs up the leadership ladder, and he worked very hard at it, at the expense of the suffering of others. His wife was nicknamed "WGM" by the children because she had curly hair and red cheeks, typical of women from Gansu Province, and it was said she was going around saying that one day when her man is sitting in the "first chair" of the Petroleum Company, she would "fix up" the "cadres" one by one. When that big talk reached the ears of Sourpuss, who was in fact the one who occupied the "first chair" of the Company, he was not happy. He was very zealous, but lacked two of the "three steel plates" that Cyanide had. I later visited Altai in the early 1990s and twice encountered "WGM" but we did not exchange greetings. Both she and her husband, among others, had gone out of their way to make life miserable for us and many others during those years, and seeing her again just brought back unpleasant memories. I think both of them, and the other persecutors, felt a sense of "loss" because they had not managed to label us with any tag that would permanently stick. But after that, they still took it out on us in different ways whenever they could.

One day when my husband was out of town on a business trip, Cyanide made it his business to monitor the Kazakh boy, Murat, who delivered water to me. Murat was a little slow because he had had brain surgery in Shanghai for a tumor, and every day he delivered water to the company and to the three families living in the same courtyard. We bought ration tickets for the buckets of water that we would be supplied, and Cyanide took it upon himself to see that Murat did not give me more water than I had given him tickets. How petty can one get? The day that I flared up at him was an especially cold one, and I had asked Murat in for a cup of hot tea. Murat had always been treated like an idiot after his brain surgery which had left a big scar across his scalp, and he had been slow to begin with.

Cyanide waited outside my door while Murat had his tea and warmed himself. And when we came out, Cyanide told me that I could not have more than two buckets of water from Murat a day because if I took more than two buckets, Murat would have to make an extra trip. I blew up. I told Cyanide to mind his own business. I called him all sorts of names that I had been calling him to myself over the past few years, and enumerated all the bad things that he had done to us and to others.

People from the office came out to see what the ruckus was, and for a fleeting moment I felt ashamed of myself for the outburst. But too much had been bottled up inside of me and this man had pricked my balloon, so now I let him have it.

I shamed him for picking on me when my husband was not home. Why couldn't he be a man and pick on someone his own size and sex, I said. His pettiness and meanness were typical of his illiteracy, I charged, and if he had the time to go around looking for people to pick on why couldn't he use the time instead to learn to read and write properly so that he would be fit for the leading position that both he and his wife craved.

I think having the audience of people from the company office encouraged me somehow, but I had taken so much with a bowed head for so long that the eruption was inevitable. He couldn't use his fists on me anymore because the time for struggle sessions was over. And what was more, what I accused him of was what everybody knew him to be. A few of the men from the office tried to pull him away, but he held his ground and wagged his finger at me, saying that he had no time to waste talking to a "woman." I had to laugh. It was his own fault for having too much time to waste, and he was talking to a woman, a woman who was no longer afraid of him or any others of his kind.

He did try to get even with my husband later on. But not everyone who had had a hand in making life miserable for us continued their hostility after my husband was reinstated in the Business Department, in a more lowly position than previously, this time in the transportation section. The company had bought several seven-ton Isuzu oil tankers and someone had to manage them together with the other tankers, a maintenance group consisting of several mechanics and repairmen, and a roomful of spare parts for the vehicles. He was called on to do the job.

Many of the people in the workplace had been very hostile, but most of them had just been going in the direction the baton pointed and did as they had been told to do. It seemed strange to me that my husband did not feel awkward working with them again after how he had been treated. I once asked him about it, and his response was, "Why should I feel awkward when I had done them no wrong?"

One day, my husband bought a piece of sheet iron for 8 yuan to make an oven. A ready-made oven (*dohofka*) of the same material would have cost around 15 yuan from the local tinsmith. We had seen how useful it was in other people's homes, but decided we could save half the expense if it was home-made. First he drew the plan with a compass and ruler, then it was transferred onto the sheet iron. We borrowed the necessary tools and bought the required number of rivets, and a few days later we had a brand new oven with a double-layer door, two deep trays, and enough material left over for two dustbins, one big and one small. We were delighted with the bargain. In other words, the tinsmith charged 7 yuan for his workmanship for the oven with two shallow trays, depriving the customer of two dustbins. Later we discovered that our trays were one-third deeper than the ones the tinsmith made.

An oven is a must in winter for households in that region. Aside from the usual baking, it could be used to warm food, and when not in use, the door was left open so that the heat could warm the room. The oven was fitted into the back of the renovated brick stove so that the flames from the fire in front would circulate once around the outside of the oven before going into the zigzagging flue in the "fire wall" and finally going out the chimney. In winter, we took sponge baths in front of the open oven door to keep ourselves from freezing from the cold.

Some people from the office came to see our new oven, and remarked at how clever and hardworking my husband was. One of them, a man several years our junior who had been anything but kind to us in years past, asked my husband if he would make one for him if he bought a piece of the same sheet iron. My husband came home and told me about it, and I made it clear to him that if he did bring a piece of sheet iron home and make an oven for that man, I would be strong enough to render the sheet iron useless. I still had a lot of anger in me which my husband could not understand. He seemed to have more pity than anger for those who had treated us so badly.

A few women from the office and neighborhood remarked at

how well and fast I knitted, when they saw me knitting for my Kazakh neighbors in exchange for half a liter of milk a day, and jokingly asked if I would knit for them. I treated those remarks as jokes. I was still angry at them. As time wore on, some of my anger wore off, although the wariness stayed. It is useless to carry a grudge against any one individual because it was not entirely that individual's fault, but the system's. I consoled myself with the belief that many people had to trim their sails to the wind in the hope of future promotions, applications for Party membership, and other considerations for their own survival. Later events proved that such people came out "winners" as they were smoothly promoted to higher positions because of their keen "adjustability".

Nothing could prove me, or my husband, or many, many other people, guilty of what we had been accused of. On the contrary, my husband's being not good enough to join the rest of the staff in "stop production to engage in the revolution" and keeping the company operating during that time proved to have been the correct thing to do. In other words, the rest of the people, under the leadership of Sourpuss, Cyanide, and his lackeys such as SKM, CL, and many others who had been so active in "stop production to engage in the revolution" had been in the wrong. That was hard for them to swallow. But for us, not having been proven guilty did not mean that we were innocent either. At that time, and perhaps to a certain extent, even now, as I am writing this, people are guilty unless proven innocent, and not the other way around, as is accepted in most enlightened societies in the world. True, there were no more struggle sessions, at least for the time being, proved to be a very welcome respite, but would the calm last? Past experience showed us that it could be just another "lull" before yet another storm. The Cantonese have a saying which fits the predicament of people like us to a "T", The system "has someone by the hair to yank back and forth at will" is the literal translation.

Life continued on as usual. It was now 1972, the children were growing and the pinch of poverty was that much more intense.

A neighbor in the courtyard kept hens, and many of them were brooding, in the mood for hatching babies. Hens stop laying eggs when they get into the "heat" of wanting to squat in their coop and hatch, even if there is no egg under them. Everything is done, short of killing them, to get them out of the "urge". They are doused with cold water, chased around the yard, hung on a pole by one leg... anything to get them out of the nest so that they will begin to lay eggs again. Nothing works, until eventually they get over it and start laying eggs again.

One neighbor had an especially stubborn hen who would do nothing but sit in her coop. I suggested that she lend me the hen to hatch instead, and she did. I borrowed ten eggs from another neighbor and put them under the hen. A week later, I inspected each egg with a light bulb and found that there was hope as there was a spot and a dark shadow in each of them. After more than three weeks, chicks emerged. Of the ten chicks, less than half were males. We took very good care of them and made sure that at night no cats or other animals could get to them. Over the next few months, we ate all the roosters except the handsomest of the bunch which was a leghorn with snow-white feathers, long yellow legs, and a red, red comb. We nick-named him 'little son in-law', and he began to monopolize his "harem". No other rooster could go near the hens so long as he was around, and he was always there.

The next spring, the hens began to lay eggs. It was such an exhilarating experience for me to gather three to five eggs a day! It meant that we could improve our children's diet, and we were eager that one of our hens would also get the urge to hatch so that we could have another batch of hens. Then tragedy struck. A fowl epidemic wiped out all the chickens on our street in two days and we were left with nothing. Such a fowl epidemic raged once a year, in different parts of the town. The local vet center would offer shots to be injected under the wings, but it was usually too late to save the chickens. The improper burial of a dead chicken usually led to a vicious circle of more chickens dying, and it just went on and on until there were no more chickens around or the virus was spent.

Christmas of 1972 was a good one in that my spirits had been uplifted by President Nixon's China visit. The USA was still considered evil, but it was the lesser of two evils in comparison to the Soviet Union, which was our top enemy. Not long after that, I received a hand-copied script of an American movie that reputedly had been given to China by Henry Kissinger. I can't recall its name, but I do remember something about the story which entailed a string of misunderstandings between several people, and a few deaths. The story was that A killed B thinking the latter was responsible for the death of someone closely connected to him (or her), while in fact B was his "savior", and C was the culprit whom A had mistaken for "savior". I think it had a message.

Another thing that made that Christmas a good one was that every employee received a long overdue raise, however minimal. We had been in dire straits for a long while, and badly needed something to boost our morale. Both of us had lost quite some weight during the past couple of years because of what we had gone through. I was having problems with my teeth. For the first time, I realized what "getting long in the tooth" meant. My gums had shrunk, exposing the roots of my teeth so that they were very sensitive. A few teeth had to be extracted because the cavities were too big to be filled. Not having a job meant that only half of my medical care costs would be covered, and dental care was not included except for the extraction of teeth. Medical care, even though primitive, was a luxury for us and had been neglected and things just worsened with time. I was advised to treat my insomnia with Chinese herbal medicine instead of Western medicine. Having always been in good health in my youth, the thought of downing bowlsful of bitter, black ooze three times a day was enough to make me feel sicker than ever before. The medicine did not do any good and made me lose my hair. I was really at my wit's end. It seems that the past was catching up with me, and all that pent-up frustration and anger was now showing through in my physical condition. I was turning into a wreck even though neither of us had to attend struggle sessions any more, and for housewives even political study had been canceled.

The Petroleum Company transportation section needed new drivers for their newly-acquired oil tankers, and CL, the one-time lackey of Cyanide, who was now working as a repairman instead of just a worker rolling oil drums at the station, wanted to be a driver, and took the required written tests needed for a license. He scored higher marks than some of his colleagues who took the test with him, but he had failed in the road tests whereas all the others passed. In spite of the rule that one had to pass both written and road tests to qualify for a driving license, Cyanide insisted that CL be given a Jiefang tanker and be allowed to make the twice-weekly trips to Dushanzi and Karamai so he could practice for the next road test. My husband refused to comply because it was too dangerous to have CL on the road with a truck full of oil, but Cyanide went to Sourpuss and insisted that my husband's refusal was "class revenge" because of what had happened during the Cultural Revolution. Sourpuss, Cyanide, and CL were all Party members and my husband was not, and in that day and age, one arm could not out-twist three arms, especially three "red" arms.

CL abused the "trust" of his superiors and on his very first trip careened off the road and rolled the truck down a hill. The truck would have exploded had it happened on his way back when it was full of gasoline. The truck was repaired, and all was quiet for a few months with CL back working as a repairman. But after he saw the other drivers coming back with sacks of melons in the summer, and coal in the winter, he started to clamor for another chance at driving.

The trucks and oil tankers on their way to Dushanzi or Karamai passed the Hoxtolgay coal mines where coal could be gotten for a few yuan a sack because it was directly from the pits with no transportation added, and also passed by many state farms in Wuerhe where vegetables, and melons abounded in the summer and were very cheap. Drivers usually brought back sufficient coal for their families for the winter at a sack or two each trip, and enough vegetables and melons so that neighbors and friends could also benefit. Again, my husband's decision to not let CL drive a truck was overruled and this time he was assigned a truck to make trips to the lumber areas up in the mountains to transport logs down to Altai.

The trips were made with a convoy of several trucks. On one trip, my husband was in the last truck so he could make sure there were no stragglers. The trip up the mountains, the loading and the return were relatively smooth, and he breathed a sigh of relief as the convoy drove back into Altai town. But as his truck turned the corner on to the main street, it was confronted with the line of trucks braked to a stop. My husband got down from his truck and walked up along the line of trucks, only to discover that exactly half the cabin of CL's truck had been flattened and the man who had sat next to him, XS, was crushed flat as a pancake from the waist up. CL had driven straight into the truck in front of him which had stopped by the roadside near the driver's house.

Jiefang trucks were about 3.5 meters long, and the logs were at least four meters long, with half a meter or more sticking out. CL had swerved too late and drove into one of the logs jutting out of the back of the stopped truck straight into XC, who was killed instantly. XS had recently remarried because his first wife did not give him a child. He left behind elderly parents, a sister, and his new wife. CL, unscratched, was taken away by the police.

Sourpuss and Cyanide arranged for the funeral, and CL was given a minimal sentence which he served out of jail because a few days after the accident his wife was diagnosed with bone cancer in one leg. She had been limping for a while. As her health deteriorated, CL took her home to Henan to die, and came back with a new wife to take care of his bunch of children. After his sentence, served out of jail, was over, he was allowed to drive again. This time much more carefully, I think. But however careful a driver is, there will always be the possibility of a something going wrong. On one of his trips he had a flat tire, and he used a hydraulic jack to prop up his loaded truck so he could change the tire. But as he crawled under the truck to check the tire, the hydraulic jack snapped, and the truck crushed him to death. That was the end of CL.

In February of 1973, thanks to the back-pay from the raise my husband got, and with help from Auntie Ellie and friends overseas, I returned to Shanghai to get medical care. I took the two children along because my husband had a business trip to Shanghai scheduled a few months later, in May. By then, my father was back home from confinement, and so were Dr Tu and Chum. My father and many of his generation, having weathered so many political movements, quietly told me that this last one had been the worst by far. Like me, my mother who was also a housewife, had to attend struggle sessions with the lane people, and was also dragged through hell and high water.

When I visited Dr Tu, I was saddened to find that he was no longer himself. He seemed very remote, and had a glassy stare in his eyes. He could not take care of himself. He had never been the kind of man my father was. My father could not function without my mother who had to take care of his clothes, his meals, his everything, whereas Dr Tu had been very self-sufficient and independent. He had had wonderful teeth, and now he had to wear dentures and was not accustomed to them. In short, he was a different person altogether. Chum was more or less unchanged, at least superficially. I asked about the fate of people we used to know, and was surprised how little was known because during those years, few kept in touch for fear of guilt by association.

As usual, there were horror stories, and almost every family had at least one member who was involved in some way in the Cultural Revolution. No one will really ever know to what extent the Cultural Revolution affected the mentality of the Chinese people, and how long it would take for them to get over the trauma. Again, the physical wounds received during the "unprecedented ten years" healed quicker and better than the psychological ones. I am positively sure that the nightmares from that decade will haunt us Chinese people for years to come.

One thing the Cultural Revolution did accomplish was to antagonize the people who had the most to contribute to the development of the country. Many who had had parents who returned from overseas in the 1950s, left the country for good in the early 1980s when things started to loosen up. Unlike parents of Dr Tu and Chum's generation, who had wholeheartedly supported Premier Zhou Enlai's call to have their children who were overseas return and serve the country, these children, now the parents themselves had learned their lesson the hard way, and many, many of them did all they could to get their children out of the country for fear that perhaps in the future their children would have to go through what they themselves had gone through. History has been known to repeat itself, and they didn't want to be in the audience during its repeat performance. Since their parents' and their own patriotism had been abused, they decided why bother, I guess.

Different people had different "hangovers" from those ten years, and some of them can be inherited. It is true that important government officials who had been persecuted during those ten years have been rehabilitated, but that accounts for only an iota of all those who underwent sufferings of different degrees during that period. What about the general public? We had so many political movements prior to the Cultural Revolution that another movement to round up the persecutors of that period would not have been an excess in any way, and it would, for a change, have been a welcome one. Instead, excuses were provided to get them off the hook and few, if any, of the persecutors who did not have the name of a VIP on their list of victims got away with whatever they had done. It seems that the value of one's life is in direct proportion to one's status. That the persecuted remained silent for the most part and let "bygones" be "bygones", that no official attempt was made to make those who did wrong to realize their wrongdoing, and that no encouragement was given to the persecuted to expose their persecutors - all this is not understandable unless taken as a sign of reluctance to have the root of the evil traced to the source which abetted all the chaos. Perhaps voluntary collective amnesia is what it is.

It has been many decades since the Cultural Revolution took place, everything about it is already so much blood, sweat, and tears under the bridge, and we now have more important issues to deal with than to "go over the old accounts". But avoiding an issue does not make it go away. Time is doing away with those who have that issue, and that is being taken advantage of. Whenever there is a TV interview with someone who had suffered during those ten years, they refer to it with pain too severe to dwell upon. When asked about those years, their lips quiver, their eyes get misty, they choke back a sob, and underneath it all, is a sense of utter helplessness. And with time, that helplessness turns to resignation. It really is difficult to know whether to call that a "merit" or "demerit" of the Chinese people. It definitely is a "merit" from the perspective of the system, because it means one worry fewer, and tracking down those who persecuted their fellowmen in the CR would be a huge project, China being such a big country, and the numbers involved being so great. The "demerit" is the message it sends of indifference. "You were persecuted during the Cultural Revolution? Well, who wasn't? Too bad for you."

For us, in those years, no news was bad news. Whatever we read in the papers and saw on TV was mostly good news. It was what we actually saw happening around us that was bad. The overall decay in morals, in work ethics, corruption, violence, drugs, crime, sex, and what-have-yous. But statistics tend to compare all these bad things with their rate in the U.S. and other Western countries where the population is much smaller and the rates are much higher, so in spite of everything, we look good.

In late February of 1973 we travelled to Shanghai. We took the plane from Altai to Urumqi because the children only needed half tickets, and the travel expense amounted to the same as if we had gone by bus which would have taken us three days with two nights in indescribably dirty inns and awful meals. The airfare per person then was 36 yuan. Then we took the train from Urumqi and again the children only needed quarter tickets. My daughter was less than five years old, and had never left Altai prior to the trip. Everything was new to her. On the train, next to our car was the soft sleeper section where several pot-bellied army officers were, and she got to be friendly with them. One of them asked her in which place she had grown up, a question that she had never encountered before, her reply got them in stitches, it was equivalent to "I grew up in patches" because she really did grow up in hand-me-downs from her brother, and most of them were badly patched.

My parents saw my husband for the first time after twelve years of our marriage. I married when I was of age, and needed no permission from my parents, and in fact they were not even notified until I was actually married even though they did know that I was going to marry someone by the name of Gong Wenbin. In the years that followed, there had never been any unfavorable mention of him in my letters home because we got along very well and he was a good husband and father. There is a Shanghai saying which literally means that when a mother-in-law sees her son-in-law, the more she looks at him, the better she likes him. The old saying that one 'loses a son when he marries, but gains a son when a daughter marries' rings true in many cases. Another reason for their taking to my husband could be that since he could not remember his own parents because he had lost them in infancy, he treated mine with special courtesy. For the first time in his life, he now had people he could call "Father" and "Mother." My mother compared him favorably with her two other sons-in-law, who lived in Shanghai.

Shanghai had not changed much in the eight years since I

had last been there except that the facades of the buildings in our part of town had gotten 'facelifts' because of President Nixon's visit. I spent my days going to the dentist's and the Zhongshan Hospital where my sister worked and where I could have access to medical care. One lady doctor who checked me looked so familiar that I swore I had seen her somewhere before, but just couldn't remember where or when. I mentioned it to my sister, and she told me that the doctor was Wang Guangzhen, sister of Wang Guangmei, wife of Liu Shaoqi, Chairman of the country, one of the chief targets during the Cultural Revolution. This doctor had had a private practice on Yuan Ming Yuan Road in earlier years, and that was just one street away from where we lived in Shanghai. No wonder!

We stayed in Shanghai until July before returning to Altai. That we could make the trip without having to ask permission from anyone meant that we were "off the hook", and with the overall political climate improving, I felt very hopeful. I was sure that there would be great things to look forward to. First of all, I could resume my correspondence with Auntie Ellie, Chum, and other friends, and secondly, I could be working again. I had with great expectations upon our return from Shanghai, and every day I prayed that something would happen to end my now eleven years of unemployment, as our needs were greater with the two children growing, and even with my husband's modest raise it was still a struggle to provide a reasonably nutritious diet for everyone. So instead of waiting for a job to come my way, I went out to look for one.

In those days, the government was the only employer, and if that door was closed, all doors were closed. All my attempts at seeking employment failed and I became more frustrated than ever before. I couldn't even get a job as a street cleaner. I knew a very cheerful and fat Uygur woman by the name of Amerahan who had gotten a job to sweep the main street in Altai, and I asked her if another woman was needed for the job because there were other streets that needed cleaning. She went and inquired for me, and came back to say there was a position available, but I was deemed unemployable, and eventually the opening went to another person. It made me so angry. I could not think of a more menial job to ask for as outhouses were all cleared by nearby communes and one had to be a commune member to qualify for that work.

Once again, I began to sink into the slough of despondency. Physically, I was in a better state than a year ago, but mentally, I was not. I would cry for no reason, and often in the middle of the night, waking up for no reason at all but to wail heartrendingly. Every few months, I would feel all choked up again so that swallowing food was a problem, and only with a good cry, always in the middle of the night, could I gain temporary relief, only to have it build up again in a few months. I could not explain what I was crying about, or crying for, but I had to cry myself hoarse to earn any relief. I was in fear of losing my sanity. Somewhere in the back of my head this quotation surfaced: Those whom the gods destroy, they first make mad. (Years later I found the correct version - Whom God would destroy, He first sends mad). My unexplained bouts of crying were very annoying and disturbing to the children and my husband because the next day I would go around with eyes swollen to the size of peaches, and people would look at me queerly, and neighbors would ask the children if their parents had had a fight.

My husband could not understand why I was frustrated when he had never once confronted me about my unemployment, and after all, he had not gone through any less than I had. In fact, he had gone through much more during those years and all on my account, so why all the tears? That terrible urge to weep, to cry out loud, to literally wail myself hoarse every now and then, however exhausting it was, just could not be suppressed, much as I wanted to.

A military VIP by the name of Pei (Fei) Zhouyu was said to be visiting Altai. I wrote a letter detailing my tale of woe, hoping to hand it to him personally. I think other people in Altai were doing the same thing, but I had no success in encountering him even though Altai was such a small town. I did not give up, though, and instead began writing to Premier Zhou Enlai and sending my letters through registered mail to the State Council. I wrote in English, letter after letter telling him of my troubles and all that had happened and was happening in Altai, the scandals concerning the different prominent people, and the lawlessness. All the letters were written in English because I was afraid that they would be opened and read by the local Post Office people and handed to the authorities which would surely land me in the slammer. In 1975, I received a small piece of paper from the State Council telling me that my letters had been forwarded to the Xinjiang Uygur Autonomous Region Government, and that it would ask the local Altai Government to deal with my problem.

The boomerang knocked me off balance for a while because I knew, knowing them for what they were, that if the problem was referred to the local authorities, nothing would ever happen. I had been in Altai for nine years now, who knew how much longer I would be there? There was no light at the other end of the tunnel. I went to the local government with that sheet of paper from Beijing and found some local VIPs, but all I got from them was a shrug of the shoulders. They claimed that my employment problem was not a Cultural Revolution problem as I had been unemployed several years before that, and therefore they could not correct a problem they had not created. They had enough problems on their hands as it were. My argument was that my problem was not one left over from the KMT Government in pre-Liberation days, and since we had had the same government since 1949, the only logical place for me to go for resolution was that government, the one and only employer in the whole country. Have we not always prided ourselves that no unemployment exists in China? So my having been unemployed for the past dozen years or more must clearly be a gross mistake, and that was why I was asking for a job. The fact that I saw other women, some illiterate, being given jobs and I was not, even if I begged, was more than upsetting to me.

SKM, that detestable torturer of the Petroleum Company from the Cultural Revolution, went on home leave and came back with a wife, a strapping, fresh-faced young woman from Shandong Province. He bragged to all who would listen that his wife was the daughter of a high-ranking cadre from the air force, and a lot of other baloney. They eventually had three children. Sourpuss took to her immediately and was very helpful in finding her employment, but the night before she was to report for work, she was reportedly caught engaging in illicit sexual activities with a man who was not her husband, and her employment was canceled. No, that job was not given to me either even though I was no less qualified for it than she was. To make things easier for them, Sourpuss had SKM and family transferred to another Petroleum station in Karamai where no one knew of them, but it seemed that she was even more active there than she had been in Altai, and one day SKM returned from work to find her gone with all her things, leaving the children with him. She left behind no note and he did not know where to go to find her. Three years later, she returned, and this time took all her children with her while SKM was away at work.

Old Man Geng, that "progressive mangliu" was run over by a horse-drawn carriage while crossing the street. His ribs were broken, piercing his lungs and liver, and he lay in hospital dying from internal hemorrhage. It was an open secret that his elder son's wife detested him because he always goaded his son to beat her up for having "insulted" or "disrespected" him. He would push his son into their room and stop the door with his body and call out to his son that if he were a good and filial son, he would beat his wife for having treated his father wrongly. To satisfy him, his son would take off a shoe and beat it on a table while his wife 'howled'.

When the time for his funeral came, the wife of the elder son was supposed to be among the chief mourners, and her duty was to dress in hemp and white cloth, and most of all, to wail, as the Shandong custom called for. This daughter in-law, a very outspoken and saucy woman, remarked to her friends that she was so happy the old man was dead that she could sing and dance the whole day, but that she could not cry, let alone wail, at the funeral. Someone gave her a tip and said that she could sprinkle red pepper on her handkerchief and rub her eyes, causing them to tear, and since she would be covered in hemp at the funeral procession, she could yell out in a loud voice and pretend to be wailing. So it was a strange funeral procession with some on-lookers having a hard time suppressing wide grins as they knew she was pretending. After all, Altai was a small town, and everyone knew everyone else's domestic affairs.

After Premier Zhou Enlai died, I had no choice but to go to the Regional Government in Urumqi. Writing letters was no use now that there was no one to write to. I hitch-hiked to Urumqi in the spring of 1976, with that small sheet of paper from the State Council. To my surprise, the government building and all its halls were covered with big character posters, and all the rooms in the buildings were empty. There wasn't even a guard at the gate. I could not find anyone to talk to. I went back the next day, and after walking through the building and putting my head into each of the offices, I finally found one with someone behind a desk, I told him my problem and showed him the sheet of the paper I had in my hand. He looked at it and wrote a note, addressed it to the Altai Prefectural Government, and referred the problem to them and asked me to go back to Altai to wait for news. I did as I was told. Nothing happened. Years later I was told that someone from the Altai Government had gone around town with the stack of letters I had written to Premier Zhou Enlai, looking for someone to translate them into Chinese so they would know what was in them. I wonder if those letters are still in some desk drawer in the Altai Government now.

The Petroleum Company was given a hilltop on which to build its new office and housing for its staff, and day laborers were needed to level the hilltop before any construction could take place. Many women, wives of men working for different companies under the Commercial Bureau, had never been employed and their men took the initiative to contract the work to their wives, under the auspices of the housewives organization. I asked to join them, and did so after Sourpuss gave the nod. We were paid 2.50 yuan a day for an eight-hour work day. One-tenth of that was deducted for the housewives organization, for what purpose I did not know and dared not question.

Altai has only a short season of frost-free days, and the outdoor work began in mid-May and had to end in early October, at the latest. Once the temperature reaches near-freezing point, all outdoor work such as construction with adobe or kiln-baked bricks is stopped. We used steel rods to pry loose the boulders heaped on the hill and loaded them onto push-carts to dump further down, thereby leveling the hill as we progressed with the work. After the first week I was made team leader, because I was working very hard. Most of the other women were people I remembered from the struggle session days. I was not comfortable working with them, and certainly did not want to work like them. They chatted and gossiped endlessly, and it seemed that once they lips moved, their hands had to stop, there was no coordination. A few of them had bound, later loosened, feet and were only there so that they could get paid. They could not carry anything heavy, and they got away with it. As for me, I was so thrilled to be actually working again, that I did as much as I could, and enjoyed every minute of the back-breaking work. I was surprised at how physically strong and energetic I was. I now ate like a horse and slept like a log. Gone was my insomnia and urge to cry. I just wished that the work day was longer than eight hours.

After the hilltop was leveled, construction began. I was in the team of four people who went with the four-ton Jiefang trucks to the kiln to load bricks to take to the construction site and unload. We had to make two trips each morning, which meant loading and unloading eight tons of bricks. We used clips that would pick up four kiln-baked bricks at a time. Loading sun-dried adobe bricks was the most strenuous task because each adobe brick weighed eight kilograms. Each brick was tossed up to the person standing on the truck to stack them, and catching each one was another strenuous task. If the truck could not get near to where the adobe bricks were stacked, they would have to be loaded by 'relay', with several women standing in a line but within a throw's distance from each other. We would throw the adobe from one to another to be loaded on the truck. The person standing nearest the truck would have to throw the eight-kilo brick up to the one standing on the truck who would catch it and stack it. The work was back-breaking, but, somehow the job managed to get done.

Mixing up the plastering for the walls was a job for men

because wet mud mixed with chopped up hay could only be mixed with the men wearing high rubber boots stamping on it. But we carried the mixed plaster in buckets on the ends of a shoulder pole and walked up a plank to the roof of a house.

Every day was a physical challenge, but because I was so happy to be working again, I did not feel the exhaustion until I went to sleep at night. I was dead to the world as soon as my head hit the pillow. It was too bad that the fall came early, and we had to call it quits for the year because outdoor work of that kind could not be done in below-zero weather.

The year 1976 was a bad one with many deaths of national leaders in Beijing. We, like the rest of the people in the country, did not know what to expect. Were things going to get worse? Could they really get any worse now that it was at its worst, as far as we could see it? A million other questions remained unanswered. There was all the talk about the "Gang of Four", and we only knew as much as the newspapers carried, which wasn't much. By then, editorials had lost any credibility, but for the first time we realized that there was a power struggle going on up top. Being in Xinjiang, and in Altai at that, where "the heavens are high and the emperor is far away," it was very difficult to know what was actually going on in the rest of the country. What the newspapers printed could not be relied on and all news was good news. The bloated figures of agricultural production during the late 1950s was a good example. There was great disparity between what the newspapers said and what people were talking about in private. We could only believe half of what we heard and read, and drew our own conclusions.

We had started another coop of chickens after the fowl epidemic was over, and by now had around ten laying hens. Life was passable in that we could count on gathering four to five eggs a day, sometimes even more. I took in knitting in the winter, and even baby-sat for a neighbor who had had a quarrel with her mother-in-law and left her child with nobody to care for it. I also started to write letters more frequently and to subscribe to a publication called *Shikan* (Poetry Journal) and tried my hand at translating some politically satirical verses by Ci Beiou, for practice, to send to Chum. Some people in my husband's office thought that I was being "high falutin'" subscribing to that quarterly, actually I picked it only because it was cheaper than other monthly publications.

I wrote down all the hymns and popular songs I could remember, and while I could sing them, to myself of course, I could not do anything creative in English aside from my limited letter-writing. That had to be limited because it was an expense, and too many letters would also cause suspicion. But the urge I felt to do something in English was so strong that I had a hard time suppressing it. I could speak and sing to myself which I had been doing all along, but what I needed most of all was oral communication in the language.

The local bank in Altai had been given a battery-operated Casio calculator by its general office in Urumqi, but the operation manual gave instructions in several languages but not in Chinese. Since it was known that I had been suspected of being a CIA spy and knew English, one man from the bank asked me to translate the manual for him. I did so, and the calculator was put to use. Then the local hydropower station imported a Japanese-made Nissan diesel generator, and again the manual was in English and not Chinese, and I was approached to translate it, free of charge, of course. I did, and the machine worked. I felt so good about it that I walked on air for a few days afterwards. It felt good to be able to render a service.

Our work on the construction site ended in early October

when the weather got cold, and it was to be suspended until the next May. My neighbor, a Hui-Kazakh woman who was a typesetter for the local newspaper, had to go to Urumqi for her annual lead-poisoning check up, and she asked me to take care of her son and her family cow. I was to baby-sit the child during office hours when the father was away. The boy was only about four years old, but spoilt rotten. But whenever he was with me at our place, he was normal and behaved in an acceptable way, and we treated him like we treated our two children; we did not pamper him. As soon as he was back at his own home, he would act up and be out of control.

Each morning and evening, I was to milk their cow. One milking would be mine and the other would be theirs. While she was gone, our two children had any amount of milk to drink because one milking was more than half a bucketful. After less than a week, the boy began to miss his mother, and asked why she wasn't back yet. She returned after ten days, and I was discharged from my duties. My daughter asked, "Why is she back so soon?" Evidently she missed the daily bowls of milk.

That same neighbor's sister-in-law, H, was getting married to Y. It was an arranged marriage. H was only in her teens while Y was in his late twenties, if not early thirties, and the two had only met once or twice prior to the wedding. The girl's trousseau and presents from relatives and friends were all hung up on laundry lines in the room for the guests to inspect and comment on. When the guests began to arrive, the custom was for the people on the groom's side to smear the face of the bride's father with soot, and make him ride a donkey backwards.

The food, aside from the usual candies, "bawsak" (fried pieces of bread), cube sugar, and sunflower seeds, there would be pilaf and other edibles such as fried cakes. Usually the older people would be the first batch to eat, males and females in different rooms, and after that the younger people. And when the eating is over, the bride would be taken to her husband's home. As at every wedding, a master of ceremonies was invited to oversee the whole affair, and, for good luck, the person selected would usually be a happily married man.

At this wedding, the emcee was another Hui by the name of Ma. He was the father of three little girls, the two younger ones were twins who were still using diapers, and his wife was the adopted daughter of the old Kazakh couple who had been our neighbors in our first neighborhood. Ma had married once before, but was childless, and his present wife was at least ten to fifteen years his junior.

The custom was that after the reception at the bride's parents' home, in H's case her brother's home, people from the groom's side would come to fetch the bride, and people from her side would not let her go unless a required sum was paid. The bride got on the truck with other people from her side of the family, and the last to get on was Ma, the emcee. As the truck started to pull away through the gate of our courtyard, two people suddenly jumped out and stretched a rope across to stop the truck to demand the gift of money. The driver stepped on the brakes, causing everyone in the truck to fall back, and Ma, being at the very end of the truck, fell to the ground, landing on the back of his head. He was helped to his feet but his head sagged, and blood was dripping from one ear. The groom had the driver take him and Ma to the hospital and while everything possible was done to save him, Ma died on the third day. His skull had been cracked by the sudden fall and he suffered cerebral hemorrhage which took his life.

So before the marriage could be consummated, a funeral took place. It was a terrible tragedy for both families. The deceased left behind a young wife and three small daughters, the wife had been sterilized after the twins were born, no longer able to have children, which also meant that her chances of marrying again were next to nil. The ill-fated marriage was marred from the first day because it unintentionally caused the death of Ma. A year later the couple's first born, a beautiful baby boy, was discovered to be deaf and therefore mute, like the groom's late mother had been, so people said. When the second child was about to arrive around four years later, the older boy was left with relatives living a few houses up the hill from us. One day he was playing with sled in their yard, and slid his way downhill to a frozen pool of water into which he plunged and drowned, unable to call out for help. The couple's second child was another son, also born deaf and therefore mute. They took him to Beijing to the best hospitals to see if there was anything that could be done to correct his hearing, but with no effect. The boy had an enormous amount of nervous energy and was uncontrollable in many ways. Later they sent him to a school for the deaf and dumb in Urumqi. He grew up to be a tall teenager, good at drawing, which was the thing he liked doing most. The couple stuck together through all the tragedies which had begun on their day of marriage.

I had been asked to help out with the kitchen work at H's wedding, and I made the mistake of not asking what exactly was involved in kitchen work. I naturally picked the heaviest job, that of kneading the dough to make fried pancakes which the Hui call "*you xiang.*" I rolled up my sleeves and scrubbed my arms up to the elbows, and was just about to start mixing water into the flour when an old lady let out a scream and literally fell on me from behind. I had forgotten that I was a "*kapir*" (infidel), and should not have had a hand in making anything that was edible for Muslim people, especially since it was food for a wedding reception. It was very embarrassing. After that, I stayed away from all the food and only helped in washing the bowls and

341

dishes after each batch of guests had finished. The elderly Hui were much more fundamentalist than any Kazakh I had known.

There were two Swatownese men who worked for companies under the Commercial Bureau whose wives had committed suicide inside a matter of a year or so. One of them, who worked in a barbershop, hanged herself, and the other, a very good-looking young woman who worked behind a counter in the local department store, jumped into an abandoned well in the courtyard where they lived. Both women left behind young children. It was evident that both had died because of family quarrels or because their husbands had been abusive. Instead of making inquiries into the deaths, there were rumors that they had belonged to a "Plum Blossom Party" that was supposedly headed by former KMT President Li Zhongren's wife, and LSQ's wife WGM was also rumored to be one of the members. There was no law to protect women from domestic violence, even though these two women were also government employees and on equal footing with their husbands, but no one stood up for the dead, and they were thousands of miles away from their kith and kin in Guangdong Province. Before long, both men remarried, and their new wives were also from the Guangdong countryside.

Old customs take a long time to die out. Even though the "four old customs" had been supposedly eradicated at the very beginning of the Cultural Revolution, their remnants resurfaced in different forms and under different guises. The Cultural Revolution had also brought on a lot of 'new' customs which became unwritten laws. For example, no photo studio would take a picture of anyone without that person wearing a Mao badge, the bigger the better. And at the same time, no one would ever think of taking a picture at a studio without wearing a Mao badge as it would serve as evidence of dissent. There is no record to show how much aluminum was used to make Mao badges during those years, and how much money people spent to buy those badges at the sacrifice of foregoing other much needed things, such as food. You either bought the badges or suffered the suspicion of being a 'bad element.'

As for the Little Red Book, and the songs – excerpts from the Little Red Book that everyone was singing – they reminded me of church days. I was almost sure that someone in Beijing who came up with the idea of printing the book and the writing the songs had learned it from the Protestant Church. The Little Red Book was like the 'New Testament', and the songs were the choruses we had sung in both Sunday School and the Youth Group. The idea was the same, putting the quotations to music made them easier to remember. The way the leader was deified made the Little Red Book that much more like the New Testament, and the songs that much more like Sunday School choruses.

Each family had to make at least one embroidered picture of Chairman Mao, and the money for the colored thread needed for the embroidery would be deducted from the pay. My husband was responsible for the embroidery, which was done with a syringe needle with a hole punctured at the head, very much like that of a sewing machine needle, and the thread was pulled through the hollow part of the needle. The embroidering was done at the back of the cloth where the picture of Mao was traced using carbon paper, and the finished product, the front, would be a fuzzy-looking pile. All one needed to do was to jab the needle at the picture again and again. To me, it was like voodoo, but saying that would have landed me in jail. The picture was done on a piece of blue gingham, and then framed and hung in the room, more for inspection than for any other purpose. Each family had several sets of Chairman Mao's Works, and more than several poster-size pictures of him. Many believed that the more pictures one had of him on the walls, the more patriotic one was. Few, if any, in Altai have ever heard of the second Commandment, I think.

In late May of 1977, my son's headmaster heard that I knew English, and he came to the construction site where I was working as a day laborer to ask me if I would consider standing in for their English teacher who had just begun her maternity leave. They would pay me 1.5 yuan a day, 75 fen less than what I was earning as a day laborer. Since the frost-free season in Altai is very short, and we cannot do any outdoor work once the weather gets cold, I calculated that teaching would not be limited by the temperature and classes would not be canceled even if it rained daggers, so I decided to give it a try. But when the school principal asked me if I knew grammar or international phonetics, I had to tell him honestly that I knew neither, and he questioned how I could claim to know the language when I didn't even know the two most important things about the English language. This headmaster himself knew no English. But because it just would not do to let the students stop their English lessons for the fifty-six days their teacher's maternity leave, he reluctantly agreed to let me have a try. I think I spent a month just correcting the pronunciation of the students. I left the day before the teacher returned to her job, and went back to my construction site work that paid 75 fen more than teaching.

I went to see the doctors at the local hospital to have my backache treated, and saw a stack of dust-covered xeroxed copies of *Clinical Pediatrics*, a *JAMA* publication, on the desk of one of the doctors, and asked if I could borrow a copy or two to read. He could see from my case history that I was a local, and would probably return what I borrowed, and lent them to me. The head doctor of the hospital, surnamed Wei, felt his subordinates needed English lessons, and was beginning to teach them in the evenings from tape recordings. When I heard this, I volunteered to do the job even though during the day I was working as a day laborer. He agreed. I returned from my job early each evening, washed the dirt off my face and out of my ears, grabbed a bite to eat, put on a clean jacket and went to the hospital to teach. Unfortunately, the lessons were discontinued after a short time when the weather turned cold and the days shortened.

A month or so later, the headmaster of my son's school came to ask me to teach at his school again, but by then many people had told me a lot about what was being said of me by the other teacher and how the students were being criticized for speaking English with a queer accent, among other things. I frankly told the headmaster that much as I had needed the job, unless he could find someone in Altai whose English was better than that of both the teacher and myself to allow for a fair evaluation, I would not work with someone who thought I was a fraud, just because I had been a housewife for so many years. By now, I had resumed my regular correspondence with Auntie Ellie and Chum and other people, and felt really bad that I had no good news to tell any of them, in spite of the fact that the Cultural Revolution was supposed to be over, the 'Gang of Four' were being dealt with, and things were starting to look up again.

I went out to work as a day laborer again in May of 1978 because there was no other work for me. We were still leveling hills to make ground for the construction of the Petroleum Company Office Building. A few days later, a teacher from the No.1 Middle School came to the construction site to ask if I would consider teaching English lessons for the 7th, 8th, 9th, and 10th graders in his school. They had no English teacher and had never had English in their curriculum. I made sure it was not another short stint as losing 75 fen a day amounted to something over time. He promised me that I would be given a six-month period to prove myself, and that if I met their standards, they would consider giving me long-term employment as a regular teacher. By then, I had already been jobless for sixteen long years. I bent over backwards to meet their requirements, and was very hopeful that I would have a permanent job after the six months' trial period was over. But I was wrong.

When the six months were up, I asked if my performance was satisfactory, and the answer was that the six-month trial period would be extended for another year, because six months was too short a time for them to evaluate me. I felt short-changed because they did not keep their promise and could not point out what was not to their satisfaction. My difficult experiences before and after becoming unemployed in 1962 created in me an aversion to people in leading positions, and that aversion will probably remain with me to the end of my days. The headmaster of that school proved himself to be another one of that kind. I came home and had a good cry, because I was at my wits' end. I didn't understand why nothing worked out. Then something in me snapped. I sat down, tore out a sheet of paper from my son's exercise book, and wrote my tale of woe (in English) and addressed it to the Dean of the Foreign Languages Department (assuming there was one) of Xinjiang University in Urumqi (again, assuming there was such a school), and mailed it. I returned to work the next day, feeling absolutely down in the dumps.

A week or so after my letter was mailed, I received a telegram asking me to go for an interview, but no sender was named. Just by luck, my husband had to make a business trip to Urumqi, and with that telegram in hand, he went to Xinjiang University, found the Foreign Languages Department, and looked up the Dean and asked if that telegram had been sent by him. The Dean acknowledged it, and asked him, among other questions, if my spoken English was as good as the written. My husband had to confess ignorance of how good or bad my English was since he did not know the language himself, but he did say that I would come for an interview immediately now that he knew who I should look for when I came.

With that news, I told the headmaster of the No.1 Middle School that since I was not good enough to merit permanent employment, I was leaving. I think he thought I was bluffing until he saw me clearing out my desk. When he saw that I was serious, he said he would give me the permanent employment I wanted if I promised not to leave. I found out later that I could have had the permanent employment if he hadn't promised my employment permit to another person who was the wife of one of the teachers. Not wanting to burn my bridges, I told him that since he was willing to give me permanent employment, he could save it for me until I returned from Urumqi. I borrowed 50 yuan from a neighbor and bought an air plane ticket on the morning flight to Urumqi with only a toothbrush and a face towel in hand. One of my Urumqi friends took me to Xinjiang University because I did not know where it was.

A senior teacher interviewed me. The Dean and all the teachers in the department were surprised that someone from Altai could speak understandable English. I had not once spoken English to anyone in Xinjiang since arriving in 1956, except to Delia and her husband, because I had never met anyone who professed they knew English or could understand spoken English. During the interview, a senior teacher asked me some questions in English, and I responded appropriately. But once the floodgates were opened, I could not be stopped. It was so good to be able to meet someone who could speak and understand English again. After we had spoken for a while, I was told to stay behind then and there.

I went out to long-distance call my husband and told him

to send my things out with the next truck that was coming to Urumqi. Before noon of the same day that I had left Altai, nearly everyone in town knew that I had found a job in Urumqi, at Xinjiang University, even though it took another two weeks before formalities were completed and I was officially employed again, after an interval of a few months more than sixteen years.

My arrival at Xinjiang University was, appropriately, December 23, 1978, the beginning of longer days and shorter nights.

9

THE YEARS SINCE 1978

I HAD THOUGHT that after I had been interviewed, I would be told to return to Altai to await their decision. That was why I had only brought along a toothbrush and a face towel. I had intended to hitchhike back, or at least get a free ride home with one of the company trucks. Of the fifty yuan I had borrowed, thirty-six yuan had gone for the plane ticket, and what was left had to see me back home. The Dean borrowed a folding cot and some bedding for me, and I was given a small room to myself. There was little time to think clearly because everything had happened so fast, and being told to stay behind was the last thing that I had expected.

I had to go through the formalities of taking an examination which included translations of English into Chinese, and vice versa, of prose and non-prose, listening comprehension, and last but not least, actual classroom teaching with all the senior teachers present to evaluate me. I was told to teach a lesson from a textbook that the finishing class, the '76 class, otherwise known as the last "worker, peasant, soldier" class, had used.

I had never taught at this level before, not in the real sense of the word. The text that I was to trial teach was a long article from the English newspaper, *The Guardian*. I remember the headline to be something like "Socialism in Sham, Capitalism in Reality." I asked the Dean what was expected of me since I had no idea how English was taught at this level, never having had a formal college education myself.

A well-meaning senior colleague gave me some tips, and at the same time showed me an exercise book of hers with lesson preparations. I was shocked at the amount of work involved in teaching just one lesson. Several sentences were used to illustrate the use of each new .word or phrase. I would not know which word or phrase would be considered "new" to the students, so almost every word uttered in class was written down and then read to the class. I went to the Dean and told him that I was not up to it. The teaching approach was much too confining for me. What if I had a better idea of how to use a word or phrase after everything had been written down? My Dean assured me that there was no one set way to teach, that I could do as I saw fit, and that after all, it was just a trial. His words put me at ease.

The room I stayed in was only a few steps away from the classrooms. One day, a student, a tall, good-looking girl, asked me if my name was 'Margaret'. I was very surprised, and I said 'yes', and asked her how she knew. It seemed that the university president, ZY, a friend and patient of this girl's father who was an orthopedist at the local Medical College Hospital, who was also the long-time neighbor of Delia and Julian, my first friends in Xinjiang. I had lost contact with them after I left Urumqi in 1962, but had heard through various channels that both of them had been dragged through the coals during the Cultural Revolution days, especially Delia. Well, it seemed that on one of ZY's visits to the orthopedist, in the course of their conversation, ZY mentioned, what to him seemed a 'strange' and 'laughable' thing, that 'a housewife in Altai' had written to the university to seek employment. When this piece of news was repeated to their neighbors, Delia and Julian, Delia wondered aloud if it could have been Margaret. To make a long story short, I was very glad to learn that both Delia and Julian were still in town, and were still in their former jobs. Within a short time, I was in contact with them again after a break of more than sixteen years.

Needless to say, it felt good to be working again after so many years, and this time, doing something that I had never done before, teaching English. Or at least, attempting to do so. Never having had a formal higher education myself, I had little idea of what I would be dealing with. I knew only that I would type. I had learned to type very early on a typewriter my father had bought at a second-hand store in the Central Arcade on Nanking Road in Shanghai. That was decades ago, but I had kept it up by 'typing' on my belly or thighs whenever I was writing an imaginary letter, or 'singing' a hymn or song.

The school authorities, on the recommendation of the department, had to approve my employment on the paperwork that would be submitted to the Education Commission for its final approval. The Dean took me to the Administration Building of the university and we entered an office of one of the departmental administrators. She asked me the usual questions of how old I was and so on. She counted on her the fingers of her hands approximately how many years I could work before retirement to see if it was worthwhile to employ me. I felt very insulted. She didn't like me from the beginning, but fortunately, she was not in direct charge of me. It turned out later that she retired at least a dozen years earlier than I did.

I was asked to spend most of my time sitting in front of a mike and taping lessons from textbooks for the different teachers, which their students would then listen to. I was also asked to teach students how to speak, and I taught them some songs from the musical *Sound of Music*, and other songs that I had learned as a young girl in Shanghai. In those days, the textbook used was called *Essential English*. It was British, and the books did not come with audio tapes.

The first class to graduate was the one which was enrolled in early 1978 after a lull of ten years during which all formal college education was stopped because of the Cultural Revolution. This group of students is referred to as the Class of '77, the first batch of college students to enter college through an entrance examination since the mid-1960s. One of the arguments for closing down higher education during the 'unprecedented ten years' was that 'the more knowledge a person has, the more reactionary he is.' So only "worker peasant soldier" students had been enrolled in short three-year courses, the greater part of which was spent in 'learning from the peasants and workers' by going to either the countryside or factories and doing anything but learn English, or whatever their majors were. These people later had to take remedial courses to qualify them for undergraduate status. I have no idea what the selection standards were, but when regular students began to be enrolled, many of these "worker peasant soldier" students displayed an inferiority complex.

Higher education had suffered a lull of ten whole years during the Cultural Revolution but I was just in time to teach the first two classes of 'real' students. When the first class graduated, I had a falling-out with one of the senior professors because he was unhappy that I had failed some of his pet students for cribbing during finals. I was convinced that I had done the right thing, but even the Dean did not stand up for me. When one of the professor's pet students threatened to beat me up and to smash the window panes of my apartment, he was not reprimanded. Neither was I given an apology for that student's disgraceful behavior. Had I not been staying on the top floor of a five-story walk-up, his threat would have become reality. So I decided that it would be wise to leave the department and teach elsewhere. It was evident that the ten years of lawlessness during the Cultural

Revolution among the younger generation was still having an effect on some of them.

Teachers, regardless of the level at which they were teaching, were still considered by a minority of the students to be 'stinky No. 9s' – a derogatory term for intellectuals. But the majority of the students treasured their chance at higher education, especially the older ones who were generally referred to as the *lao san jie*, meaning students who had graduated from high school prior to the Cultural Revolution, in 1966 or a little earlier. Many of them had been sent to the countryside or factories for re-education, to 'learn' from the peasants and workers, some of whom were already married with children. When higher education resumed, many of them passed their entrance exam into universities with flying colors, and more than a few had school-age children when they themselves belatedly entered university. Many of these students later proved to be the 'cream of the crop', and are now quite successful in their own fields of interest, either in China or overseas.

It was unpleasant to work in an atmosphere of hostility from one of the senior professors whose pet students I had failed. One day, in the reference room of the department, in the presence of many colleagues, he called me names for what I had done. He condemned me to 'hell', saying 'there are no incompetent students, only incompetent teachers.' I was much too shocked to respond, and looking back, I am glad that I had been rendered speechless by his insulting outburst. If I had responded, an argument would have ensued, and the man had been known to use his fists. I once helped to disengage him when he had a physical confrontation with another senior professor over the use of the definite article in naming countries.

Since I was 'incompetent', I decided to look for work elsewhere. It so happened that someone from the newly-established Swatow

(Shantou) University was in Urumqi scouting for teachers, and he got to hear of me. But I was hesitant about such a move because there were many restrictions on residence permits, and Xinjiang University had given me and my two children residence permits to live in Urumqi. This was very precious because there are strict rules about moving to it from other places in the region.

My chance to leave the Foreign Languages Department came when some of the very best students from the university's departments of Biology, Chemistry, Physics, Geography, Mathematics and others stayed on after graduation as teaching assistants while pursuing their graduate degrees, and they needed someone to help improve their English. This batch of students had spent one semester with the professor in question and I was approached by a professor from the Mathematics Department to take over the job for the second semester of the students' English course. It proved to be a turning point in my teaching career at the university.

It was an exhilarating experience for me to be with aspiring young people whose main concern was not how many marks they got on a test but what they had learned, and whether what they had learned would be useful to them in their own studies and work. The year I spent with them was a very rewarding one for all of us. I learned as much from them as they had learned from me, and very congenial friendships developed which have lasted to this day.

Thanks to the reform and opening up in the early 1980s, the government began to send students to foreign countries, especially to the United States, to pursue their graduate studies. The students in my class were talking about the great opportunities that would be available to them if they went overseas, and were very motivated in their English learning. Students from the Biology Department were further motivated when the CUSBEA (China-U.S. Biology Education Admissions) program reached the Northwest of China. Of the six admissions allocated to the entire Northwest, half of them went to three students in our Biology Department because they had not only passed their subject test, but their English proficiency test, as well.

The first biology student who passed the CUSBEA admission test had to be sent to the Guangzhou English Language Center (GELC) on the campus of Zhongshan (Dr Sun Yat-sen) University to receive further language training in order to pass yet another language proficiency test before going to the U.S. As chance would have it, our department sent me to the same university for a one-year refresher course, as a consolation because of the above-mentioned unpleasant experience in the department.

It was a pleasant change to be on the Zhongshan U campus, especially since one of my former students was studying there. The American teachers at GELC were very impressed with the student, partly because he had come from such a remote place. Students in major cities such as Beijing, Shanghai and Guangzhou had the advantage of having native speakers teach them English, but out in the boondocks of Xinjiang, such a luxury was not so easily available. But what we needed was not so much native-speaking teachers but more up-to-date teaching materials. University students in major cities were already taking the Test of English as a Foreign Language (TOEFL), which was a must if students wanted to go to the U.S. for further studies. But here in Urumqi, all the books we had on English learning were obsolete, especially for non-English majors.

Xinjiang was not opened to tourism until mid-1979, and even then the places that foreign tourists were allowed to visit were relatively limited. In fact, our department became part of the tourists' itinerary in Urumqi. At that time, many of the tour guides at the China Travel Service were former 'worker peasant soldier' students of our department. In October 1980, a group led by a professor from the School of Religion at U.C. Berkeley came to my class to talk with the students. Having native speakers come for talks was always a highlight with students and a good chance to test the students' language skills.

Among the tourists in this group was Dr John Scott Everton of Yarmouthport, Massachusetts. As the group was about to leave, Dr John Scott Everton gave me his address and asked me to write to him. I did. It was through this correspondence that I learned about the United Board for Christian Higher Education in Asia and its China Program.

In late 1983 or early 1984, the regional Education Commission invited the British Council to send three teachers to Urumqi to run a short intensive English language training course. Young teachers from all the higher education institutions in Urumqi and other cities of Xinjiang had to take a preliminary test to qualify for admission to the course. My class of young teachers all took the test as well as young teachers from local and out-of-town medical colleges and other institutes. When the day for the results to be announced came, one of the administrators assigned to oversee my class was reluctant to go to the Medical College to see the roster, fearing that our students would not pass. So I went with a young teacher of our Biology Department who had taken the test to copy down the names. We were most pleasantly surprised to see that one and all from our class had passed with very good results, which also meant that there would be no room for young teachers from other schools if the British teachers insisted on sticking to the original number of people in the class. But they added a class, making it possible for the teachers from other schools to benefit from the course as well.

While the students were on that course, I began to write to

the China Program of the United Board for Christian Higher Education in Asia, asking for assistance. I needed newer textbooks and also simulated TOEFL tests to train my students. When the books came, I typed out each test individually, then stenciled, printed and stapled them so that each student could have a copy.

Most of the students were Han, living in Xinjiang because their parents had either volunteered to work in Xinjiang like me, or worse still, were transferred to the region to work. So none of them were here voluntarily and all could see the disadvantages of being in Xinjiang, a land so remote from other parts of China with fewer chances to improve themselves either through further studies or working in good jobs. The result was that these students, who were bright and mature, valued their time in school and wanted to learn as much as possible, many of them with an eye toward overseas study. But first, they had to learn authentic English language skills in listening and reading comprehension and in writing, and not only in terms of grammatical analysis of each sentence as the language was then usually taught.

It was a great joy to work with motivated students in the physical sciences, and pretty soon the materials I had on hand had been used up and I had to keep on looking for more. The class consisted of around thirty-two students, as that was the number of booths in the audio lab, and I was the sole teacher teaching a majority of the classes, amounting to four to six hours a day. I had an assistant who improved his language skills at those classes and left for the United States to study and never returned. The same thing happened to the second assistant and to the third. From then on, it was a one-woman show until my retirement in 2002.

POSTSCRIPT

LOOKING BACK OVER the sixty-two years I have been in Xinjiang (I left Shanghai on September 29, 1956 and I am writing this in early 2019), I feel that for all my life, I have been a round peg in a square hole. In other words, and to put a positive spin on it, I have had the opportunity to move around and experience a variety of things which most people do not because they stay in the same environment their whole lives. I have milked cows, collected cowpads, taken in knitting and worked as a day laborer. I have taught, done interpretation and translation. I have done whatever I had to do. As the Cantonese say, a person who is alive will not let his bladder burst (活人不能叫尿憋死). Not all of the roles I have played have been enjoyable, but I had to go through with it in order to keep sane and alive. Adaptability played a big part in this. I am not saying that I am special, as there are people, lots of them, in Hami, Urumqi, Changji, Burqin, Beitun, Altai and wherever else, who have known no other way of life than the one I was thrown into in Xinjiang. But I was not a local and had to adapt and get used to it rather than accept it as normal life.

The campaign to get these young people out of the cities (to systematically depopulate them?) was very widespread, and nearly every family had some child or children sent to Xinjiang, Inner Mongolia, the Northeast or to Xishuangbanna in Yunnan. Only the lucky ones got to be sent to Chongming island on the outskirts of Shanghai. When the Cultural Revolution was over, these youths clamored to go back to where they had come from, but by that time they had already spent several years out in the wilderness, and many had married local people and had children, so there was a lot of cleaning up to be done. Some families thought these young people had gone for good, and especially in places like Shanghai, one less person meant more room for everyone else, and housing was a big, big problem (don't I know it!). So not all families welcomed back those who had been away for so many years. Some parents had died in the interim, and their siblings, now married with families of their own, would certainly not accept the long-lost sibling back to live with them. The result was that many of these unlucky 'left-outs' became mentally disturbed, especially the uncommitted ones who were still single and had never really adapted themselves to their surroundings.

Anyway, the generation that went through that chaos is dying out, but that doesn't mean that that part of history should be wiped out also. It has been a hard life – not that I am complaining, simply stating a fact. Someone asked me recently if I owned any jade and I had to reply that I do not. Come to think of it, I have never had any jewelry, not even a wedding ring.

Can I be blamed for being paranoid where what is meat today can be poison tomorrow? If China ever recovers from that aftermath, it will be after my generation is gone.

Strange, I have no 'good old days' to look back to. Tough life, it was, but I survived it.

China is our motherland, not step-motherland although at times many innocent people have been treated as step-children. While the days described in this manuscript no longer exist, I want to remind myself and the younger generation that the present came at a price paid with much blood, sweat, and tears by the older generation. Days when law-abiding citizens had nowhere to plead their innocence because there was no due process of law, and one's life was practically in the hands of the leadership of the work place if you happen to be employed, or then in those of the police or the local residents' committee.

Not only are the days no longer in existence, so are the places. I have revisited many places that I had lived in and discernible in this book, and little of what I saw remains. The improvements in the past four decades has been a chance to wipe out the past which had brought us little credit. Physical signs are easily changed, and mental impressions perish with a person's death, so that with time nothing will remain from which we can learn precious lessons so that the past will not be repeated.

We are citizens of China, but we are also citizens of the world, and we are due all the rights and freedoms that all such citizens should enjoy. The days when some people are more 'equal' than others should be forever gone. If only all those who have died falsely accused could live to see the great changes, their ghosts would be comforted.

It is now exactly forty years since I first recommended myself to Xinjiang University which was gracious enough to employ me. I had little formal education, and it can be almost considered a miracle that instead of using me as a typist as I had wanted to be, the school used me as a teacher, and eventually gave me all the promotions due. I have been extremely lucky to have had enlightened superiors who gave me the freedom to do all that I did in my work, with no interference at all, and I pride myself on making the acquaintance of the cream of the crop among the college students of Xinjiang who attended my language-training classes, the majority of whom are now overseas. (there are many of my former students working in Washington, D.C. and countless others who are tenured in universities across the

United States). Xinjiang may have been far and remote in the past, but the number of her educated who are now overseas are many. Whenever I am in the U.S., which has been five times in the past few years, I always make an effort to visit at least a few of them. No, I have not used the school's money for these travels as I think it should be spent on young teachers who are the future pillars of the school, although very unfortunately, nearly all those who have been sent out on government funds have never returned.

I want to thank the United Board of Christian Higher Education in Asia for its generous help in getting the needed materials to begin my language-training program in the early 1980s, and for including me in their list of visiting scholars for their China Program in 1996, to spend a year on the campus of a university in the United States. And also thanks to the Phillips Foundation for the funding in 2002 to allow me to spend a year as a visiting scholar in the U.S. And last, but not least, to thank the late Dr. and Mrs. Ben Smith for their help in obtaining a scholarship for me in 1986 at the University of the Pacific where I spent a year.

Last but not least, I want to thank the folks who sent me boxes of books which helped me to continue my education and enrich the language-training work I was doing. Many of these folks are no longer living, but while they are gone, they are not forgotten because they contributed to a worthy cause. The past should never be forgotten. It should be remembered in order to better appreciate the present, which so many take for granted.

About The Author

Margaret Sun was born in Shanghai in 1935, and has lived in the Xinjiang region of northwest China for over 50 years. She was unemployed for many years, but obtained a job in the late 1970s teaching English at Xinjiang University. She is now retired and lives in Urumqi. She has two children and two grandchildren.